Public Sector
Governance
in Australia

Public Sector Governance

in Australia

Meredith Edwards · John Halligan · Bryan Horrigan · Geoffrey Nicoll

Australian
National
University

E PRESS

ANU
E PRESS

Published by ANU E Press
The Australian National University
Canberra ACT 0200, Australia
Email: anuepress@anu.edu.au
This title is also available online at http://epress.anu.edu.au

National Library of Australia Cataloguing-in-Publication entry

Title: Public sector governance in Australia / Meredith Edwards ... [et al.]

ISBN: 9781921862892 (pbk) 9781921862908 (ebook)

Notes: Includes bibliographical references and index.

Subjects: Public administration--Australia--Decision making.
               Intergovernmental cooperation--Australia.
               Australia--Politics and government.

Other Authors/Contributors:
               Edwards, Meredith, 1941-

Dewey Number: 320.60994

Cover design and layout by ANU E Press

Contents

Part I. Context and Framework

Part II. Rise of Corporate and Public Governance

Part III. Key Issues

Acknowledgements

The research for this book was carried out with generous public funding from the Australian Research Council (ARC), which we acknowledge and appreciate for providing the basis for undertaking this ambitious project. Hopefully, in helping to advance the knowledge, understanding, and practice of public sector governance in Australia and elsewhere, this book justifies that support.

Financial and in-kind assistance was also provided by the ARC Linkage Project's industry partners: the Australian National Audit Office, the Australian Government Department of Finance and Administration, CPA Australia, Deloitte Touche Tohmatsu, and MinterEllison Lawyers. In addition, sponsorship funding was provided to the project by the Australian Public Service Commission. The project was ably supported by these industry partners and benefited from their input and commentary. The four academic co-authors remain solely responsible for the views that are expressed in this book.

Research for this project involved extensive interviews with heads of government departments, agencies and bodies, and public servants in central agencies who have had roles in public sector governance. These interviews were supplemented by case studies of governance in several agencies. Six issues papers were produced,[1] and a range of articles, chapters and papers. This material was supplemented by final interviews that reflected the changing interpretations and practice of public governance up to 2011. We wish to express our appreciation for the time that was given to the project by numerous senior public servants.

The project was started by the four principal investigators at the University of Canberra: Professor Meredith Edwards, Professor John Halligan, Professor Bryan Horrigan and Dr Geoffrey Nicoll. During the project's tenure, Professor Edwards was made professor emeritus and Professor Horrigan moved first to Macquarie University and then to Monash University as the Louis Waller Chair of Law. The University of Canberra has provided a supportive environment for

---

1 Issues Papers, nos 1–6, Corporate Governance ARC Project, University of Canberra:

Meredith Edwards and Robyn Clough 2005, *Corporate Governance and Performance: An Exploration of the Connection in a Public Sector Context.*

John Halligan and Bryan Horrigan 2005, *Reforming Corporate Governance in the Australian Federal Public Sector: From Uhrig to Implementation.*

Meredith Edwards 2006, *Appointments to Public Sector Boards in Australia: A Comparative Assessment.*

John Kalokerinos 2007, *Developments in the Role of the Chair in the Private and Public Sectors.*

Australian National Audit Office and CPA Australia 2008, *Monitoring and Reporting Financial and Non-financial Performance of Australian Government Organisations.*

Meredith Edwards 2008, *Participatory Governance.*

the project. Monash University, the University of Canberra's Faculty of Business, Government and Law and the ANZSOG Institute for Governance provided final research and editing support.

Several researchers and staff have contributed to the project: Dr Richard Grant served as project officer in the initial stages; Roberta Dowd was indefatigable as the main project officer; Dr Robyn Clough provided valuable research assistance; and Chris Tabart combined project, research assistance and editorial work with enthusiasm and competence. The work of Claire Baddeley is also appreciated for material that was collected for use in chapters 4 and 5. Joseph Valente worked tirelessly and expeditiously on editing and research support for the final manuscript.

The partners, and many others, have had to wait longer for this book than was originally anticipated. However, rather than publish on the cusp of change and transition through recent governance and electoral cycles, this book is being released when the way ahead in the 2010s, in academic and policy terms, is becoming clearer in some respects, while still uncertain in others.

Abbreviations

ABC	Australian Broadcasting Corporation
ACCC	Australian Competition and Consumer Commission
AFMA	Australian Fisheries Management Authority
AGRAGA	Advisory Group on the Reform of Australian Government Administration
ALP	Australian Labor Party
ANAO	Australian National Audit Office
ANU	Australian National University
ANZSOG	Australia and New Zealand School of Government
APA	Airline Partners Australia
APRA	Australian Prudential Regulation Authority
APS	Australian Public Service
APS Values	Public Service values in the PS Act
APSC	Australian Public Service Commission
ASIC	Australian Securities and Investments Commission
ASX	Australian Securities Exchange
ASX CGC	Australian Securities Exchange Corporate Governance Council
AWB	Australian Wheat Board
CAC Act	*Commonwealth Authorities and Companies Act 1997 (Cth)*
CEO	chief executive officer
CFAR	Commonwealth Financial Accountability Review
COAG	Council of Australian Governments
DEWHA	Department of the Environment, Water, Heritage and the Arts
DFAT	Department of Foreign Affairs and Trade
DIMA	Department of Immigration and Multicultural Affairs, formerly Department of Immigration
Finance	Department of Finance and Deregulation (DFD), formerly Department of Finance and Administration (DFA)
FMA Act	*Financial Management and Accountability Act 1997 (Cth)*
FOI	freedom of information
GBE	government business enterprise
GFC	global financial crisis
HCA	High Court of Australia
HIP	Home Insulation Program

IAPP	International Association for Public Participation
ICT	information and communication technology
IDC	interdepartmental committee
MAC	management advisory committee
NPM	new public management
NRM	natural resource management
OECD	Organisation for Economic Co-operation and Development
PBS	portfolio budget statements
PM&C	Department of the Prime Minister and Cabinet
PPP	public-private partnership
PS Act	*Public Service Act 1999 (Cth)*
RBA	Reserve Bank of Australia
RBB	Reserve Bank Board
SBS	Special Broadcast Service
SCAG	Standing Committee of Attorneys-General
SRA	shared responsibility agreement
Treasury	Department of Treasury
UK	United Kingdom
WEA	Wheat Export Authority

Introduction

This book examines public governance in the Australian Commonwealth public sector, especially from the late-twentieth century to the early twenty-first century. This a period in which public governance has been informed and influenced by the principles and actions of private sector corporate governance but also, more generally, by how government departments and agencies, in their decision-making processes, increasingly relate to other government bodies and to organisations outside the government sector.

There are at least three strong reasons for the interest in the topic of public sector governance. One reason is the trend toward a general acceptance by government of the need to include more players in decision-making processes and to find new means of dealing with public policy questions. Another reason is the extent of the public sector's incorporation of private sector and market experiences. A final reason lies in renewed attention to the role of government in an era of increased political, socio-economic and environmental interconnectedness, which is demonstrated worldwide through particular governmental responses to collective challenges, such as climate change and the 2008–09 global financial crisis.

This book concentrates on the Commonwealth level of government. Focusing primarily upon this level provides a common point of reference for those studying or engaged in governance, given the similarities and differences across all Australian jurisdictions. It also matches the focus that rests on the Australian Government within much of the literature (e.g. Keating, Wanna and Weller 2000) and key governance reform initiatives. Most importantly, the gradual expansion of Commonwealth power under the Australian Constitution, at the expense of the states and territories, makes the Commonwealth level of government pivotal in governance initiatives that are influential across levels of government in addressing cross-jurisdictional concerns, such as water management and conservation. So, this book also offers comparative insights for those charged with reviewing, reforming, or otherwise studying governance at other levels of government within Australia or in other countries.

Governance reform and terminology

From the 1980s, public sector reform drew on private sector ideas and practices in moving from traditional public administration to a public management approach. The language of corporate governance was transferred to the public sector as both an expression of that and through the need to revisit how to provide a corporate basis for transforming organisations in rapidly changing environments. This marked the first stage, in the 1990s, of the public sector's appropriation of corporate governance models that drew on corporate law and governance in the sector's design of legislation for statutory corporations and agencies (i.e. the *Commonwealth Authorities and Companies Act 1997* (CAC Act)), as well as in major governance reviews of the early twenty-first century (e.g. Uhrig 2003). Governance modelling of the public sector upon the private sector also developed within a broader system of multi-level points of entry for enhanced central coordination and control of public sector bodies (Halligan 2006; and MacDermott 2008).

As the thinking about corporate governance in the public sector matured and the fixation on the private sector passed, at least in public administration, the term 'public governance' also came into use. The differences in values between the public and private sectors, and in the dynamics of the relationships with shareholders and stakeholders, necessarily affected the automatic transference of ideas. The most notable conversion was that of the Australian National Audit Office (ANAO) which, having been the primary advocate of corporate governance within the public sector, in 2003 adopted 'public sector governance' for its guidelines.

In addition, 'governance' has entered the parlance of practice as a generic term that covers the internal workings of government as well as its interactions with others beyond the public sector itself. Within the rubric of governance, two applications reflect the activities and organisational basis of public agencies. Core corporate governance principles apply most directly to government enterprises, particularly public authorities with a board and other attributes that correspond to a private sector organisation. But there are also applications more generally to public organisations throughout the public sector, including departments of state.

The Australian Government currently uses both corporate and public governance concepts. For example, the Department of the Prime Minister and Cabinet refers to corporate governance as the process for directing and controlling agencies. The ANAO lists governance principles that cover accountability, transparency/ openness, integrity, stewardship and leadership. This book seeks to examine these various elements within a general conception of governance that illustrates the interconnections between organisations, levels and sectors.

Contemporary governance landscape

The contemporary governance landscape in Australia has a number of regulatory landmarks and reform milestones. The regulatory landmarks in the late-twentieth and early twenty-first centuries include the package of legislation for the governance framework (especially the CAC Act, *Financial Management and Accountability Act 1997* (FMA Act) and *Public Service Act 1999* (PS Act)), as well as the official governance guidance that has been produced in various forms by the Department of Finance and Deregulation (Finance), ANAO and other government agencies. Under official policy, public organisations can be formed under the FMA Act when they are departments of state or other budget-funded agencies, while the authorities or companies of the outer public sector are regulated under the CAC Act.

The reform milestones of the twenty-first century's first decade, which have significant governance implications, consist primarily of two government reports that examine Australian Commonwealth public administration: the *Review of the Corporate Governance of Statutory Authorities and Office Holders* (Uhrig review) in 2003 and *Ahead of the Game: Blueprint for the Reform of Australian Government Administration* (*Ahead of the Game*) in 2010. While there are additional reforms of discrete aspects of Australian Commonwealth public administration, these two reports have been pivotal in setting governance frameworks for the Commonwealth public sector as a whole, with flow-on implications for governance structures and arrangements at the organisational level for public sector bodies.

Each report reflects different conceptions, reform phases, and central government priorities for governance. Similarly, each report presents major challenges in creating and administering public sector bodies for the ends that they serve in a new era of governance. The reform of organisational governance structures and arrangements that is signalled in these two reports continues in aspects of the Commonwealth Financial Accountability Review (CFAR), which Finance began in late 2010 and continued to pursue as this book went to press in 2012. The major public discussion paper to have been released as part of the CFAR in early 2012, *Is Less More?: Towards Better Commonwealth Performance* (DFD 2012b), takes the improvement of governance arrangements for a whole-of-government financial framework to a new level. In several chapters, this book takes into account the connections and disconnections between these governance reform milestones.

Orientations and audiences

As this introductory discussion shows, governance is a subject that can be studied from multiple disciplinary and work-situated standpoints. The concepts, regulation and practices of governance draw insights from public administration, management and law. This is reflected, for example, in the multidisciplinary backgrounds of the book's co-authors. Governance is therefore relevant as a topic of study by academics and students in many different courses and fields of research, and by those engaged in the work of governance both within and outside the formal structures and processes of government. To assist the book's various audiences, it contains key tables and figures, case studies and other examples, and relevant insights and models for reform that have been derived from experience internationally.

In addressing public governance, the co-authors are also mindful of what it has not been possible to cover within this book. Sub-national government only appears in the relationship of state and territory government to the Commonwealth government. Under revitalised notions of cooperative federalism, this is an increasingly important interaction in its own right. While the political executive is ever present, it is not at the core of this study, even though in practice it is the pivot of public governance in its governmental dimension. The significance of the political executive is evident as the source of policy initiative, the political dynamic and democratically based leadership, as well as a source of the limitations of good and effective governance. There are of course other studies that consider these matters as well as governance in sectoral terms (e.g. Brown and Bellamy 2007), and the increasing importance of the civil society aspects of governance (Osborne 2010).

The analysis of governance directions in this book focuses mainly upon developments in the last quarter of the twentieth century and the early stages of the twenty-first century. In particular, this analysis takes into account the approach to governance of John Howard's Coalition government from 1996 to 2007, as well as the Labor government's handling of public governance issues under the leadership of both Kevin Rudd and Prime Minister Julia Gillard to the end of 2011. As CFAR continued into 2012, this book also positions this major official initiative and its governance implications within the broader timeline of governance reform.

Structure

The first part of the book examines the context and frameworks of governance in its relevant forms. Chapter 1 explores several dimensions of governance as a baseline for its discrete explorations in subsequent chapters, including the different meanings and the growing use of more expansive and inclusive conceptions. Chapter 2 then examines the rise of corporate and public governance, considering in particular the evolution of official principles and practice that has occurred during the last three decades. Chapter 3 considers the defining tensions that arise in the assimilation of corporate governance with public sector governance more generally. This is informed by evidence-based assessment of the underlying tensions.

The second part addresses governance in the public sector, with chapters that focus upon discrete features of governance, including system governance, departmental governance, board governance, and participatory governance. Chapter 4 focuses upon central government and cross-government activity. This is followed by two chapters on distinctive organisations and their governance: chapter 5 which explores governance of the departments of state, and chapter 6 which considers board governance of authorities and state-owned companies. Chapter 7 explores the way in which citizens may be engaged in the policy process.

The final part looks at key challenges for governance design and implementation. Chapter 8 is concerned with how to create or restructure public sector bodies and chapter 9 explores crucial issues that arise in appointing CEOs and directors to boards of authorities and bodies.

The book concludes in chapter 10 with a review of directions in public governance in Australia and overseas as a result of various challenges, in particular those that arise from the demands of integration within central government and collaboration across the public sector and with other sectors. It highlights the increasing permeability of government boundaries and the implications of this for public accountability.

Part I. Context and Framework

1. Dimensions of Governance for the Public Sector

Governance is concerned with how societies, governments and organisations are managed and led. Importantly, this includes how they structure and otherwise order their affairs, make decisions and exercise powers, and manage their relationships and accountabilities. Official governance frameworks and standards, which have been developed across sectoral and geographical boundaries, contain commonalities and differences in their illumination of key governance concepts, principles and applications. These features are not developed in a social, political and legal vacuum; they reflect underlying values, practices and other norms of governance, they are enshrined in the governance architecture and arrangements for Australia's system of government and public administration, and they are responsive to the evolution of governance thinking and practice over time.

Accordingly, this chapter explores the basic concepts and facets of governance and its governmental architecture, primarily as they relate to the Australian Commonwealth public sector, but with relevance for other Australian jurisdictions and comparable Westminster-based systems. It provides a connecting thread between underlying governance values and other norms, levels and components of governance, and the significance of looking at governance from a series of societal, governmental, sectoral and organisational perspectives. In doing so, it offers a glimpse of how emerging changes and limits to key aspects of the system of governance in the twenty-first century present challenges for the Commonwealth level of government and its public sector system. Finally, it introduces central themes of 'horizontal' and 'vertical' governance, 'hard' and 'soft' forms of governance, and other analytical tools for understanding, regulating and practising governance. This chapter's discussion of these different dimensions of governance serves as a foundation for the analysis of governance in later chapters.

The problems of 'governance-talk'

'Governance' has several meanings, a range of elements and sectoral contexts, and a variety of dimensions and forms. These differences are not reducible simply to matters of terminology. For example, the focus of governance for governments and others trying to coordinate mutual responses to national or global public policy problems is very different from its focus for any particular organisation in administering its own affairs or playing a role within a larger enterprise. Similarly, the origins and manifestations of governance vary across national, sectoral and organisational boundaries. Moreover, the focus of the study and practice of governance also varies according to the institutional or individual standpoint from which governance is examined.

This problem in talking about governance is exacerbated when its literature and official governance reviews offer only partial glimpses of the full complexity of governance. The normative evaluation and operational implications of alternative governance approaches and options for government can only be assessed holistically if the right number and combination of governance aspects are captured. So, every account of governance must be assessed according to how it relates to the whole picture of governance, both generally and for the purpose at hand. In particular, this affects scrutiny and evaluation of the governance frameworks outlined in the literature as well as landmark governance-related reforms within government (chapter 2).

At the same time, if it is viewed primarily as a mass of complex and interactive layers and applications, governance risks losing its conceptual and operational effectiveness as an organising concept. The different discussions of governance throughout this book show that there are important levels on which discrete considerations of governance are both possible and necessary. The governance of organisations in the public and private sectors has different contexts and features, for example, and can be discussed sensibly in each case without escalation at every point to their interactions with each other or society as a whole. The present point is simply that those interactions also demand attention where they are relevant, and that discussions of governance and its applications are incomplete without appropriate attention to them.

The next part of this chapter therefore commences with a taxonomy of governance and orders of analysis that can be brought to bear in understanding the true complexity of the concept in the contemporary Australian Commonwealth public sector. This is followed by a categorisation of the different values and other norms that infuse the political and legal infrastructure for governance at this level of government, only some of which are captured explicitly in legislation that is focused upon public sector values. Together, these opening parts serve as a platform for understanding some of the key drivers and features of evolving governance reform in this country (chapter 2), the resultant tensions in the political and legal architecture of governance (chapter 3), and their collective implications for governance interactions at central, organisational, and stakeholder levels within the Commonwealth public sector (chapters 4–7).

Meanings and components of governance

Framing the taxonomy of governance

Most commentators now accept the futility of trying to develop an ideal one-size-fits-all definition or model of governance, as well as the importance of systemic, jurisdictional and other underlying contexts for the usefulness of any definitions or models of governance that are used. Just as there is no single and universal theory of corporations across disciplines, so too 'there is no one theory of governance in political science and public administration' (Chhotray and Stoker 2009: 26). Nor does law or any other discipline supply such an overarching theory of governance.

At its most basic level, governance covers 'the management of the course of events in a social system', whether such systems are conceived in organisational, sectoral or broader terms (Horrigan 2010: 49; quoting Burris et al 2005: 30). In that sense, the governance of systems embraces their structures, internal and external interactions, and modes of decision-making and other behaviour. In this vein, Chhotray and Stoker formulate an all-embracing definition of 'governance' as follows (2009: 3):

> Governance is about the rules of collective decision-making in settings where there are a plurality of actors or organisations and where no formal control system can dictate the terms of the relationship between these actors and organisations.

In short, governance is concerned with how and why systems of all kinds are constituted and operated.

Beyond the commonly agreed position that all kinds of governance across the public, private, and community sectors require attention to core elements such as performance and accountability, each of those features also has different levels of meaning, application and context, about which there is relatively less consensus. Finally, all conceptions and definitions of governance-related concepts are contingent upon the particular scholarly, regulatory or other perspective that governance observers and participants bring to their governance standpoint or role (e.g. OECD 2002).

Recent debate about governance has focused on the extent to which it is government-orientated (as distinct from society-centric and, thus, involving non-state participants), relationship-focused (as distinct from hierarchical and authority-based), and network-centred (as distinct from organisation-based). The question of which of these models or orientations best suits the twenty-first century governance environment is problematic because each provides different insights into different dimensions of governance. In other words, they each reveal part of the broader complexity of governance within and beyond government.

All of this reinforces the central point that governance within a public sector context comprises different orders of governance — governance of a public sector body, within a whole-of-government approach to governance, sometimes across levels of government, and often involving governance interactions beyond the public sector. To foreshadow a later discussion, these different orders of governance are themselves underpinned by 'horizontal' and 'vertical' dimensions of governance, as well as manifested through 'hard' and 'soft' forms of governance.

Different concepts of governance

As governance is a multi-dimensional concept, the term 'governance' is used differently depending upon the frame of analysis, the standpoint of the observer and the particular sector or aspect under scrutiny. Understood from an organisational perspective, for example, the corporate governance of a public sector body connects to other orders of governance at governmental, societal and organisational levels.

The concept of 'the state' as a nation (with associated governance and regulatory dimensions) can be contrasted with the concept of self-governing states and territories in a federal system of government, as exists in Australia, Canada and the United States.[1] As the role of the nation-state has changed under the pressures of new governance and the new regulatory state (chapter 2), so too must our understanding of the nature and forms of governance. Governance is increasingly responsive, for example, to multi-stakeholder standard-setting, non-state engagement in policy networks, external and independent monitoring of government, and the pressures of participatory governance and deliberative democracy (e.g. Chhotray and Stoker 2009: 48–51). One of this chapter's themes is that there are connections between different senses of governance, state-centric and society-centric standpoints on governance, and the engagement of state and non-state actors in the ongoing evolution of democratic mechanisms.

As the Australian Public Service Commission (APSC) acknowledges in its assessment of the new environment for public sector performance and accountability, the old governance model of 'hierarchical modes of decision-

---

1   Unless the context suggests otherwise, references in this chapter to 'the state' and associated terms and contrasts (e.g. 'non-state influences') are references to the nation-state, rather than to a particular Australian state or territory, such as the state of Victoria. The use of terms such as 'the regulatory state' and 'non-state influences' signals the emergence of a distinct body of cross-disciplinary regulatory studies that focuses upon the distinct and related regulatory roles of both state and non-state entities (e.g. corporations).

making', 'sequential approaches to problem solving', and 'single points of accountability' no longer fits all governmental functions and must adapt to accommodate 'new public policy implementation models' that are more 'collaborative' and be otherwise responsive to policy challenges that straddle traditional departmental lines of authority (APSC 2009b: 1–2). This view of governance in transition also reflects aspects of vertical and horizontal governance.

In this way, governance now engages multiple institutions and participants in multiple governance interactions. Various governance systems containing 'a plurality of actors' interact with one another in a series of 'interconnected governance networks', employing multiple mechanisms for distributing, wielding, and rendering accountable the exercise of power in society. At this level, governance focuses upon 'the mechanisms (institutions, social norms, social practices)' through which social goods such as 'democracy, honest and efficient government, political stability and the rule of law' are 'instantiated' in such systems (Burris et al 2005: 30–1).

The outcomes of the Governance Stream at Australia's 2020 Summit, for example, focus in part on 'the need to strengthen the participation of Australians in their governance'. This occurs in part through the development of 'innovative mechanisms to increase civic participation [and] collaborative governance to strengthen civic engagement and trust, facilitate "deliberative democracy" and strengthen citizen engagement' (PM&C 2008: 32–3). In turn, this idea of citizen engagement has thematic links with collaborative governance within government (chapters 4 and 5) as well as participatory governance with societal stakeholders (chapter 7).

Nation-states and governments remain central to all systems of governance, regulation and responsibility (Bell and Hindmoor 2009), but there are ongoing fundamental changes in how governments engage with the people and how the people hold those who wield institutional power accountable. So, while governments therefore remain firmly at the helm in their own right or, alternatively, at the centre of networks that are devoted to national and global public policy development, non-state institutions and actors are increasingly coming to the fore, especially through multi-stakeholder standard-setting initiatives and extra-governmental mechanisms of societal scrutiny (e.g. Keane 2009: 688–89). This development also relates to democracy's evolution to embrace such features, as is considered later in this chapter. Indeed, as this chapter shows, there are strong connections between governmental and non-governmental stakeholders, their involvement in different democratic mechanisms, and various orders of governance and their underlying values.

A number of different but related governance concepts are therefore discussed in the following sections, including: (a) *public* governance (extending out from the government sector to the private and community sectors); (b) *public sector* governance (i.e. governance of the administration and business of government); and (c) *corporate* (or organisational) governance (i.e. the governance of particular bodies in particular sectors). Each of these concepts of governance, which are represented in Table 1.1, can be viewed from national, comparative or global perspectives.

Table 1.1: Governance concepts

Level of analysis	Macro	Meso	Micro
Description	Public governance	Public sector governance	Corporate governance
Focus	Society ⇦	⇨ Government ⇦	⇨ Organisation

The close relationship between public governance, public sector governance and corporate governance sits within the broader framework of other societal and global governance, as is outlined earlier in this chapter. Farrar explains the relationship between the different orders of governance as follows (Farrar 2008: 6–7, quoting respectively Keasey, Thompson and Wright 1997: 2; and Cioffi and Cohen 2000: 307, 313):

> In a wide sense, corporate governance includes 'the entire network of formal and informal relations involving the corporate sector and their consequences for society in general'. It can be seen as 'the nexus of law, markets, public and private hierarchies, and national and international political economies'. It is capable of subsumption under broader concepts of contractual and social governance. Every country approaches corporate governance from the background of its own distinctive culture ... In any study of corporate governance we must, therefore, look at other systems and consider the evolving norms of 'global' corporate governance. Indeed corporate governance provides a good perspective for viewing some of the contradictions in globalisation.

An understanding of governance in the Commonwealth public sector requires comprehension of at least some of these related governance concepts, both in their own right and in how they relate to it. As outlined in what follows, the sharpest point of distinction for present purposes is between 'corporate governance' as conventionally understood and what is described as 'public sector governance' in official or suggested governance frameworks at more than one level of government in Australia (ANAO 2003c: 5–6; Weller and Webbe 2008: [4.2.4]). This point draws support from the statement by Patrick Weller and Simone Webbe that 'different constitutional, legislative and environmental considerations steer variances in the respective practice, and results, for corporate governance and public sector governance' (2008: 28). Thus, the different conceptions of governance offer insights on different parts of the complex whole that is 'governance'.

Public governance

Public governance occupies a central place in this scheme of governance-related concepts. It focuses upon governance within the public domain at large, including but not limited to the function and operation of government. This acknowledges that governance in the public sector covers broader processes extending beyond the formal structures of government (e.g. Davis and Keating 2000). Public governance, therefore, embraces not only governance as it relates to the institutions and business of government, but also government's engagement with non-government parties in the governance process. Considered from this perspective, the general notion of 'governance' (and 'governing') is conventionally associated with 'the processes that create the conditions for ordered rule and collective action within the public realm' (Chhotray and Stoker 2009: 71).

In the age of 'new public governance' (chapter 2), for example, governance in the guise of 'public governance' can be broken down into subcategories such as 'socio-political governance' (i.e. governance of societal relations), 'public policy governance' (i.e. governance of the public policy process), 'administrative governance' (i.e. governance of the business of government), 'contract (or third party) governance' (i.e. governance of public procurement and contracted service delivery to the people), and 'network governance' (i.e. governance through state and non-state networks that are engaged in policy-making and public service delivery) (Osborne 2010: 6–7). Collaborative governance, which is raised in chapters 2, 4 and 5, might also be added to this list, given its operation within and between levels of government, and even beyond government (e.g. participatory governance: see chapter 7), as well as its relationship to some of these governance spheres (e.g. network governance). Public sector governance also straddles several of these spheres.

As such, public governance embraces relations between different governments and societies as well as relations within the one society and level of government. In this sense, it captures 'that other sense of "governance" … which sees our communities "governed" through complex interactions between the public (government), private (market) and civil (third) sectors, emphasising the importance of constructive networking between these sectors' (Wettenhall 2005: 42). More broadly, the debate between 'society-centric' and 'state-centric' views of governance (Bell and Hindmoor 2009: 71) can be seen as part of a wider evolution in ideas, forms, and tools of governance that remains a work-in-progress on multiple levels, not least in the public sector (Chhotray and Stoker 2009: 16–26).

This particular conception of governance can also be viewed within the broader perspective of global public governance, in which transnational government networks operate as the hubs of a series of interconnected networks, which involve governmental, business, and community actors who are all engaged 'in the pursuit of a larger conception of the global public interest' (Slaughter 2004). The point in common is that public governance is integrally involved with government, but also transcends government at both national and international levels.

Despite public governance's increased attention to governance networks that involve a range of actors (Rhodes 1997), the state-centric perspective has remained highly influential, and covers several approaches: top-down authority and control (e.g. law and coercion), network steering by government, policy and regulatory instruments (focused on effectiveness and efficiency) and the role of institutions (Peters and Pierre 2000: 37–46). Operating within this frame, 'governance' is regarded as 'the tools, strategies, and relationships used by governments to help govern' (Bell and Hindmoor 2009: 2). This more discrete and government-focused notion of governance resonates particularly with public sector governance and its focus upon the 'steering' role of government in society (chapter 4).

Public sector governance

Public sector governance focuses attention more discretely upon governance within the public sector generally, or a designated level of government in particular. This is distinct from the broader conceptions of 'public governance', which were considered in the preceding section. Governance within the formal system of government remains a distinct dimension of governance in its own right. It deserves separate consideration.

Public sector governance concentrates upon governance as applied to the governance of organisations within and across the government sector, including different levels of government and their interactions with one another and other societal groups. So, public sector governance is not limited to governance as applied only to the formal administration of government, largely through the executive branch of government. In the context of the system of government and public administration that lies at the core of public sector governance, the 'steering' role of government is paramount (chapter 4), not least in terms of the 'capacity of government to make and implement policy — in other words, to steer society' (Pierre and Peters 2000: 1).

In material that has been endorsed by the Australian National Audit Office (ANAO), Prime Minister and Cabinet (PM&C), and APSC, 'governance' is defined in the context of Australian public administration as 'the set of responsibilities and practices, policies and procedures, exercised by an agency's executive to provide strategic direction, ensure objectives are achieved, manage risks and use resources responsibly and with accountability' (ANAO and PM&C 2006: 13; APSC 2008). This definition of governance straddles corporate governance (see discussion below) and public sector governance. Similarly, the ANAO framework for public sector governance also straddles these different conceptions of governance, as follows (ANAO 2003c: 6):

> The term 'public sector governance' has been chosen to focus this guide on the governance arrangements for public sector organisations at the Commonwealth level in Australia, as outlined in the definition below.

> Public sector governance has a very broad coverage, including how an organisation is managed, its corporate and other structures, its culture, its policies and strategies and the way it deals with its various stakeholders. The concept encompasses the manner in which public sector organisations acquit their responsibilities of stewardship by being open, accountable and prudent in decision-making, in providing policy advice, and in managing and delivering programs.

Considered from within the system of government, Commonwealth governmental bodies are responsive to one or more sources of public sector regulatory influence, according to their organisational type. This system of monitoring and review includes portfolio oversight and extends beyond the Commonwealth public sector and its members to other components of the executive arm of government (e.g. auditor-general, ombudsman, and other mechanisms of administrative review).

However, considered from a broader governance perspective, Commonwealth governmental bodies are also increasingly subject to an array of public scrutiny and influence. So, this system of monitoring and review also extends to other arms of constitutional government (e.g. judicial review and parliamentary committee scrutiny) and, even further, to the non-government sector and community as well. To the extent that this reflects enhanced scrutiny of government and input into public policy and standard-setting from organisations and communities outside of government, it resonates with the tension that exists between state-centric and society-centric views of governance. It also connects with the concerns of monitory, deliberative and participatory democracy (Gutmann and Thompson 2004; and Keane 2009), as discussed later in this chapter.

Corporate governance

Corporate governance in the public sector focuses upon the governance of organisations in that sector, as well as upon the governance of their relations and interactions with others, both within and beyond the sector. In official governance guidance for Australian public administration, terms such as 'public sector governance' and 'governance' in the context of the centre of government are often contrasted with those such as 'corporate governance', to avoid 'any perceived ambiguity concerning the application of the term "corporate" to "non-corporate" public sector organisations' (Barrett 2003: 5).

By way of comparison with the private sector, the Australian Securities Exchange Corporate Governance Council's (ASX CGC's) *Corporate Governance Principles and Recommendations* state that corporate governance 'encompasses the mechanisms by which companies, and those in control, are held to account' and 'influences how the objectives of the company are set and achieved, how risk is monitored and assessed, and how performance is optimised' (2010: 3). Here, the ASX CGC also draws upon the HIH Royal Commission's view of corporate governance (which is considered, along with other authoritative definitions of corporate governance, in chapter 2). Still, as the ASX CGC also acknowledges (2010: 3): 'There is no single model of good corporate governance.'

The perception of standard corporate governance elements such as performance, conformance and accountability is affected by the prism of constitutionalism, managerialism, or any other organising theory of public administration that holds sway from time to time (chapter 2). Contemporary understanding and use of core corporate governance concepts such as 'accountability' occur against a background of recent governmental reform history in which 'arguments about independence, accountability and efficiency are endemic to the "new managerialism"' (Bottomley 1994: 529). Public law's concern with judicial review of administrative action has similarly meant grappling with the forces that are unleashed by 'new managerialism' (Bayne 1991: 17).

As this connection between governance trends and elements confirms, the literature on governance at the organisational level strongly identifies it with at least the elements of performance, legal and policy compliance, and multiple accountabilities. To these can be added factors such as assurance, management and planning, as well as leadership, ethics and even fairness (e.g. Barrett 2003: 7–8). Based upon authoritative governance guides for Australian public administration (e.g. ANAO 2003c: 13–15), a more nuanced cataloguing of governance elements might further divide them into groups of substantive elements (e.g. conformance, performance and accountability), qualitative elements (e.g. fairness, integrity, leadership and ethics), structural elements (e.g. management, committee and advisory structures) and functional elements (e.g. planning, resourcing, management (at several levels), monitoring and reporting).

Commonwealth bodies that are responsible for its oversight describe corporate governance as providing 'a framework for the management and accountability of key decision-making bodies' (DFA 2001). A more expansive conception involves integrating 'the main elements of corporate governance within a holistic framework, which are communicated effectively throughout the entire organisation and underpinned by a corporate culture of accountability, transparency, commitment and integrity' (Barrett 2002b).

Considered mainly from the organisational perspective placed within a wider public sector context, the APSC views agency governance as follows (APSC 2010a):

> While there is no 'one size fits all' approach to governance, it is important to realise that effective governance will contain the following building blocks:

- 'strong leadership, culture and communication';
- 'appropriate governance committee structures';
- 'clear accountability mechanisms';
- 'comprehensive risk management, compliance and assurance systems';
- 'strategic planning, performance monitoring and evaluation';
- 'flexible and evolving principles-based systems'; and
- 'effective operation across organisational boundaries'.

However, there are limits to simply listing or cataloguing governance elements at an organisational level. First, each of governance's key elements has multiple guises. Management embraces management of risks, personnel, resources, and relationships. Accountability not only embraces internal and external constituencies and mechanisms, but also embraces different functions such as monitoring, evaluation, and review.

Secondly, their meaning and application are each subject to sectoral nuances. The organisational and regulatory architecture for the accountability of corporations in the private sector differs in important ways from that which applies to organisations in the public sector. This is illustrated by the difference between accountability to shareholding ministers of state-owned enterprises and accountability to shareholders who hold and trade shares in a regulated stock market (chapter 2). Similarly, the kind of stakeholder consultation and engagement that is followed within government circles in the development and implementation of public policy (chapter 7) differs from the kind of stakeholder engagement that characterises publicly listed companies under prevailing standards of corporate governance.

Thirdly, under some conventional notions of governance, there is a tendency to limit too narrowly the relationship between owners, managers, and constituencies. In the private sector context, this means conceiving of governance only in terms of the relationship between a company, its board and management, and its shareholding 'owners'. In the public sector context, equivalent narrowing occurs when governance attention is focused solely upon the relations between a department's or agency's governing body, its CEO, and relevant ministers of state (Barrett 2003: 5). Such a limited conception of public sector governance risks overlooking the governance significance and nuances of 'the systems, processes, policies and strategies that direct operations, assure quality, monitor performance, and help manage [board and CEO] obligations to stakeholders' (Barrett 2003: 5).

Finally, simply listing or cataloguing elements of governance in the abstract says nothing about the relationship and synchronicity between those elements. In other words, it is one thing to identify elements of governance and something different to show how those components relate to one another in a coherent and workable notion of governance. Focusing upon the related notion of corporate governance in primarily a private sector context, Steven Cole suggests that a conception of corporate governance whose crux is the alignment of its different components (Cole 2002). According to his view, corporate governance involves the organisational systems and processes that align the roles and responsibilities of managers with the corporation's internal and external relationships to produce strategic, measurable and otherwise accountable outcomes. This produces a holistic view of corporate governance, especially from the practical perspective of those responsible for governing an organisation.

These limits to the listing of corporate governance elements in the abstract can be contrasted with the beneficial emergence of principle-based frameworks for corporate governance. Examples already exist of principle-based frameworks of corporate governance for public sector bodies and environments, to be compared and contrasted with those that now prevail for listed public companies in Australia (e.g. ASX CGC 2010), New Zealand, the United Kingdom and elsewhere. The Independent Commission on Good Governance in Public Services in the United Kingdom, for example, identifies 'six core principles of good governance' in its *Good Governance Standard for Public Services*. According to this standard, the requirements of 'good governance' include the following six elements (OPM and CIPFA 2004: 5):

- 'focusing on the organisation's purpose and on outcomes for citizens and service users';
- 'performing effectively in clearly defined functions and roles';
- 'promoting values for the whole organisation and demonstrating the values of good governance through behaviour';
- 'taking informed transparent decisions and managing risk';
- 'developing the capacity and capability of the governing body to be effective'; and
- 'engaging stakeholders and making accountability real'.

Such principle-based frameworks across the private and public sectors are characteristically seen as more flexible and less prescriptive than rule-based frameworks, therefore allowing more room for customisation to particular organisations and other circumstances. The distinction between principle-based and rule-based standards also corresponds to that between soft and hard law. The relationship in each case is also interdependent given, for example, the significance of governance legislation for ancillary governance guidelines and principles within each sector.

The use of principle-based standards within the Commonwealth public sector is evidenced by the frameworks underpinning the Commonwealth Financial Accountability Review (CFAR) and the Australian government's governance guidelines for Commonwealth government business enterprises (GBEs), both of which were released in 2011. For example, the former rests upon principles of 'comprehensiveness' (e.g. clarity of objectives and accountabilities), 'flexibility' (e.g. technological adaptability) and 'user-friendliness' (e.g. ease of understanding and accessibility) (DFD 2011a), and the latter is underpinned by a common set of key principles of governance responsibility and accountability for all Commonwealth GBEs (DFD 2011b). Both, however, are also supported by relevant governance legislation for the sector.

From governance conceptions to governance planes and forms

In summary, the relation and nuances between public governance, public sector governance, and corporate governance in the public sector extend beyond mere grammatical differences, to express differences in scope, orientation and context as well. These three different conceptions of governance can be compared and contrasted with official and other authoritative definitions of governance (especially corporate governance) in the wider literature (chapter 2).

Just as analytical distinctions can be made between these related governance conceptions, so too can analytical distinctions be made between different planes and forms of governance. Two major analytical distinctions are commonly made in the literature — one between 'horizontal' and 'vertical' planes of governance, and the other between 'hard' and 'soft' forms of governance. These distinctions and their significance for the Commonwealth public sector are outlined next.

The relationship between these governance conceptions, planes and forms is two-fold. The governance planes and forms apply to each of the different conceptions of governance discussed here, and therefore transcend any particular sector or jurisdiction. In addition, any governance model that purports to approach the full complexity of governance in the contemporary business of government must pay some attention, at least, to these different conceptions, horizontal and vertical planes, and hard and soft forms of governance, to which this chapter now turns.

'Horizontal' and 'vertical' governance

As applied to government, the notions of 'vertical' and 'horizontal' governance apply to relations within and across different levels of government. In addition to governing itself, for example, a public sector body might liaise with other agencies within the same government (under a whole-of-government governance framework), its equivalents in other levels of government (as in cooperative federalism), and its counterparts in other countries (as in trans-Tasman cooperative regimes and other regional initiatives). Moreover, it might have governance interactions beyond the government sector. This more expansive notion of the 'horizontal' and 'vertical' dimensions of governance is a theme that underpins several chapters in this book.

The distinction between horizontal and vertical governance can be viewed successively from system-based, sector-based and organisation-based standpoints, with network-based governance cutting across one or more of these standpoints. The usefulness of this distinction as an analytical tool for understanding important features of governance is evidenced by its incorporation in official guidance from the APSC on the overall responsibility and accountability framework for the Commonwealth public sector. As identified in key guidance for the Australian Public Service (APS), for example, 'the traditional model of accountability describes a vertical chain that provides a continuum of accountability relationships between the electorate, the Parliament, the Government and the public service', which is matched by administrative law developments that 'have extended and strengthened the horizontal accountability of public servants and Ministers' (APSC 2009b: 6). The APSC also states that 'public servants are accountable mostly through a vertical and hierarchical chain, but it does include some horizontal accountability to external review bodies', and also adds that 'other horizontal accountability arrangements are emerging' (APSC 2009b: 8).

In its most basic and conventional form, the distinction between horizontal and vertical governance refers to the notional vertical line that exists between the inner governance of an organisation and those to whom it is ultimately answerable (e.g. ministers and the centre of government), together with the notional horizontal line of outer governance relationships for organisations with others in the public sector and beyond. This simple horizontal-vertical governance dichotomy is packed with underlying nuances about the shifting core of essential governmental activity, the rise of non-state influences upon public governance, the swinging pendulum between centralisation and fragmentation of executive government control, and both the relevance and limits of hierarchical chains of institutional authority and accountability (Chhotray and Stoker 2009: 18–23; Bell and Hindmoor 2009: 85–9).

The distinction between horizontal and vertical governance has relevance for other modes of governance, such as participatory and networked governance. The relationship between these various modes of governance is a key feature of contemporary governance frameworks for the public sector. As confirmed by the initial public discussion paper for the CFAR, which was released in early March 2012, 'traditional models for delivering public services, based on vertical and hierarchical governance and accountability, need to be complemented by participative and networked arrangements' (DFD 2012b: 7). This is critical in meeting a number of CFAR's possible outcomes, including 'an opportunity to develop a more coherent, portfolio-based governance framework, which rebalances devolution and accountability' (DFD 2012b: 88).

Viewed beyond their application within a single organisation, these horizontal and vertical planes of governance can also extend outwards in a series of concentric circles of coverage. This wider coverage includes: horizontal and vertical interactions within one level of government (e.g. 'public sector governance': ANAO 2003c); horizontal relations between levels of government (e.g. COAG agreements); governance interactions between multiple organs of government at national and transnational levels (e.g. 'horizontal government networks' and 'vertical government networks' across 'disaggregated' nation-states: Slaughter 2004); and governance interactions between governmental and non-governmental institutions and actors. These various planes of governance are present, for example, in the institutional governance tensions that are identified in chapter 3, the nature of participatory governance as outlined in chapter 7, and the society-centric and other conceptions of governance canvassed in this chapter.

'Hard' and 'soft' governance

Connections exist between horizontal and vertical planes of governance, on one hand, and 'hard' and 'soft' forms of governance, on the other. In managing horizontal and vertical governance from organisational and other standpoints, much depends upon the successful marriage of the external and internal influences upon an organisation's governance, and the hard and soft aspects of governance. This necessity reinforces the holistic nature of governance.

The distinction between hard and soft governance throws light on the complete set of factors that characterise well-governed organisations, including not only formal and structural aspects (i.e. 'hard' governance factors) but also behavioural and relational aspects (i.e. 'soft' governance factors; e.g. Edwards and Clough 2005). In terms of the private sector, leading empirical studies of effective boards bring both hard and soft factors together, for example, in a complete picture of board efficiency and effectiveness that embraces board structures, membership and skills mix, and processes and behaviours (Leblanc and Gillies 2005: 139; see chapter 6, in this volume, further on board governance). Similarly, in terms of the public sector, the formal (e.g. structural) features of institutional governance architecture, such as legislated whole-of-sector governance requirements (e.g. the *Public Service Act 1999 (Cth)*, *Financial Management and Accountability Act 1997 (Cth)*, and *Commonwealth Authorities and Companies Act 1997 (Cth)*), differ from the informal features of governance (e.g. organisational governance practices and cqnduct).

This distinction between hard and soft governance can also be elevated at a systemic level to a distinction between the formal institutional and regulatory architecture and associated 'rules' that govern decision-making for collective entities such as corporations and governments, on one hand, and their less formal counterparts in ordering and otherwise influencing 'collective decision-making' and behaviour, on the other (Chhotray and Stoker 2009: 3–4). In this way, the distinction between hard and soft governance parallels the distinction between 'hard' law (i.e. legislation and court judgments) and 'soft' law (i.e. other forms of regulation, such as official codes and guidelines).

Important connections also exist between governance and regulation, the horizontal and vertical dimensions of an organisation's governance, and hard and soft forms of governance. As explained by Chhotray and Stoker (2009: 23–24), these connections matter in terms of organisational autonomy, regulatory guidance and performance outcomes:

> Governing by regulation from a governance perspective is about one public organisation aiming to shape the activities of another [in] the rolling out of a governing technique in the context of complex architecture of governance. Regulation can be a soft form of governance where the regulated agency or organisation is not commanded to do something but acts with autonomy, within prescribed limits, and is held to account against the achievement of certain goals or outcomes.

Norms of public sector governance in their broader governance context

Connections between values and governance

The different conceptions, orders and other aspects of governance canvassed in this chapter both reflect and shape a variety of values that are embodied in the structures, processes and behaviours surrounding governance in its various senses. Values and other norms of conduct therefore underpin governance on many levels. Sometimes, they explicitly form an integral part of the governance framework, as in the incorporation of designated values in governance legislation and other official guidance.

In terms of public sector values, authoritative sources of governance guidance for Australian public administration, such as the ANAO governance framework, list 'accountability', 'transparency' (or 'openness'), 'integrity', 'stewardship', 'leadership', and 'efficiency' as fundamental principles and values of governance (ANAO 2003c: 8). The APS values, which were originally enshrined in the 'APS Values' and 'APS Code of Conduct' sections of the PS Act, include values as diverse as societal values (e.g. community 'diversity'), democratic values (e.g. 'the effectiveness and cohesion of Australia's democratic system of government'), governmental values (e.g. ministerial responsibility), workplace values (e.g. meritorious, non-discriminatory, and equal opportunity employment), professional values (e.g. an 'apolitical', 'impartial', and 'professional' outlook, for the provision of 'frank, honest, comprehensive, accurate and timely advice' to the government of the day).[2]

Even the revision and streamlining of the APS Values that are recommended in *Ahead of the Game: Blueprint for the Reform of Australian Government Administration* (see chapter 2, in this volume) serve value-driven aims of cohesion, effectiveness and excellence in government (e.g. greater clarity of expectations, roles and responsibilities). The recommendations outlined in *Ahead of the Game* also reflect values of integration (e.g. whole-of-government,[3] intergovernmental, and cross-sectoral initiatives), cooperation (e.g. cross-agency

---

2   Assuming that it becomes law in a form that does not differ too greatly, or at all, from the Bill introduced into the federal parliament in early 2012, the *Public Service Amendment Act 2012 (Cth)* separates and consolidates public service values into two lists — a list of 'APS Values' and a list of related 'APS Employment Principles'. The APS Values embrace being 'ethical', 'respectful', 'accountable', 'impartial', and 'committed to service', with broad descriptions of each of those values also included in the Act. The APS Employment Principles are similarly defined, with a subset of principles covering appointment and promotion on merit.

3   For example, under reforms introduced in the *Public Service Amendment Act 2012*, the responsibilities of departmental secretaries include portfolio responsibility for developing 'a strong strategic policy capability that can consider complex, whole-of-government issues'.

coordination and collaboration),[4] monitorability (e.g. regular agency reviews), efficiency (e.g. regulatory simplification and 'deburdening'), and innovation (e.g. digitalisation, flexibility, responsiveness, and adaptation). Similarly, the value-laden trends of the last 25 years of Australian public administration reflect ideals of openness, consultation, engagement and efficiency, amongst others (McPhee 2009b: 5–6).

As understandings and practices of government evolve, so too do the underlying thematic influences and emphases in governance values. Some degree of correlation exists, for example, between how society views the role of the state and the public sector governance trends that prevail from time to time (chapter 2). The shift from the welfare state to the regulatory state and, lately, to a more pluralistic and facilitative state brings with it changes in the conceptions and practices of public sector governance that themselves mark shifts in sets of values and their priorities (Osborne 2010: 2–10). Similarly, some key institutional tensions in governance at systemic, departmental and agency board levels stem, in part, from competition between different values (chapters 3–6).

At the same time, new and underlying themes of cross-institutional and trans-sectoral integration, interdependence, and shared responsibilities combine with old underlying themes of organisational capability, efficiency, and effectiveness.[5] In these ways, the values of governance, as they are explicitly embedded or otherwise fostered through public sector regulation, connect on various levels to the components and elements of governance and its institutional architecture within government and society.

Categories of governance values and other norms

This connection between governance architecture, reforms and values makes it imperative to map such values in some detail, for the purpose of discussion in this and subsequent chapters. At least four distinct but related categories of values and other norms shape the governance arrangements and supportive regulatory architecture for the Commonwealth public sector. They can usefully be summarised in the following table, in descending order of systemic breadth and governance specificity:

---

4   For example, under reforms introduced in the *Public Service Amendment Act 2012*, the roles of departmental secretaries include 'providing stewardship within the Department and, in partnership with the Secretaries Board, across the APS'.

5   For example, one of the functions of the Secretaries Board, which was established under the *Public Service Amendment Act 2012*, is 'to draw together advice from senior leaders in government, business and the community', while one of the key responsibilities of each departmental secretary is 'to manage the affairs of the Department efficiently, effectively, economically and ethically'.

Table 1.2: Categories, focus and examples of governance norms

Category of norms	Focus	Example(s)
Broader societal governance	Integration of internal and external systemic responsibility and accountability	Social trust, cooperation, transparency, contestability and monitorability (chapters 1, 7 and 10)
Liberal democratic government	Constitutional system of democratic government in Westminster-based systems	Rule of law, responsible government and sovereignty of the people (chapters 1–3)
General public sector regulation, management and administration	Reforms to the executive branch of government and its relations with other governmental branches and levels	Public managerialism, regulatory state and new public governance (chapters 2–6)
Governance-specific public sector regulation, management and administration	Regulation of governance values, structures and other arrangements for public sector bodies (e.g. PS Act, CAC Act and FMA Act)	APS Values (chapter 1), Uhrig review templates (chapters 2, 6 and 8) and official Finance governance guides (chapters 1, 6, 8 and 9)

At an overarching level, societal norms both permeate and underpin governance ideas and practices. The values of social trust and cooperation, for example, are as important for civil society as they are for the workings of government and business. Values such as these also have discrete governance implications, especially in terms of public responsibility and accountability, under both state-centric and society-centric views of governance and the tensions between them, as explored in various chapters in this volume. This category of norms informs both internal and external dimensions of public responsibility and accountability, in the sense that these values condition public responsibility and accountability through the formal institutions of government as well as through engagement of the private sector and civil society.

The norms for the governance of society as a whole have both similarities and differences with the norms that relate to the governance that operates through a system of democratic government. In each case, values such as trust, cooperation and transparency remain important, although often with different contexts and mechanisms.[6] The trust that is necessary in business transactions and professional life is not the same, for example, as the trust that voters place in elected governments. At the same time, the system of government also reflects and gives effect to particular values in particular ways.

---

6   On the importance of trust in a governmental context, see: Uhr 2005; and Braithwaite and Levi 2003. On the importance of transparency as a dominant value in business regulation worldwide, see: Braithwaite and Drahos 2000.

A series of democratic, constitutional and other values underlie notions of the public trust, public service, and public accountability, which infuse systems of government and their governance arrangements (e.g. Finn 1993; Hood 1998; Finn 2010). Whatever the ongoing normative and operational significance of these organising principles for the framework of government today (Finn 2010: 350), they have a powerful legitimising and standard-guiding influence over what the people expect from their governments and how governments should themselves behave.

Within the system of government, the connection between governance and values is reflected in constitutional and legislative arrangements, such as the Australian Constitution's incorporation of the rule of law and the reference to ministerial responsibility in the APS Values. In addition, the values associated with liberal democratic government must accommodate and adapt to democracy's own evolution. The tension between contemporary democracy's state-centric manifestations (e.g. the institutions of representative democracy) and its society-centric forms (e.g. deliberative democracy) also impacts upon governance and its manifestations (e.g. network, collaborative and participatory governance).

The governance of the public sector is also discrete from governance within the broader system of government. In terms of the public sector as a whole, there is general regulation of public sector management and administration, which is underpinned by a series of sectoral values, some of which are explicit and legislated (e.g. APS Values) and some of which are implicit and reflected in governmental behaviours and processes (e.g. public service conventions and protocols). Indeed, the APS Values cut across both general regulation of the APS and the governance of particular Commonwealth public sector entities. More broadly, norms of public sector regulatory infrastructure are also located in public accountability laws (e.g. laws of judicial and administrative review, freedom of information and privacy) and general laws that apply to governmental and non-governmental organisations alike, at least to some degree (e.g. governmental liability under the *Competition and Consumer Act 2010* (previously *Trade Practices Act 1974*)).

Accordingly, the Commonwealth public sector also contains within it a discrete set of governance-specific laws and official guidance, from both whole-of-government and organisational perspectives, with underlying values and principles that are grounded in the prevailing notions of good governance. Here, the main governance-specific legislation consists of the FMA Act, CAC Act and PS Act. Together, these acts supply the primary legislative framework for regulating the governance of Commonwealth public sector bodies of all kinds, in terms of governance structures and values, financial and reporting responsibilities, and other governance responsibilities and arrangements.

Other major governance-specific frameworks and policy initiatives in this category include the governmental adoption of most of the recommendations of the *Review of the Corporate Governance of Statutory Authorities and Office Holders* (Uhrig review) and their extension throughout the Commonwealth public sector (chapter 2). These recommendations are supplemented by ANAO frameworks and guides on governance, together with what the Department of Finance and Deregulation (Finance) describes as 'principles for helping determine the most appropriate structure and governance arrangements for Australian Governmental bodies' (DFD 2007, as outlined in DFD 2005b) as well as other official guidelines on governance from Finance (e.g. DFD 2011b). These are important sources of governance principles and related norms.

At a final level, in descending order from societal, governmental and sectoral governance, we reach the organisational level of governance. All of these levels of governance have their associated values and other norms. Some of these norms integrate, at an organisational level, the governance norms that operate from a whole-of-government perspective, including sector-wide norms such as the APS Values. Some of them reflect effectiveness, efficiency and other values that are derived from official governance templates (e.g. the Uhrig review templates) and other official guidance (e.g. DFA 2005b), while still others are more organisation-specific in nature. These organisation-specific values are derived from sources as various as particular organisational statements of expectation and intent, organisational charters and missions, and other aspects of organisational design and strategy. Good organisational governance at this level can also model good governance values and practices from other organisations within the public sector and beyond.

In short, viewing governance in these societal, governmental, sectoral and organisational terms reinforces the connection between cross-cutting spheres of governance and their associated values. These cross-cutting connections between governance and values are demonstrated by a series of accountability mechanisms from the inner and outer public sector to wider society. These accountability mechanisms and the borders that they transcend also offer insight into governance as a multi-dimensional system of interdependent parts. The final part of this chapter considers key aspects of this interrelationship between governance architecture and its underlying norms in more detail. In particular, it illustrates how changes and limits to this architecture and its norms create challenges for the Commonwealth level of government and its public sector system.

Governance changes, limits and challenges

The form and substance of governance in Australia and other Anglophone countries is integrally connected to the prevailing system of democracy and government.[7] Neither that system, nor our understanding of its features and limits, remains fixed forever. Accordingly, there are progressive insights about this system and its ongoing evolution that any serious study of governance must accommodate. Three such insights bring together many of the themes underpinning this chapter, and serve as a platform for the analysis of governance in later chapters.

First, the forms and institutions of democratic government are evolving to accommodate new societal expectations and mechanisms of public engagement and accountability. Governance must adapt to contemporary democracy's transition from a primary focus upon majoritarian democracy, which is characterised formally as rule by majority vote in parliament, to embrace what is variously termed 'government by discussion' (Sen 2009: 324), a 'partnership conception' of democracy (Dworkin 2011: 5), and governance through multi-order monitoring of all institutional exercises of power over the people in the new era of 'monitory democracy' (Keane 2009: xxxiii). So, too, are the organs and actors of democratic government exposed to enhanced standards of public contestability, deliberation and justification in their official decisions and actions, under related notions of 'deliberative democracy' (Gutmann and Thompson 2004).

Democratic norms are also the subject of continuous conceptual recasting and operational application to changing circumstances. For example: democracy is now concerned as much with respect for individual freedoms and human rights as it is with majoritarian rule; responsible government and ministerial responsibility are both affected by the party-based system of government; and popular sovereignty and the rule of law are still works-in-progress in their application to the contemporary complexity of executive government and the legal conditions for exercising public power on behalf of the Australian people (Finn 1995: 7, 13, 20). Electoral outcomes are another and increasingly volatile dynamic in recent democratic history, in light of the transition from majority government to minority government and post-election coalition formation in the United Kingdom, Australia and other Anglophone countries. The relations between government and the people change as the understanding and practices of representative democracy change too.

---

7   Governance has many systems. The system of democracy and government discussed here is only one such system. Another is the public sector governance system discussed in chapter 4.

The central idea in this new era of participatory, deliberative and monitory democracy is that governance and regulation in democracies now involves interactions between state and non-state actors, greater accountability to the people for what governments do, and enhanced means of public engagement and monitoring in the democratic process. This includes societal standard-setting, norm-shaping and regulatory influence beyond simply their governmental forms in policy-making and law-making. It also includes discrete and sometimes shared responsibilities across the public, private, and community sectors (and even national boundaries) in developing and implementing public policy and regulation, steering and ordering societal behaviour, and monitoring and calling to account the use and abuse of institutional power. This evolution of democratic governance has clear connections to other aspects of governance, as explored in this and other chapters.

Secondly, the public trust is connected to democracy's evolution and resultant impact upon governance, in the following sense. The public trust remains a central concept that underpins the system of government, accountability to the electorate and democracy's evolution to embrace meaningful public engagement beyond periodic elections. This is why talk of the public trust in law and government remains meaningful and action-guiding, rather than merely aspirational or even passé.

At the very least, this central concept requires that those who are governed are enabled to give their fully informed consent to the exercise of power over them by governing institutions and public officials (Funnell 2001: 149). In constitutional and legal terms, the public trust informs official standards and behaviours including those enshrined in public sector codes and other regulation (Finn 2010: 330–39, 350). In political terms, the UK Nolan Committee's mid-1990s warning against improper financial relationships between non-government parties and politicians reflects deeper concern about safeguarding the public against breaches of the public trust invested in elected representatives (Committee on Standards in Public Life 1995; Finn 1995).

The core principle is that those in government who are invested with political and legal power exercise that power for and on behalf of the people, whatever the ultimate foundation for this public trust. This grand theme of making the people the masters and not the servants of public power permeates the conferral, conditioning and proper use of that power over people's lives. Consider, in this context, the governance significance of recent legal recognition of the sovereignty of the Australian people as the ultimate source of constitutional authority. If the people are the source of all democratic power, for example, those institutions and public officials who wield such power do so on trust from and for the people, and are accountable to them through various electoral, agency-based and Westminster-style mechanisms (Finn 1994: 227–28, 234–35).

Finally, these ideas and mechanisms of public trust and accountability also make it necessary to consider how Australia's system of government and public administration sits within a broader tradition of Westminster and other influences (Rhodes et al 2009). This common reference point for convergence and divergence across systems of government means that Australia and countries such as the United Kingdom, Canada, New Zealand and others can look to one another for models of good governance regulation and practice (Finn 1995; Halligan 2003a, 2007a; Wettenhall 2005; and Rhodes et al 2009). The reform of Australian public administration that is foreshadowed in *Ahead of the Game* (see chapter 2, this volume) acknowledges the comparative lessons from other jurisdictions (AGRAGA 2010: 64). Using governance comparisons and lessons across jurisdictions to model governance reforms is another theme in several of the following chapters, as is Australia's debt to the influence of Westminster-based ideas and conventions of government.

In what is sometimes called the 'Washminster' model (e.g. Thompson 2001), Australia's system of government combines aspects of the American system of a written constitution, separation of powers and bicameral legislature with the British system of responsible government, ministerial accountability and Westminster conventions. At the same time, there are questions of lingering legal and political significance about the extent to which Westminster notions are actually enshrined in the Australian constitutional structure, the apparent non-applicability of such notions to Australian innovations in the use of statutory authorities and state-owned enterprises, and the resultant challenges to core tenets of associated doctrines such as individual ministerial responsibility (Finn 1995: 12–13). Together, they serve to highlight 'the limits, limitations and uncertainties of "Westminster" theory and practice' (Finn 1995: 12–15, 22–9). Similarly, residual questions remain about the consistency of Westminster-style machinery and doctrines with the progressive tightening of public accountability measures that involve administrative review, the public service and corporate governance (Bottomley 1997).

In other words, what is suitable under Westminster conventions for the governance of a public service within a unitary system of government that is based upon a constitutional monarchy, an unwritten constitution and the ultimate supremacy of parliament does not necessarily translate fully to contemporary Australian democratic, constitutional and political conditions. Even after 100 years of Australian constitutional jurisprudence, the High Court of Australia is still hearing cases that explore the extent to which the doctrines, prerogatives and conventions that relate to the Crown in right of the UK government remain applicable to Australia's constitutional system of government.[8]

---

8 E.g. *Australian Competition and Consumer Commission v. Baxter Healthcare* (2007) HCA 38; *Pape v. Commissioner of Taxation* (2009) HCA 23; and *Momcilovic v. The Queen* (2011) HCA 34.

An alternative to the view of an inevitable erosion or dilution of Westminster principles of responsible government and good public administration is the view of 'traditions under challenge that reshape reform as reforms reshape them' (Rhodes et al 2008: 472). In characterising recent developments in Westminster-based systems, one set of public sector management commentators characterises developments variously in terms of 'innovative ways of combining past traditions with new organising principles of governance', and 'a convergence of traditions as Westminster-derived jurisdictions wrestle with new challenges to their understanding of governance', The result has been that a series of models co-exist in some form of layers and sedimentation (Halligan 2010d). In the words of Rhodes et al, 'it is not a question of "in with the new, out with the old", but of "in with the new alongside key components of the old"' (2008: 474).

Conclusion

As presented in this chapter, governance in the public sector is the product of different orders of governance within society and their underlying norms, all of which impact upon one another to varying degrees. The design and practice of governance in the contemporary public sector manifests itself through 'hard' and 'soft' forms of governance that infuse the 'vertical' and 'horizontal' governance interactions of public sector bodies, with multi-textured governance relationships across and within different levels of government as well as with others beyond government.

All of this occurs within an overall system of governance that itself draws upon and interacts with other systems of societal, democratic and legal governance. None of these things are captured fully for their own purposes or adequately for overall evaluative purposes by focusing on select governance models (e.g. government-centric models), features (e.g. structure and performance) or outcomes (e.g. financial probity) to the exclusion of others that are of equal significance. At the same time, different concepts of governance — especially public governance, public sector governance and corporate governance — retain their own settings and features that demand attention in their own right.

Accordingly, this book's chapters collectively develop and present a kaleidoscopic view of governance as a multi-level systemic, holistic and reflexive enterprise. It is *systemic* in the sense that different components contribute to a system with a coherent overall focus upon a unit of governance (e.g. a nation, its public sector, or bodies comprising it) that itself interacts with other systems of governance. For example, the governance of each public sector body is conducted within a system of governance for the sector as a whole, which itself sits within wider systems of political, legal, and socio-economic governance (chapters 1–7).

Next, governance is *holistic* in the sense that it is a multi-layered and multi-textured enterprise, to be considered and practised on a range of levels that are distinct from and yet also related to one another. For example, both the design and implementation of governance arrangements for particular public sector bodies and the appointment and staffing at senior levels for public sector bodies must be understood within a broader system of federal public sector governance that is observed from central, organisational, and community stakeholder viewpoints (chapters 4–9).

Finally, governance is *reflexive* in the sense that its values, practices and other features both shape and are shaped by their surrounding environment, through multiple points of interconnectivity. For example, the different phases of Australian governance reform from the late-twentieth century to the early twenty-first century have an impact upon different central and agency conceptions of governance (chapter 2), just as the governance of particular kinds of public sector bodies is responsive to both state-centred and society-inclusive dimensions of public governance (chapter 3). This reflexivity extends from systemic and institutional levels to organisational and individual levels too, with the accountability of public servants evolving to include their internalisation of public sector values and professional ethics, in addition to the norms served by traditional external scrutiny (APSC 2009b: 6).

Such a view of governance means that the more that we can appreciate how the different aspects of governance bear upon one another, the better that we can understand and practice it in all of the discrete ways that matter to those engaged in the work of governance, especially the business of government. Accordingly, our understanding of Australian public administration and its changes over time cannot be compartmentalised away from these influences.

Understanding public governance, public sector governance and corporate governance on their own terms as well as in relation to one another is essential for the discussion of different aspects of governance in this and the following chapters. Using this opening discussion as a platform, the next chapter explores in more detail the evolution of the different forms of governance that are related to Australia's system of government and the role of public administration in it.

2. Rise of Corporate and Public Governance

This chapter examines the emergence of governance as a primary concept during the last three decades and the ways in which two different forms of governance — corporate governance and public governance — have risen to prominence in the Australian public sector. To understand the significance of this it is necessary to explore the context of public sector reforms, and specific policy and reform agendas. The changing theories and broader conceptions of governance that were considered in chapter 1 assist with this task.

The intersection of the public and private sectors has been a fundamental and under-researched dimension of changing governance. The connections between the public and private sectors that have been so central to reform over the last three decades build on a much longer history as governments have turned to business for advice about efficiency and economy. There are two streams within this relationship. The first is the transfer of private sector ideas and techniques to the public sector (ranging from different modes of management to the corporatisation of functions and marketisation). The second is the flow of assets and various forms of outsourced activity from the public sector (this includes variations on privatisation). Underlying the relationship are the shifting boundaries between government/public concerns and market/private concerns.

Prior to the term 'governance' coming into vogue, the nomenclature used for similar concepts was that of government and public administration. This nomenclature provides the backdrop for mapping movements in the emphases of public sector governance, which are examined in this chapter in terms of three phases of public sector reform over the last 30 years. Reflected in these phases we find distinctive modes of governance emerging during different decades: corporate management in the 1980s, corporate governance in the 1990s and public governance in the 2000s. The pattern for the 2010s is still emerging during a period of turbulence and uncertainty.

Three phases in public sector reform

The Australian experience can be summarised with reference to the phases of reform and the decade in which they became significant during the reform era (from the early 1980s) (Table 2.1). Managerialism (Pollitt 1993; Zifcak 1994; Considine and Painter 1997; Halligan 2007b) best reflects the first phase in which management became the central concept and reshaped thinking as part of a paradigm change. This was succeeded by a phase that, for a time, came close to the mainstream depiction of new public management (NPM) (Hood 1991), in which the market element was favoured and features such as disaggregation, privatisation and a private sector focus were at the forefront. In turn, NPM was followed, although not displaced, in the 2000s by integrated governance (Halligan 2006).

The sequence of reform has run from administration to stages that have been dominated first, by management, then markets, and then performance-based governance. The Australian tradition has been administrative rather than managerial; the latter being historically more closely identified with the commercial arms of government than the core public sector. In each of the three reform phases it is possible to distinguish elements that applied particularly to the departments of state and those that pertained to statutory authorities, corporations and companies (Table 2.1).

Table 2.1: Reform phases 1980s to 2000s

Reform dimension	Managerialism	New public management	Integrated governance
Central concept	Management (based on private sector)	Market	Performance management to demonstrate results
Reform focus in core public service	Financial management improvement	Outsourcing	Whole-of-government
Reform focus in outer public sector	Corporatisation and government business enterprise (GBE) companies	Privatisation Public–private	Uhrig review (2003) and rationalising public bodies/authorities
General trends	Paradigm change to results management	Devolving and disaggregating	Integrating and strengthening centre
Public–private trends	Importing private sector concepts/ techniques	Exporting assets and functions. Importing corporate governance ideas	Renewal of public sector as the centrepiece of governance
Public engagement	Reassessment of relationship and costs of public provision	Service delivery to customers	Citizen-centric policy and delivery

Managerialism

The initial period of reform in the 1980s displaced traditional administration with a package of reforms that were based on management. Over about a decade, a new management philosophy was developed and implemented, which replaced the emphasis on inputs and processes with one on results (Halligan and Power 1992).

The main elements of the reform program (under a Labor government) focused on the core public service (including commercialisation, decentralisation and the senior public service) and improving financial management, followed by corporatisation and later privatisation. The Financial Management Improvement Program (FMIP) dominated the reforms of the 1980s. The Australian focus on results, outcomes and performance-oriented management dates from this time, although the emphasis then was on program budgeting and management. The flagging reform momentum in the mid 1980s produced new directions that were linked to an emerging micro-economic reform agenda, the most significant element being the major reorganisation of the machinery of government (for details see Campbell and Halligan 1993; Zifcak 1994; Halligan 1997).

A central element of reform was creating more business-like operations in the public sector. The movement towards corporatisation that occurred from the late 1980s, through either GBEs or incorporation as companies, produced significant changes to the status of major organisations (Halligan and Power 1992: 109–10).

New public management

The first phase of this reform era displayed incipient NPM in several respects, but the dominant theme was management improvement. The commitment to neo-liberal economic reforms that existed in the 1990s, following the advent of a conservative coalition government, led to the public service becoming highly decentralised, marketised, contractualised and privatised.

This new reform stage became most apparent with the increasing acceptance of the need for market-oriented reform by the mid 1990s. A major impetus for the application of market principles came from the National Competition Policy Review (1993), which was a flow-on from the micro-economic reform agenda that emerged in the mid 1980s. The Commonwealth and the states agreed to implement its recommendations, including competitive neutrality between the government and the business sector, and the structural reform of public monopolies to allow competition between providers within sectors. By the mid 1990s, the Australian public service was again in transition as the pressures for further reform intensified. The new agenda centred on competition and contestability, contracting out, client focus, core business, and the application of the purchaser/provider principle.

Market principles were applied first to the outer public sector and subsequently to the core public service. The private sector and market forces were closely related: the exporting of responsibilities to the private sector and/or making the public sector subject to market disciplines; and the importing of business techniques combined with attempts to replicate market conditions internally. Several tiers of markets became accepted within the public sector, the main distinction being between the internal (or activities within the public service involving purely public transactions, such as user charging) and the external market (or public–private transactions, such as contracting out). A more significant dimension of management reform occurred in instances where there was a major organisational transformation (corporatisation or privatisation: Wettenhall 2001), although this was normally within the broader public sector. The national focus on improving competitiveness, and the emergence of a Council of Australian Governments, produced an agenda for rationalising and decentralising the delivery of services within the national public sector.

The agenda also covered a deregulated personnel system; a core public service that was focused on policy, regulation and oversight of service delivery; and contestability of the delivery of services with greater use of the private sector. A major financial management framework was introduced with budgeting on a full accrual basis for 1999–2000, implementation of outputs and outcomes reporting, and extending agency devolution to budget estimates and financial management.

The devolution of responsibilities from central agencies to line departments (responsible for specific functions) was highly significant in the late 1990s and resulted in a diminished role for central agencies (Halligan 2003b). As a result, the Australian Public Service Commission's (APSC) role was modest while the Department of Prime Minister and Cabinet's (PM&C) interventions were constrained and it was no longer providing overall public service leadership. The role of the then Department of Finance also contracted substantially.

Integrated governance

The new phase, integrated governance, which began in the 2000s, had an impact on relationships within and the coherence of the public service, delivery and implementation, and performance and responsiveness to government policy. Four dimensions were designed to draw together fundamental aspects of governance: resurrection of the central agency as a major actor with more direct influence over departments; whole-of-government as the new expression of a range of forms of coordination; central monitoring of agency implementation and delivery; and departmentalisation through absorbing statutory authorities and rationalising the non-departmental sector. A centralising trend within the Commonwealth system was also identified within specific policy sectors. In combination these provide the basis for integrated governance (Halligan 2006).

These trends placed greater emphasis on horizontal relationships through cross-agency programs and collaborative relationships. At the same time, vertical relationships were extended and reinforced. The whole-of-government approach was centralising in that central agencies were driving some policy directions across agencies and the public service. The result was the tempering of devolution through strategic steering and management from the centre and a rebalancing of the positions of centre and line agencies.

An underlying element was political control: the use of programs to improve financial information for ministers; greater emphasis on strategic coordination by cabinet; controlling major policy agendas; the abolition of agencies and bodies as part of rationalisation and integration; and monitoring the delivery and implementation of government policy. These measures increased the potential for policy and program control and integration using the conventional machinery of cabinet, central agencies and departments as well as other coordinating instruments.

The intensity of the Australian reassertion of the centre and the ministerial department resulted from both system shortcomings and a response to the threat of uncertainty, which favoured the security of a stronger centre. A core principle of the 1980s was to require departments to manage as well as to provide policy advice. The language of the mid 2000s came to emphasise effective delivery as well as policy advice with the latter defined in terms of outcomes (Shergold 2004b). Departmentalisation was expressed through absorbing statutory authorities and reclaiming control of agencies that were managed by hybrid boards that did not accord with a particular corporate (and therefore private sector) governance prescription.

Underlying change, then, was a mainly state-centric focus on sorting out the architecture and processes of systems to provide for more effective government. Less apparent was thinking and action about external relationships. Those concerns were evident in the whole-of-government agenda, and the rhetoric intensified about citizen engagement and collaborative governance (O'Flynn and Wanna 2008), but the Commonwealth government had yet to centre public governance more clearly within societal processes.

Modes of governance at the system and agency levels

A different mode of governance has emerged during each of the last three decades, reflecting the tone and content of the then reform agenda: the narrow concept of corporate management in the 1980s, corporate governance in the 1990s and two variants of public governance in the 2000s. Their relationship to the reform agenda discussed above is indicated in Table 2.2. The society-centric notion of collaborative governance indicates general discourse about, and official aspirations for, public governance in the 2010s that has yet to be properly reflected in reality. Nevertheless, *Ahead of the Game: Blueprint for the Reform of Australian Government Administration*, which is discussed later in the chapter, gives the idea of collaborative governance a more substantial foundation in public governance. At the very least, collaborative governance involves aspects of wider societal accountability, shared intra- and intergovernmental governance accountabilities (chapter 1), and participatory governance and stakeholder engagement (chapter 7).

Table 2.2: Reform agenda and agency modes of governance

Period	Public management reform agenda	Governance mode
Pre-reform	Public administration	Machinery of government
1980s	Managerialism	Corporate management
1990s	New public management	Corporate governance
2000s	Integrated governance	Public governance (state-centric)
2010s	Collaborative governance	Public governance (society-centric)

The first phase of reform had embedded management and more commercial thinking, whereas the second phase placed increasing emphasis on markets, contracts and disaggregation. Labor governments favoured the public sector but pushed it towards the private sector; the Coalition government favoured the private sector but recognised the need to maintain a strong core public service.

A focus on corporate thinking as a means of binding new management systems and processes produced the more powerful combination of corporate governance, only to be supplanted but not entirely succeeded by public governance, the second version of which points to the more inclusive reform agenda of collaborative governance.

In terms of the organisational focus, three public sector reviews need to be noted. The first was the Dawkins/Walsh reforms of the 1980s (Wettenhall 1988), which sought a specific refocusing of relationships between ministerial departments and authorities. The second was the revision of legislation governing public bodies in the 1990s, which lead to new Acts — the *Financial Management and Accountability Act 1997 (Cth)* (FMA Act) and the *Commonwealth Authorities and Companies Act 1997 (Cth)* (CAC Act). The third was the *Review of the Corporate Governance of Statutory Authorities and Office Holders* (Uhrig 2003) which lead, in the 2000s, to more generally integrated governance, and is discussed later in this chapter (see also chapter 8 on the implications of the Uhrig review for governance design). These reviews had an impact on the role, constitution, numbers and significance of public bodies.

Finally, it is worth observing that a distinguishing feature of much reform is that it has been comprehensive, and involves different phases and modes of governance over time. There is now international acceptance that, through the reform process, no one model dominates and that layering, sedimentation and hybridisation have occurred. Recent analysis of patterns of change indicates that successive phases of reform have added new governance frameworks rather than replacing old ones (Christensen and Lægreid 2006) and that coordination and integration have co-existed with disaggregation (Richards and Smith 2006). Public sector systems such as that in Australia display several tendencies concurrently as they have wrestled with different demands to deregulate and regulate, devolve and control.

Ultimately, one reason for governments pursuing contrary actions is that contradictions exist between reform agenda (Aucoin 1990). Where once it was appropriate to articulate and operate within a single coherent model, this has become increasingly difficult. The consequence is hybridisation, which involves multiple modes of governance that may be exchanged or combined with variable results.

Rise of corporate governance

Corporate governance in government must be understood and practised within a variety of related systems and dimensions of governance. It is neither fully derived from, nor transposable to, the private sector. At the same time, an understanding of some key comparisons and contrasts between the two sectors is important, for reasons outlined in chapter 1. Throughout the 1990s, private corporate governance held some sway over public sector management (Table 2.2) and it is largely as a result of experience that was gained during this period that each sector continues to have governance insights for the other. Contemporary governance challenges often engage both sectors, and therefore presuppose awareness of the governance dynamics in each. Private sector notions and experiences still exerted residual gravitational pull in the public sector at the outset of the twenty-first century (e.g. Uhrig 2003), although they were less influential on public service agenda by the end of its first decade (e.g. Moran 2010a).

In the private sector, a number of forces for improved corporate governance can be traced from the late 1980s through to the 1990s. These forces continue to identify some of the most distinctive features of corporate governance today. The initial stimulus for improved corporate governance stemmed in the late 1980s from the failures of private law and regulation that became so evident, internationally, in the collapse of many major corporations. Given the rapidly inflating asset values of the 1980s, many entrepreneurial and highly leveraged shareholders were able to take control of corporate boards and, with this, the control of major corporate assets. The corporate role of the 'owner', who commonly filled the roles of both chief executive and chairman of the board, remained ill defined. The roles of other directors sitting on the board were also poorly defined, so that much of the corporate governance debate throughout the 1990s involved the separation of the roles of the chairman and chief executive, and the clarification of the roles of non-executive directors and specialist board committees.

The era was marked by a shift in legislative style to provide more prescriptive processes for board and corporate decision-making, thus providing checks upon the discretionary power of the board. Reinforcing these legislative developments, voluntary codes and practice guides further clarified the roles and responsibilities of individual directors and specialist board committees such as the audit and remuneration committees. Commonly, these processes also involved a clearer supervisory and regulatory role for the Australian Securities and Investments Commission (ASIC). These developments have provided the backbone for both corporate 'self-regulation' and 'co-regulation'. Good examples of these prescribed processes include those for company officers declaring their material personal interests in transactions and for the approval of directors' remuneration reports by the general meeting.

In addition to a more prescriptive legislative approach to the processes of management and corporate decision-making, clearer obligations upon directors and executive management were also added to assist ASIC in its regulatory role, together with an array of new civil penalties that were designed to aid ASIC in dealing with company officers who contravened the law. Many key elements of corporate governance that were introduced over this period had the effect of highlighting deficiencies in corporate law and regulation, which became evident throughout the 1990s in the articulation of voluntary codes of practice. By the end of the 1990s, the market and market judgments of corporate governance practice had also come to provide important non-judicial elements in the public assessment of corporate management decisions and the exercise of corporate powers generally. As part of this process, in 2003, the Australian Securities Exchange (ASX) finally released its *Principles of Corporate Governance* (ASX Corporate Governance Council 2003).

The impact of these key developments in modern corporate governance is now well understood. A less well-appreciated influence upon the evolution of corporate governance in the private sector was the rise of large, publicly responsible shareholders, such as superannuation and investment funds, to displace small, individual shareholders in public companies. It is arguable that this circumstance brought corporate governance in the private sector closer to public sector and public governance. The activism of these shareholders, particularly in the late 1990s, refined the measures of corporate and management performance and established a clearer link between good corporate governance practice and superior corporate performance. While this activism has waned since the early 2000s, a period that has seen the codification of shareholders' voting policies, pension and investment funds remain an important force in determining corporate policy on issues such as director remuneration and other aspects of board governance that attract public attention. Most significantly for the evolution of public sector governance, pension fund shareholders are in essence trustee investors and they are themselves responsible for maintaining significant social obligations. Thus, their influence as trustees continues to broaden the responsibilities of corporate management beyond their more narrowly conceived legal obligations to the company.

Over the last 20 years, the four most enduring legacies of corporate governance in the private sector have been: first, the incorporation of a number of statutory, voluntary and market checks upon discretionary management power through the refinement of the responsibilities of board members and the processes of decision-making within the corporation; secondly, the embedding of corporate self-regulation and cooperative regulation rather than 'command and control' styles of regulation; thirdly, the adoption of voluntary codes and practice guides to supplement corporate law and regulation; and fourthly, a greater reliance upon the market for public assessments of corporate governance practice and corporate performance.

Corporate governance's contribution to public sector governance

Within the framework that was established in chapter 1, it has been seen as convenient to consider corporate governance as a subset of public sector governance, public governance and governance more generally. At the same time, however, corporate governance has provided both one impetus for the governance debate in the public sector and the foundational principles and codes of practice on which public sector governance is based. In recent decades, the public sector has adopted many of the ideas and practices of private sector management and corporate governance (Horrigan 2002; Edwards 2002; Nicoll 2002; Ahn, Halligan and Wilks 2002), which have covered language, forms, structures and practices, in moves to enhance goals as various as management efficiency, stakeholder representation, organisational responsibility, and overall public accountability (Halligan 1997; Barrett 2002a; Edwards 2002). This process has been apparent across the full range of agencies, from departments of state, statutory authorities to government corporations (Wettenhall 2000, 2001; Thynne and Wettenhall 2002).

Perhaps the most obvious influence of the private sector is seen in the adoption of the corporate form itself, and with this a corporate-style board with autonomous power approaching that enjoyed in private corporations. The adoption of Commonwealth companies, and the incorporation of the same law and directors' liabilities that are applicable to corporations incorporated under the *Corporations Act 2001*, may have suggested a reason for importing also the corporate codes and corporate governance practice that were developed for private corporations throughout the 1990s.

While the link between corporate failures in the private sector, board dynamics, and bad corporate governance requires closer analysis, the elements and impact of corporate governance provide one focal point for assessing organisational performance and accountability (Heracleous 2001; Bhagat and Black 2002; Edwards and Clough 2005). Together, organisational and individual performance constitutes a key component of corporate governance, on any definition of it that applies across sectors. At the same time, differences in values across the public and private sectors, and in the dynamics of relationships with shareholders and stakeholders across both sectors, all affect the degree of corporate governance transposition from one sector to the other (Bottomley 2000; Barrett 2002a, 2002b; Horrigan 2003). This has implications for performance measurement and evaluation too, not least because of the different context for public sector performance.

Given the origins of corporate governance conceptually and operationally within the private sector domain, the transposition and transmutation of corporate governance to government is anathema to some. Yet, applying the term to aspects of the relationship between organisational governance and government has a tradition within government and academia in countries like Australia and the United Kingdom. The strong common emphasis upon components of corporate governance such as accountability, conformance, performance and assurance, in both the public and the private sectors, also indicates points of convergence that exist across the two domains.

Corporate failures expose gaps in the law and regulation of corporate boards

In the United Kingdom, the failure in the early 1990s of media owner Robert Maxwell's company and the international bank, Bank of Credit and Commerce International (BCCI), spurred the publication of corporate governance codes and practice guidelines throughout that decade. In many respects, the United Kingdom took the lead internationally in promoting corporate governance reform and articulating the principles of corporate governance throughout the period.

In Australia, the collapse of Rothwells Ltd in 1987 provided the impetus for a decade of corporate law reform and the examination of the legal duties of directors. This initial period of law reform was accompanied by great public interest in better defining the roles and responsibilities of non-executive directors, chairmen and chief executives more generally. With the collapse of Enron Corporation in 2001 and the passage of the Sarbannes–Oxley Act (2002) in the United States, the royal commission investigating the collapse of HIH Insurance extended reforms in corporate governance to include examinations of the functional roles and liabilities of senior executive management operating below board level (HIH Royal Commission 2003: 130).

The early codes and practice guides that built upon the 1992 Cadbury Report were framed as voluntary codes, emphasising corporate management ethics and providing guidance for directors and management in practice. By the end of the 1990s, however, driven by the growing power of pension funds and investment managers, these codes increasingly linked corporate governance practice to improved corporate performance and began to incorporate a wider range of corporate social obligations and responsibilities to stakeholders other than shareholders.

Towards the end of the 1990s, the different aspects of these expanded codes were consolidated internationally in the Organisation for Economic Co-operation and Development's (OECD) *Principles of Corporate Governance* (1999). Accumulated codes and practice guides were adopted in 2001 in the United Kingdom by the London Stock Exchange in its *Combined Code*, and by the Australian Securities Exchange (ASX) in 2003 in its *Principles of Corporate Governance* (ASX Corporate Governance Council 2003).

Corporate governance within a private sector context was authoritatively defined in the landmark Cadbury Report in the United Kingdom in 1992 (CFACG 1992). Many later regulatory, organisational, and academic definitions of corporate governance across sectors and jurisdictions take their lead from the Cadbury Report. Indeed, its definition probably sets more of the tone and structure of contemporary definitions of corporate governance than any other single source. According to the committee, which was chaired by leading company chairman and corporate governance expert, Sir Adrian Cadbury: 'Corporate governance is the system by which companies are directed and controlled' (CFACG 1992: 2.5). What follows in that definition has become a classic statement of the formal and structural components of corporate governance (CFACG 1992: 2.5–2.7):

> Boards of directors are responsible for the governance of their companies. The shareholders' role in governance is to appoint the directors and the auditors and to satisfy themselves that an appropriate governance structure is in place. The responsibilities of the board include setting

the company's strategic aims, providing the leadership to put them into effect, supervising the management of the business and reporting to shareholders on their stewardship. The board's actions are subject to laws, regulations and the shareholders in general meeting.

Within that overall framework, the specifically financial aspects of corporate governance ... are the way in which boards set financial policy and oversee its implementation, including the use of financial controls, and the process whereby they report on the activities and progress of the company to the shareholders.

The role of auditors is to provide shareholders with an external and objective check on the directors' financial statements, which form the basis of that reporting system.

For anyone concerned with corporate governance in the public sector, what is striking about the Cadbury Report's crystallisation of corporate governance is how many of its features are tied not only to the 'hard' structural and formal aspects of corporate governance, but also to the institutional arrangements and management practice of the private sector.

In Australia, a more recent consideration of corporate governance occurred in the Report of the HIH Royal Commission, following the collapse of one of the country's largest insurers, HIH Insurance Ltd. A significant addition made by Royal Commissioner, Justice Owen, to the development of corporate governance in Australia was his consideration of the roles and responsibilities of executive management below the level of the board. Owen observed that 'corporate governance' refers to the control of corporations and to systems of oversight and the accountability of those in control', and 'Many publications describe corporate governance in terms that emphasise the structures, systems and processes in existence to ensure that an entity is properly directed and controlled'.

To this point, his analysis conforms to the Cadbury conception of corporate governance, but Owen (HIH Royal Commission 2003: xxxiii) then embraces the formal, behavioural, and relational elements:

Corporate governance ... describes a framework of rules, relationships, systems and processes within and by which authority is exercised and controlled in corporations. Understood in this way, the expression 'corporate governance' embraces not only the models or systems themselves but also the practices by which that exercise and control of authority is in fact effected.

These extended insights on corporate governance embrace both the 'hard' and 'soft' aspects of governance, which were mentioned in chapter 1, while their context remains firmly fixed in the private sector.

The OECD Principles formalise codes and 'relational' responsibilities

A significant extension to the Cadbury Committee's conception of corporate governance was apparent in the OECD's *Principles of Corporate Governance* (1999). The importance of these principles lies in the new international standards in corporate governance that they established. A distinguishing feature of the OECD principles is the description of corporate governance in terms of a series of 'relationships' between those involved in or affected by decisions, rather than in terms of corporate law and traditional constitutional board powers. This confirms the interest of shareholders, and even stakeholders, as participants in corporate decision-making. The OECD (1999: 11) principles define corporate governance as:

> a set of relationships between a company's management, its board, its shareholders and other stakeholders. Corporate governance also provides the structure through which the objectives of the company are set, and the means of attaining those objectives and monitoring performance are determined. Good corporate governance should provide proper incentives for the board and management to pursue objectives that are in the interests of the company and shareholders and should facilitate effective monitoring, thereby encouraging firms to use resources more efficiently.

These principles have potential for application beyond the private sector to state-owned enterprises (OECD 2004a: 11). Here too are glimpses of the wider systemic dimensions of organisational corporate governance: 'The presence of an effective corporate governance system, within an individual company and across an economy as a whole, helps to provide a degree of confidence that is necessary for the proper functioning of a market economy' (OECD 2004a: 11).

The 2004 OECD guidelines refer to the range of company-specific investments by various stakeholders that contribute to a company's success (OECD 2004a: 11). A company's interests need to be assessed over the long term, and it is in a company's long-term interests to stimulate 'wealth-creating cooperation among stakeholders', thus emphasising the importance of the relationship-based aspects of corporate governance. Yet, despite the relationship-focused orientation of such conceptions of corporate governance, the context of relationship-management in the private sector, with its fundamental concern for the business of business, differs in important respects from that applicable in the public sector, with its fundamental concern for the business of government.

Corporate governance, 'self-regulation' and 'co-regulation'

Contemporary corporate governance has evolved beyond a 'top-down' and 'command-and-control' vision of how corporations are structured, managed, and controlled. Its coverage also extends beyond the relations between corporate directors, managers, and shareholders as corporate actors engaged in private ordering of private interests. Responding to canonical accounts of corporate governance that focus on boards mediating relations between corporate management and investors, four leading corporate governance scholars have argued for accountability to relevant constituencies (Bradley et al 1999: 11). Under their formulation corporate governance extends beyond:

> the relationship between the firm and its capital providers. Corporate governance also indicates how the very constituencies that define the business enterprise serve, and are served by the corporation. Implicit and explicit relationships between the corporation and its employees, creditors, suppliers, customers, host communities ... fall within the ambit of a relevant definition.

Such views of corporate governance again highlight the importance of the formal and structural (i.e. 'hard') aspects of corporate governance in tandem with its informal and non-structural (i.e. 'soft') aspects (chapter 1). They also dovetail with other authoritative, contemporary encapsulations of corporate governance that are sensitive to the importance of meaningful stakeholder relations and engagement, such as guidelines on stakeholders in the OECD's principles (2004: 46). In addition, they introduce the notion of multiple levels and forms of accountability to different corporate governance participants. Bringing all of these different levels, contexts, and forms of governance to bear, overall 'corporate governance' can be viewed in terms of the mechanisms by which organisations in all sectors conduct their affairs and interact with others within and across relevant systems and dimensions of governance.

Redefining governance in the public sector: *Ahead of the Game,* CFAR and Uhrig

Ahead of the Game and the Uhrig review represent different official attempts at the federal level, from different perspectives and times in the evolution of Australian public administration, to grapple with the interactions between basic aspects of public administration, on one hand, and influences from the external global and societal environments upon public administration, on the other. In doing so, these reports relate policy-making and law-making, regulatory oversight and enforcement and delivery of public services to core elements of corporate governance for public sector organisations and whole-of-sector governance frameworks and arrangements. They also connect those related aspects to wider influences from the external global and societal environments upon public administration.

Recent refinements to corporate governance: The Uhrig review

The Uhrig review was significant because it addressed an important difficulty with absorbing autonomous corporate entities and their boards within the public sector. The review identified the features of a truly autonomous decision-making board and suggested that such a board be restricted to use by those bodies that were most clearly able (and expected) to act independently of government.

Chaired by an experienced company director, John Uhrig, the review of governance arrangements of key agencies was announced by the Coalition government of John Howard in 2002. The Uhrig review's main brief from the government was to examine the governance structures and practices of Commonwealth governmental authorities and office-holders, especially those of particular relevance to the business community, such as the Australian Taxation Office, ASIC, Australian Competition and Consumer Commission, Australian Prudential Regulation Authority, and the Reserve Bank of Australia (see chapter 8), but also other major agencies such as Centrelink (Uhrig 2003: 105–06). Those terms of reference also established the Howard government's expectation that the Uhrig review would result in 'a broad template of governance principles and arrangements' (see chapter 8).

Importantly, extending any principles more widely than the remit provided to Uhrig was always likely to prove difficult, since the terms of reference required the review to concentrate its attention chiefly upon the eight specified administrative and regulatory entities that were considered likely to have particular impact upon the business community. These entities were quite diverse in character — they included some which were constituted as authorities and statutory agencies, some reporting under both the FMA Act and the CAC Act, and some with boards that were established for both advisory and governance roles. For these reasons, the 'Board' and 'Executive Management' templates that were ultimately proposed by Uhrig need careful consideration in their application to public sector bodies generally.

In approaching the terms of reference, Uhrig considers governance '[to be] about ensuring the success of an activity' (Uhrig 2003: 21), and then examines the proper pathway to success through good governance and the well-defined roles of individuals. Uhrig also stated the central importance of identifying the clear function and purpose of the entity concerned. In this respect, the Uhrig review thus provided a different starting point than had the Australian National Audit Office (ANAO 2003c) guidelines for governance in the public sector. Implementing the ANAO guidelines had been an issue for certain CAC bodies. While defining the role and authority of individuals within the public sector would seem a sensible restatement of agency principles for individuals reporting under the FMA Act, legislating the role and authority of a governance board within the CAC Act, without also unduly confining its authority and rationale, is a more difficult task.

Criticism of the Uhrig review

The Uhrig review approach has been criticised from many standpoints. One long-standing commentator on public administration and statutory authorities summarised the immediate post-Uhrig reaction of commentators as follows (Wettenhall 2005: 45):

Corporate lawyers have been kindest to the report, at least in the sense of proclaiming its likely strong reformative impact ... Mostly, however, commentators have been less supportive, with criticisms focusing on a variety of perceived problems such as the style of writing; inadequate consultations; excessive reliance on private sector models; subservience to business; lack of concern with relevant history, academic research and overseas experience; massive generalising from just eight cases; failure to see that government is often the problem rather than the authorities themselves.

Despite its rhetorical references to constitutional, parliamentary, and public responsibility and accountability, some critics noted the relatively light treatment of these dimensions in the review's recommendations about governance arrangements and accountability frameworks, compared to the heavy emphasis upon executive government control of public sector entities and their accountability to the executive government. In particular, some decried its scant incorporation of parliamentary accountability within its governance arrangements and frameworks, given the interdependent relationships that exist between parliament, ministers, and departments concerning the establishment and operations of statutory authorities (Wettenhall 2005).

The review was also criticised for extrapolating too simple a two-limbed template for statutory authorities from too limited a sample of investigated bodies — a deficiency that, if present, was compounded by the Howard government's extension of the Uhrig review's recommendations to all portfolio bodies. Some castigated it for overestimating what private sector lessons on corporate governance might offer the public sector, and for underestimating some aspects of the public sector that affect the easy transposition of corporate governance lessons from the private sector. Others queried the review's lack of engagement with earlier official reports and inquiries, comparative public sector developments overseas, and the wider body of governance knowledge and expertise in the national and international literature on public sector governance generally and corporate governance in particular.

Considered from a legal perspective, there is a clear tension between the apparent simplicity of the Uhrig-based twin templates for governance arrangements and the more complex reality of the law's regulation of the distribution, use, and abuse of public power. In other words, the design and implementation of both cross-sectoral and organisational governance arrangements must also navigate the public sector governance implications of public law's allocation and conditioning of public power across the executive, legislative, and judicial branches (Gath 2005: 18; Miller and Sanders 2006: 28).

While there has been criticism of the ultimate extension of the Uhrig review's recommendations beyond those governmental regulators to the Commonwealth public sector as a whole, that possibility was also foreshadowed in the terms of reference (Uhrig 2003: 105). As the main department charged with implementing the Uhrig review's recommendations, the Department of Finance and Administration produced governance guidance for other Commonwealth public sector bodies in the form of its *Governance Arrangements for Australian Government Bodies* (DFA 2005b; and chapter 8, this volume).

The new public service agenda: *Ahead of the Game*

The review of the Reform of Australian Government Administration was announced in September 2009 as a six-month process. A discussion paper was released the following month (AGRAGA 2009), and the report, *Ahead of the Game: Blueprint for the Reform Australian Government Administration* in March the following year (AGRAGA 2010). The head of PM&C, Terry Moran, chaired the advisory group.[1] Kevin Rudd's Labor government charged the advisory group with moving from incremental and stop-gap reforms to Commonwealth public administration to producing 'a more sweeping reform driven by a long-range blueprint for a world class, 21st century public service' (Rudd 2009a).

The *Ahead of the Game* recommendations directly affect departments and agencies as well as having implications across the sector. The report covered 28 recommendations in nine reform areas that were organised under four themes: citizen needs, leadership and strategic direction, public sector workforce capability, and high standards of operational efficiency. The nine reform areas

---

1   For details of the process, see the comprehensive review by Evert Lindquist (2010).

were more specific about a melange of questions, such as service delivery, open government, policy capability, a new APSC for driving change, strategic planning and agency expectations (agility, capability, effectiveness, and efficiency) (see Appendix 1). The recommendations also reflected the emerging governance significance of relations with other Commonwealth public sector bodies, non-governmental actors, and levels of government. Specific recommendations addressed the roles and responsibilities of secretaries and agency capability reviews, while others were pitched at the APS level, such as strengthening leadership, assessing the senior executive service, and cross-portfolio and sector relationships.

The overall tenor of *Ahead of the Game* was to fine-tune, and augment, systemic features of the Australian public service. The corporate governance and NPM emphases of previous public sector reform were not prominent. Instead, new themes like mechanisms of transparency, engagement, integration, collaboration, and shared responsibility joined traditional ones of efficiency, deregulation and public sector values.

Critique and aftermath of *Ahead of the Game*

Ahead of the Game picked up a number of matters that were already the subject of discussion, debate and reports within the public sector. The catalogue of items compiled in the report included efficiency dividends, revising APS values, reducing red tape, the roles of secretaries — including stewardship as a response to short-termism — weaknesses in policy making, and the consequences of different conditions of employment for joint activity. Without an 'urgent, politically "hot" reform trigger, the Moran group ... found it difficult to weave a coherent narrative that holds the disparate activity clusters together' ('t Hart 2010). This lack of a distinctive and unifying core issue or theme contributed to the mixed acceptance of the overall reform agenda.

By its nature, this was not an exercise that had the potential to generate innovations that would rank internationally. Compare the earlier creation of Centrelink, for example, which was originally hailed internationally as a multi-purpose delivery agency for providing services to purchasing departments, and for seeking customer-focused delivery that provided integrated services (Halligan 2008b). This is not to say that innovation might not emerge in the continuing implementation process, and a commitment to being innovative is evident (MAC 2010).

The report did present ideas that were new to the APS, but which were based on practice elsewhere. The report addressed the question of citizen engagement, which had been the subject of debate within governance circles for some time (Briggs 2009), and borrowed from Canada and New Zealand the technique of conducting satisfaction surveys. Capability reviews were adopted from the United Kingdom and directed at departments, but the concept was substantially adapted to Australian needs.

It is possible to see the report as an exercise in comprehensive design and maintenance, but the way that it is perceived depends greatly on the execution of its recommendations; *Ahead of the Game* was essentially the precursor to an extended reform process that is managed by the public service. It contains an agenda for change, which addresses a large range of elements and encompasses many players (in particular, two leadership groups, a new secretaries board and APS 200, a senior leadership forum for supporting the secretaries). In this respect, the era presaged by *Ahead of the Game* was not unlike the 1980s and the 2000s, except there was no roadmap then.

With the removal of Rudd from the prime ministership in 2010, the implementation process was disrupted. Prior to the 2010 elections, several processes were under way to implement the report's recommendations. The most significant was the augmentation of the APSC's powers by government endorsement of *Ahead of the Game*. It was made the lead agency for around half the recommendations and the APSC was allocated $39 million for the purpose of implementation under the 2010 budget. This sum was heavily cut by the new Labor prime minister, Julia Gillard, when she projected fiscal rectitude during the election campaign, and the funding was reduced for a succession of budgets (Sedgwick 2011a). The reform agenda has not been a priority for the prime minister, as indicated by the inattention to *Ahead of the Game* — which received a passing reference only in her 2011 Garran Oration to the Institute for Public Administration (Gillard 2011). Without explicit political support, and given some ambivalence towards the overall reform exercise within the senior public service, the implementation of *Ahead of the Game* will be constrained and selective.

Nevertheless, some discrete agendas that were derived from *Ahead of the Game* have been pursued. Of particular significance were those associated with a reconstituted APSC, which continued to be the lead agency for reform. The commission's new approach was to engage collaboratively with departments and agencies in pursuit of common outcomes. The agencies have funded the commission to provide a range of services covering leadership and skills, talent management, workplace planning and standards, and a range of staffing matters, which affect public service capacity. Special reviews have become standard and they include the piloting of capability reviews of several agencies and a system review of the senior executive service (Sedgwick 2011a, 2011b, 2011c).

The overall coordination and review of the results of reform lies with the Department of the PM&C, with a departmental network being important for both systemic agendas and agency-specific reforms. The constitution of the secretaries' board as a formal central mechanism, which is chaired by the PM&C secretary, and secretaries' performance agreements have been implemented.

The Public Service Amendment Bill 2012 proposed a legislative basis for the revised roles of a number of actors, which was foreshadowed in *Ahead of the Game*, including secretaries, a secretaries board, the senior executive service and the public service commissioner. Reformulated public service values were also to be enacted.

In addition there were two sets of recommendations for 'improving agency efficiency' (Halligan 2011b). One set addressed the need to strengthen the governance framework by simplifying governance structures for new and existing entities; and amending the governance arrangements to ensure clarity for interjurisdictional entities and that new (and existing agencies) were 'fit-for-purpose' (chapter 8). Finance was charged with reviewing 'the different categories of entities ... with a view to simplifying and rationalising them'. The department was to amend the governance policy framework and to review '(e)ntities in portfolios that could be amalgamated either due to efficiency and/or synergies in structures and tasks; and opportunities for small agencies to be incorporated into departments or other agencies' (AGRAGA 2010: recommendation 9.2).

With the second group of recommendations, efficiency was accorded primacy with arguments expressed in terms of maximising outcomes against inputs and improving productivity in a challenging fiscal environment (AGRAGA 2010). This led to Finance producing the *Review of the Measures of Agency Efficiency* (2011: 46), which proposed elements of a strategic efficiency agenda to be centred on 'Efficient structures: reviewing the shape of government and identifying opportunities for rationalising the number of government bodies'. The review recommended rationalising the number of small agencies because of inefficiencies arising from duplication and the costs of corporate services, and for the economies of scale to be derived through managing programs. The review also focused on the efficiency dividend as a mechanism having implications for portfolio management, as discussed in chapter 5.

Commonwealth Financial Accountability Review

Another inquiry of broader and greater significance, the *Commonwealth Financial Accountability Review* (CFAR), was commenced in 2011 as an internal public service consultation around a series of issue papers, which led to a public discussion paper in 2012 (DFD 2012b).[2] The issue papers ranged widely over

---

2   Twelve issues papers were released plus an overarching paper on foundations for better government. The papers were for internal circulation and feedback within the public service.

financial and related matters including governance. In some respects, CFAR is more important as a review than *Ahead of the Game* as it has resulted in extensive opportunities for consultation via a process run by a team in Finance, but the discussion paper is more reflective and thought-provoking.

The essential purpose of CFAR is to review the existing financial framework, to examine options and to develop a new framework. In doing so, the discussion paper ranges over major questions about accountability and transparency, governance, improving performance, and the handling of risk. The rationale for change, and the prompt for undertaking the review, reflects both the limitations of the existing financial framework and the need to respond to attitudinal and environmental changes concerning the role of citizens, policy complexity, technological developments, and joined-up government interdepartmental coordination. The directions being taken by Finance, which have been prompted by the significant issues raised by the CFAR process, will become apparent after the responses to the discussion document have been digested in mid 2012.

The emergence of public governance

Having reviewed the evolving corporate and public governance agenda and formulations, three strands can be seen as converging to produce new understandings of governance in its public form: corporate governance-like features that are inherited from NPM; public governance; and governance in general.

First, NPM had opened up government to new ideas and approaches. As NPM reforms were introduced into the public sector, elements of corporate governance 'began to accompany them as the default accountability and control tool advocated to replace the traditional process-based controls that historically had been used' (Tucker 2010: 3). The flow on from government outsourcing is the acceptance of third party relationships as a normal part of government. The experience with markets led government to regard non-hierarchical (ie non-bureaucratic) instruments as an option for solving a policy problem. Moreover, the policy imperatives of the last decade have increasingly required joint action and collaboration.

Secondly, as discussed in chapter 1, the rise of a broader concept of *governance* has been significant in that the role non-government organisations is recognised. It has a range of meanings and definitions in the relevant literature such as an over-arching theory of institutional relationships within society (Kooiman 1999) or self-organising inter-organisational networks (Kickert 1993) — the common element being the breadth of the application. A traditional view defines governance in terms of a governing process associated with formal structures of government. A society-centric conception sees governance in terms of networks of public and private interactions (Rhodes 1997). A new public governance perspective (Osborne 2006: 384) recognises a:

> plural state, where multiple inter-dependent actors contribute to the delivery of public services and a pluralist state where multiple processes inform the policy making system. As a consequence of these two forms of plurality, its focus is very much upon inter-organisational relationships and the governance of processes, and it stresses service effectiveness and outcomes.

The formulation that has received considerable acceptance, however, covers both the traditional and recent conceptions. Central governments remain central as the responsible decision-makers on public policy, but they are expected to use third parties and networks, to be responsive to external preferences and to incorporate meaningful interactions with citizens and civil society. In the OECD context, when it is removed from any specific national or sectoral limits, governance is defined in terms that embrace a broader set of relationships, processes and outcomes, and thus includes more than public administration and the institutions, methods and instruments of governing. It also encompasses the set of relationships between governments and citizens, acting as both individuals and as part of or through institutions, e.g. political parties, productive enterprises, special interest groups, and the media (OECD 2000). Recent agendas reflect a growing concern with horizontal relationships inside and outside government and citizen engagement (see chapters 7 and 10).

Thirdly, the official position on corporate governance in the public sector has evolved through several stages. The rhetoric from ministers and departments originally paid lip service to the concepts, but did not produce an over-arching formulation, leaving the ANAO to take up the mantle for articulating and propagating ideas. The auditor-general at that time, Pat Barrett, 'was an early and intense advocate of corporate governance: of the 139 public addresses he made between 1995 and 2005, one in three addressed public sector corporate governance and accountability issues' (Tucker 2010: 3). The ANAO also took the lead with a series of statements on corporate governance for the public sector in general and a statement of principles and better practice for authorities and companies in particular (ANAO 1999). In contrast, there appear to have been minimal contributions from government ministers, although several, such as Senator Eric Abetz (2003a; 2003b), advocated corporate governance as an approach in the public sector. According to Tony Tucker (2010: 3) these were 'isolated occurrences by individual ministers rather than a comprehensive approach endorsed by government'.

As chapter 1 has indicated, the ANAO then adopted the term 'public sector governance' when it came to issuing guidelines in 2003 for principles that covered both board agencies and government departments (ANAO 2003c). By the mid 2000s, a range of central agencies (APSC and PM&C) and integrity agencies (ANAO and the Commonwealth Ombudsman) were contributing statements and guidelines as governance failure became a central issue. In these subsequent statements, both governance and corporate governance were used in official documents, as discussed in chapter 5 (ANAO and PM&C 2006; PM&C 2009a).

The lack of a coordinated approach has, according to Tucker (2010), contributed to interdepartmental 'variations in the acceptance of corporate governance'. A different approach was adopted by PM&C (based on the Australian Securities Exchange guidelines) to that taken by the ANAO in its departmental requirements for annual reporting of corporate governance. Both approaches involved parliament, in one case an officer of the parliament, the auditor-general, while in the other, PM&C's statement was endorsed by the Joint Committee on Parliamentary Accounts and Audit. 'With such a failure of Parliament and central agencies to agree on the nature of corporate governance there is little wonder at the lack of uniformity of application in the APS' (Tucker 2010: 4).

The consequence of this history is that there is general understanding of the principles of corporate and public governance, and of the variations between different types of government organisation (particularly departments of state and authorities with executive boards), but no formal framework to put good governance into operation. Chapters 3 and 5 pick up the variations in perceptions of governance for these different public sector bodies, while chapter 4 concentrates upon the central perspective.

Conclusion

The revolution in public management of the 1980s to 1990s was the introduction and institutionalisation of public management that was based, in large part, on private sector practice. There was much debate about the merits and applications and the contradictory components (Considine and Painter 1997) but, by international standards, a remarkable level of change was accomplished and sustained in Australia (Pollitt and Bouckaert 2011; Halligan 2007b). This was succeeded by a lesser-understood 'quiet revolution' in the late 1990s to the early 2000s, through the infusion and acceptance of corporate governance as a mode of operating in the public sector, thereby continuing the application of business-like forms and practices across the public sector. In addition, the acceptance of governance as a generic term that applies at several levels, and particularly across multiple boundaries, has extended the operative and collaborative basis of government.

The public sector governance of today has absorbed these influences to produce a blend of these features. An organisation may be inclined towards public sector governance features such as private sector aspects, citizen engagement or core public service values, depending on its location and function in the system of public administration. The overall mix, though, appears to emphasise traditional public administration principles, which are discussed in later chapters.

3. Exploring Tensions in Public Governance

Chapter 3 explores a number of tensions that underlie the different aspects of public sector governance that are examined in subsequent chapters of this book. These areas of tension are firstly: those currently encountered in the relationship between politicians and the bureaucracy; secondly, those existing within the organisational foundations of central government departments; thirdly, tensions arising in the integration of authorities and companies established under the *Commonwealth Authorities and Companies Act 1997 (Cth)* (CAC Act); fourthly, tensions arising in processes of coordination and collaboration within government and between government and external groups; and finally, tensions associated with defining and adopting the broader governance concepts of accountability, corporate regulation and performance across the public sector as a whole.

One source of these tensions was examined in chapter 2, which discussed the state-centric and society-centric elements of public governance that are now sought to be integrated in a central government responsible for providing both strong leadership and strategic direction within the sector (AGRAGA 2010: 20). This integration requires the reinforcement of traditional vertical lines of accountability and responsibility and, in this respect, tensions exist in the relationship between ministers and the senior public service, in organisational aspects of government departments and line agencies (chapters 4 and 5) and in integrating bodies that have been established under the CAC Act (chapter 6).

At the same time, however, difficulties in horizontal integration across government departments and portfolios increasingly intrude, pointing to the tensions that are associated with maintaining the traditional bureaucracy while admitting flexibility in policy formation and program delivery. The society-centric elements of public governance add new horizontal elements, requiring further collaboration within government and between government and external groups (chapter 7). Collaboration is increasingly a problem for governments as it may involve those from outside the public sector in decision-making and, thus, these horizontal elements may be less formally defined. Nevertheless, they must be permitted to open central government to the influence of new ideas and collaboration with others such as academics, business and the broader community (AGRAGA 2010: 20).

Tensions in context

Tensions in public governance have existed, at least in a proto-modern sense, ever since ministers' roles were more clearly differentiated from those of departments and a variety of public organisations began to emerge.[1] Invariably these tensions are centred on boundaries and relationships, on politicians and the extent of their reach over different organisations. In addition to these tensions within government, some tension also arises in the integration of several different forms of corporate-style organisations, and their boards, on which governments have at times relied. In Australia, these organisations have included statutory authorities and government business enterprises.

For the purposes of this book, the focus is on the last decade of change and the contemporary position. Evidence of the tensions referred to above emerge from studies undertaken by the authors during three significant periods over the last ten years. Few empirical studies have captured this breadth of public sector bodies and officials in transition during the implementation of new governance measures. The significance of the interviews undertaken in this study is that they capture point-in-time reactions of high-level participants while they were engaged in these reform periods. The interviews are utilised elsewhere in the book to illustrate clear attitudes and approaches to significant structural and legislative developments that were identified within the sector.

Many of the issues that were suggested by the authors' earliest interviews in 2002 were confirmed and explored further in the more comprehensive range of interviews they later undertook, in 2005–07, with representatives of all arms of the Commonwealth public sector for the Australian Research Council–funded grant: Corporate Governance in the Public Sector. These interviews were undertaken with all federal government departments and a wide selection of statutory agencies, authorities and companies following the release of the 2003 *Review of the Corporate Governance of Statutory Authorities and Office Holders* (Uhrig review). The interviews sought to clarify the understanding of the terms 'corporate governance' and 'governance' within the Australian public sector, the value and utilisation in practice of key governance indicators for improved performance, the assumption of responsibility for the regulation of governance and the effective coordination of governance across the sector as a whole. A note on the methodology adopted for this study and the interview schedule can be found in appendix 1. Further interviews and analysis were finally undertaken in the post-Uhrig review period of the late 2000s, as the public sector landscape began to settle, and in the transitional years of the early 2010s.

---

1   For details from administrative history dating from the nineteenth century, see Halligan and Wettenhall 1990; Wettenhall 2007.

Interviews that were undertaken in 2002 with representatives of CAC bodies had confirmed the existence of manifestations of new public management and revealed difficulties in the adoption of the Australian National Audit Office (ANAO) governance principles in practice. A lack of clarity was registered in the different roles played by executive and management boards within federal government departments and agencies — given the adoption of more formally constituted 'corporate' boards under the CAC Act in Commonwealth authorities and companies. The interviewers sought to explore the ways in which CAC bodies were being utilised and adopted within the sector (Edwards, Nicoll and Seth-Purdie 2003).

The interviews suggested uncertainty as to the 'independence' of the boards and directors of CAC bodies. They also revealed uncertainty in the processes for the appointment of directors, difficulties in ensuring that the appropriate skills were represented upon the board and problems associated with the dynamics of decision-making by CAC boards in the public sector context. Overall, they suggested that significant difficulties were being encountered within the public sector in integrating the new legal concepts of board authority and individual director responsibility, which were introduced by the CAC Act, and the associated concepts of corporate governance, corporate self-regulation and performance measurement.

The interviews that were undertaken from 2005–07 sought to examine governance issues within the public sector system as a whole. Within federal government departments and agencies, interviewees asserted their strong support for maintaining the traditional legal authority and responsibility of the chief executive. At the same time, those sitting on the boards of bodies reporting under the CAC Act, which were generally conceived in law as commercially oriented and independent 'decision-making' boards, appeared acutely mindful of government policy while mostly maintaining the independence of their boards. Importantly to the coordination of governance across the system as a whole, the clear endorsement of the authority of the secretary and chief executive, and the assertions of the independence and authority of the decision-making board by many directors within CAC bodies, pointed to continuing difficulties in the integration of corporate entities and governance within the sector.

As these interviews were undertaken during the period in which the Uhrig review was being implemented, the representatives of corporations and authorities operating under the CAC Act were conscious of the possible conversion of authorities and companies to agencies. Interviewees were therefore clearly giving thought to questions such as the 'independence' of their board and the features of 'corporate' governance that were applicable to their body.

Across the sector, these interviews confirmed great diversity of opinion in the understanding of the concept of corporate governance and its application in the public sector.

Many of the elements of corporate governance that have been seen to be so influential in the private sector are often considered to be inappropriate for the federal public sector. The mechanisms for the scrutiny of public sector decision-making are seen to be far more significant checks upon the proper exercise of public powers than the regulatory controls and management checks that are associated with corporate governance in the private sector. In keeping with the strong support for the authority and responsibility of the secretary and chief executive, governance for many agencies in the public sector is seen in terms of meeting compliance and reporting requirements. Many other essential differences in the application of principles of governance drawn from the private sector, which were identified in 2002 interviews, were also confirmed in the later interviews. The processes for appointing board members, maintaining relevant skills on the board, and measuring the performance and effectiveness of governance arrangements, were all seen to be different in the public sector.

Organisational basis for the governance of public bodies

The spectrum of public bodies is summarised briefly in Figure 3.1. To the right of the spectrum lie the departments of state and executive agencies, which are the central organisational forms associated with the constitutional supremacy of parliament, ministerial and executive responsibility and the features of vertical accountability within the Westminster system. To the left lie the corporate-style bodies that have been created by parliament but influenced substantially by private corporate law. In the middle lie a mix of government and statutory authorities, which in part reflect the historical evolution of the relationship between the state and private corporations. While the CAC Act defined the legal and constitutional features of authorities and companies operating within the public sector far more sharply in terms of corporate law concepts than ever before, the features of a mixed model remain clearly in evidence. The minister, for example, makes appointments to the boards of CAC bodies, and the chief executive of several CAC bodies reports directly to the minister.

It might be anticipated that both the closeness and complexity of the relationship between government and private corporate bodies generally will continue to grow. So, too, will the exchanges between government and private corporations as new bodies evolve to meet changing circumstances. This is largely due to the fact that the corporation has proven a remarkably adaptable and convenient legal form, not merely for the conduct of private enterprise but for a wide range of other governmental and organisational purposes as well.

Figure 3.1: Commonwealth organisational spectrum and legislative basis

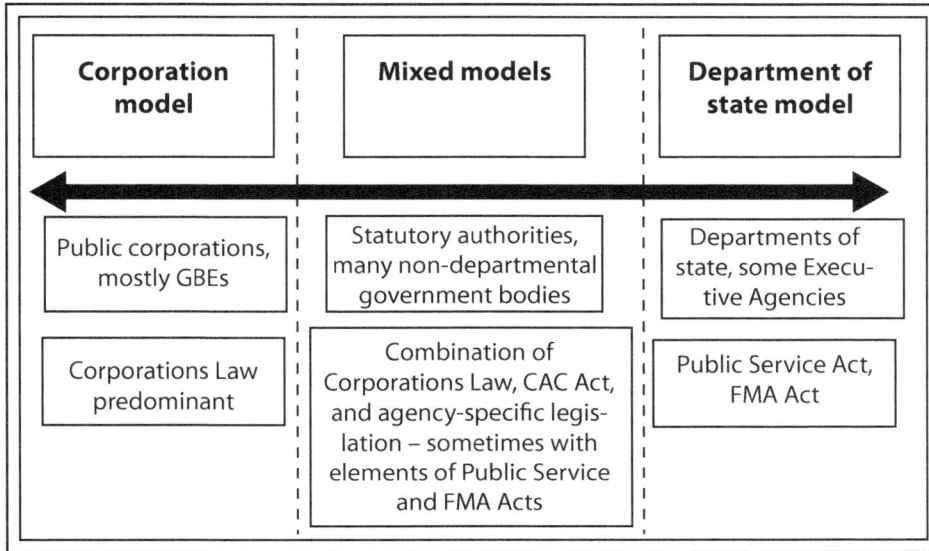

Corporation model	Mixed models	Department of state model
Public corporations, mostly GBEs	Statutory authorities, many non-departmental government bodies	Departments of state, some Executive Agencies
Corporations Law predominant	Combination of Corporations Law, CAC Act, and agency-specific legislation – sometimes with elements of Public Service and FMA Acts	Public Service Act, FMA Act

Source: Adapted from ANAO 2003c: Figure 3.

For the purposes of outlining the statutory institutional framework within which public sector governance must operate, the Department of Finance and Deregulation (Finance) has fully catalogued the bodies that are relevant to governance in the public sector in its *List of Australian Government Bodies and Governance Relationships* (DFD 2009). It also provides a regularly updated ready reference guide to this list of *Financial Management and Accountability Act 1997 (Cth)* (FMA Act) agencies and CAC bodies in a flipchart (DFD 2012a). A copy of the flipchart is reproduced in appendix 2. Table 3.1 summarises the number and types of different bodies reporting under the FMA Act and under the CAC Act.

Table 3.1: Agencies and other bodies under the FMA Act and CAC Act

111 Agencies under the FMA Act	
Departments of state	20
Departments of the parliament	4
Prescribed agencies	67
Prescribed agencies encompassing 'executive agency'	8
Prescribed agencies — statutory but staffed through departments or agencies	2
Prescribed agencies — non-statutory and staffed through departments or agencies	5
Prescribed agencies — engage staff under their own act	5
84 Bodies under the CAC Act 1997	
Statutory authorities	62
Commonwealth companies	22

Source: Chart of Agencies and CAC Bodies (Finance 2010).

Within this framework, those bodies that are most immediately relevant to the organisation and management of the business of government comprise the departments of state, departments of parliament and 'prescribed agencies' — which are named as such in regulations promulgated under the FMA Act. The essential governmental character of these 111 agencies is set by the distinctive and varied statutory requirements under which they operate. These requirements set the constitutional and operational parameters for these agencies and, therefore, they provide the ultimate point of reference when defining their roles in integrated government. There are 20 departments of state that are regulated under the *Public Service Act 1999 (Cth)* (PS Act) and four departments of the parliament regulated under the *Parliamentary Service Act 1999*. Of the prescribed agencies, 67 are also statutory agencies under the PS Act. The remaining agencies are referred to in Table 3.1.

The central importance of these FMA agencies to government, and to the business of government, is established by their capacity to receive appropriations in their own right and by the 'materiality' of 41 such agencies to government. The essential character of these bodies as government agencies is established in the FMA Act, which renders the chief executive of the agency solely responsible for the efficient, effective and ethical use of Commonwealth resources.

Tensions between the political and executive arms of government

Under the Westminster model, the relations between politicians and bureaucrats have traditionally centred on the coexistence of the neutral public service and responsible government. The embedded tension between the two elements has been kept in balance by applying well-established principles. During the last 30 years, however, an imbalance between these two branches of government has become apparent and politicians, in response to the ascendancy of the bureaucrats, have sought to expand their authority.

The continuing jostling between politicians and public servants was maintained during the last decade with the role of ministerial advisers featuring prominently as the main source of tension. A new factor became more salient as the short-term inclinations of politicians exerted continuous working pressures, thereby exacerbating relations with public servants scrambling to meet real time demands (a new meaning of responsiveness?). Measures to ameliorate the last problem came into play in the 2010s.

Organisational tensions within departments and agencies

Committees and 'decision-making' bodies within departments

Executive management boards, advisory boards and cross-jurisdictional commissions have long been utilised in government departments and agencies (Horrigan 2001: 62–6). These boards are not conceived to have independent autonomy or authority, however, and they must be considered in the context of the ultimate responsibility of the chief executive for the 'efficient, effective and ethical use' of Commonwealth property and resources. They are committees conceived to assist the departmental secretary or chief executive in the discharge of his or her ultimate statutory responsibilities. The Commonwealth Financial Accountability Review (CFAR) discussion paper *Is Less More: Towards Better Commonwealth Performance* (2012) notes that the use of boards within departments can provide a diverse range of skills and experiences that secretaries might utilise, although the paper also makes it clear that such boards do not function as corporate boards and should not affect a secretary's authority and accountability for the operations of the department (DFD 2012b: 41).

For a time following the passage of the CAC Act, these boards sometimes appeared to assume a more ambiguous place than they had held previously within FMA agencies. Despite the attempt (Uhrig 2003) to resolve ambiguities by drawing the distinction more clearly between 'governance' (or 'decision-making') boards and 'management' boards — the term 'board' continues to be used by some secretaries even though, in the context of executive government, the terminology is misleading. Management boards are essentially committees appointed by the secretary. The important consequence of conceiving boards as merely 'advisory' or 'executive management' within the overall responsibility of the departmental secretary or chief executive is that their operation is ultimately subject to a number of different mechanisms of statutory oversight. This statutory oversight of public sector boards differs markedly from the internal checks and balances upon private sector boards that are now achieved in modern corporate governance through a mix of prescribed statutory processes, voluntary codes of practice and market assessments.

The governance arrangements that have been published by Finance tend to predispose against the formation of new bodies. They begin by asking whether it is necessary to create a new body at all and whether new functions might not be best accommodated within departments (DFA 2005b: 13). They suggest that an FMA agency should be the 'preferred form' in establishing new bodies (DFA

2005b: 18). At the same time, however, Finance's *List of Government Bodies* also identifies four decision-making 'bodies' within departments. These bodies are interesting because they arise within government departments, rather than in CAC bodies. Unlike management and advisory boards, however, they sit less comfortably with the supervening authority of the secretary.

The four bodies that are nominated by Finance are: those with 'distinct functional branding', ministerial councils, joint Commonwealth–state or international bodies, and advisory bodies. Joint Commonwealth–state bodies, ministerial councils and international bodies bear scrutiny since they appear to require the representation of particular interests on the board. In this respect Finance, in its 2005 governance arrangements, suggests that governance boards should not be 'representative' boards and that such boards should not find a place within departments in which they appear difficult to reconcile with the ultimate authority and responsibility of the chief executive under the FMA Act.

In interviews, which were undertaken around the time of the Uhrig review, interviewees confirmed that boards such as intergovernmental committees and regulatory commissions might be considered to have a role beyond providing mere advice and management. When referring to the boards of Commonwealth–state bodies, regulatory, and international bodies, they spoke of the value of a collective (or even representative) decision-making board. If such boards do not sit comfortably within FMA bodies, they may be suggesting the possibilities for an advisory board of a distinctive character in the public sector.

Regulatory commissions, particularly, were not seen to fit comfortably within the FMA Act-reporting framework. Finance has generally returned such commissions to the FMA Act fold, suggesting that a regulatory body should be constituted as an FMA agency when it is required to enforce the law under enabling legislation. Further, Finance would generally discourage the appointment of particular 'representative' appointees to such FMA agencies. In the case of such commissions, good governance may prove difficult in a dynamic federal system in which some state representation may be desirable.

External appointments to management and advisory boards

It might be thought that, because of the ultimate authority of departmental heads and chief executives, the scope exists for tailoring boards with the addition of members who are equipped with the necessary external skills — effectively 'designing' the management or advisory board to provide maximum assistance to the secretary. The CFAR discussion paper notes the potential benefits in doing this (DFD 2012b: 41). This possibility, however, is said to meet with the significant obstacle in Australia that most appointments are likely to be internal appointments. Those reporting under the FMA Act expressed concerns for the appointment of 'external' (i.e. outside the portfolio) representatives on departmental boards. Executive and management boards are generally filled by internal appointees, who are all accountable to the departmental head or chief executive — and interviewees generally agreed with the view that 'nothing would ever be implemented with an independent "expertise-based" board'. External appointees may be chosen only to provide the necessary expertise or to meet the particular needs of the case. As might be expected, audit committees were cited as one important exception — a special case in which external appointments and more formal procedures were seen to be most desirable. Commissions were cited as another special case.

At the same time, those representing the boards of agencies reporting under the FMA Act also noted that it was becoming increasingly difficult to find internal appointements to the board with the appropriate skills. One reason for this was seen to be the high turnover of staff; small agencies, in particular, were seen to suffer as a result of staff turnover. These comments suggest that, despite concerns being expressed for importing external expertise, the pool of 'internal' expertise within the Australian public sector may now be too limited to fulfil the need for expertise-based board members.

Tensions in integrating authorities, companies and corporate governance

Tensions in the adoption of corporate entities and concepts of corporate governance have been recognised for some time in the literature and appear likely to persist. As noted above, the CAC Act has, more clearly than previously, defined the legal features of authorities and companies that operate within the public sector in terms of corporate law concepts. Because of this, corporatisation now raises 'in acute form' the public/private distinction (Farrar 2005: 445). The distinction is particularly marked, not only because of the different functional roles that are fulfilled by corporatised entities in the public sector (Bottomley 1994: 530), but also because of the essentially different regulatory and market frameworks that prevail in the public and private sectors (Farrar 2005: 446). So, public sector governance must accommodate differences between sectors in transposing structures and standards from one to another, as well as in developing suitable engagement and accountability mechanisms.

In terms of the recent assessment of the public sector in *Ahead of the Game: Blueprint for the Reform of Australian Government Administration* (AGRAGA 2010), the same public/private distinction seems likely to arise in endeavouring to maintain a strong central government — one that is capable of steering and coordinating the whole public sector, while also maintaining control over the outer reaches of government. In this broad sense, the 'outer reaches' of government include both line agencies, which are more removed from departmental control within portfolios, as well as the departments and agencies of other portfolios. As a result, maintaining central control invokes both vertical and horizontal (or lateral) dimensions. Chapter 7, in particular, notes the 'pressing' tension that exists today between the horizontal responsibilities of government for non-government organisations and citizens and the vertical accountabilities of the Westminster system (Briggs and Fisher 2006: 16; Fung 2009).

The key players in the effective coordination of these vertical and horizontal elements of government are first, ministers and departmental secretaries; secondly, the departmental advisory and management committees that are utilised by secretaries; and thirdly, the corporate entities and boards governed chiefly by the CAC Act. Like departmental advisory boards, the corporate boards of authorities and companies may broaden the scope for participatory governance, but their appointment processes also present greater challenges for governments because independent and external board members pose potential obstacles to lines of accountability and responsibility within traditional public sector administration (chapter 9).

Following the Uhrig review (chapter 2), and consistent with strengthening the centre, the number of Commonwealth authorities has declined and a more cautious approach has been adopted by Finance in establishing new entities (chapter 8). For some time, there have been underlying tensions in the workings of the corporate-style boards of authorities and companies — tensions that are considered in greater detail at board level in chapter 6.

Sources of tension in integrating authorities and companies

Successive phases of private sector influence have placed stresses upon the traditional vertical hierarchy of authority and accountability in public sector administration. The reasons for this are best understood through a brief consideration of the statutory framework and Finance's catalogue of government bodies, as outlined above. This framework assists in identifying the legal authority and reporting requirements of individuals, agencies and corporate bodies within the public sector. A potential difficulty arises because more recent concepts of corporate law and governance, which are associated with bodies regulated under the CAC Act, have been superimposed upon this departmental framework, thereby raising possible tensions between traditional statutory mechanisms for government accountability and more recent private sector principles directed to improving the accountability, efficiency and performance of CAC bodies.

The difficulties found in integrating corporate bodies within a public sector setting, and positioning them within a framework of individual and agency accountability in central government, arise firstly, because the corporate board is conceived as an autonomous board that is empowered and authorised to make collective decisions embracing diverse views, rather than as a single decision-making secretary or officer. Secondly, further difficulties arise in integrating corporate bodies in the public sector setting because the authority of the board remains subject to significant government controls both in law and practice.

The features of the CAC Act that are most relevant to the governance of Commonwealth authorities and companies are outlined in greater detail in chapter 6, but it may be seen in Table 3.1 that 84 authorities and companies, which lie at arms length from central government, report under this legislation. Both authorities and companies operate in a corporate form with boards of directors whose members are subject to duties cast in similar terms to those of the directors of private corporations. This statutory formulation for the structure of authorities and companies, the authority of their boards and the responsibilities of their directors and officers all suggest the difficulties encountered in their assimilation within government departments and other agencies within government portfolios.

More broadly, the quantitative performance metrics of listed corporations (such as rates of return on investment, assets or equity) as well as both 'hard' performance measures (board composition and independent directors) and 'soft' or strategic measures (such as leadership and risk-taking), which are now included in governance ranking research, are ultimately founded upon market and shareholder assessments. A difficult question then arises as to whether it is sustainable to proceed with the multiple accountabilities that are now required for both public and private entities across the system (chapter 7).

The passage of the CAC Act highlighted several related areas of tension — some of less practical significance than others. In so far as the CAC Act refers to Commonwealth companies that are subject to the *Corporations Act 2001*, and imports the principles of directors' duties from the Corporations Act, there is continuing legal uncertainty as to the regulation and accountability of CAC bodies. Questions may arise, for example, as to whether the Australian Securities and Investments Commission (ASIC) or ministerial shareholders should be responsible for the regulation of these bodies and the enforcement of directors' duties. In addition, developments in Australian corporate law surrounding directors' duties and the defences available to them will affect the interpretation of equivalent law governing the directors and officers of agencies and companies under the CAC Act. Further questions may arise as to the extent to which concepts of private corporate governance, now supervised by ASIC, should govern the constitution and processes of the board. Finally, questions may also arise as to the extent to which measures of corporate performance, founded in the private sector upon shareholder and market expectations, provide valuable performance measures for corporations operating in the public sector.

In other areas, real tensions are felt in practice. In chapter 6, the authority of the boards of many authorities and companies reporting under the CAC Act is considered in the light of the various controls exercised by government in practice. In particular, board members must remain mindful of government policy and their appointment to the board generally rests upon responsible ministers — a factor examined in detail in chapter 9. These and other factors in practice remain significant constraints upon the authority and independence of such boards. Seen in this context, CAC bodies may never have been quite as independent of government as they have sometimes been assumed to be. Nevertheless, the corporate structure of these bodies makes them at once both critical to coordination between central government and the outer reaches of government and open to the kind of collaboration with outsiders that is envisaged in *Ahead of the Game*.

Directors of corporate bodies within the public sector

Within the public sector, particular tensions are now likely to be felt by the directors of corporate bodies. These difficulties stem largely from the legal authority of the body's board, the legal duties owed by directors to the corporate body and the governmental constraints upon the body that arise in practice. Within the board, these tensions manifest in the constraints under which the directors and corporate officers themselves must exercise their corporate powers while remaining mindful of the supervening influence of government and responsible ministers. The purpose of the CAC Act is to regulate certain aspects of the financial affairs of Commonwealth authorities and companies. With respect to Commonwealth-owned or controlled authorities, the CAC Act provides detailed rules about the reporting obligations of authorities and their accountability. It also deals with the conduct of the directors and officers of authorities, and with their banking and investment obligations. For companies, the Act provides reporting and other requirements that apply in addition to those encompassed by the Corporations Act.

These provisions dealing with directors' duties provide a good example of the way in which statutory provisions, of great significance in the private sector, may seem less relevant in an Act designed to regulate director behaviour in a public sector entity. In practice, the directors of CAC bodies are less likely to be sued by shareholders or called to account by regulators for contravention of the Corporations Act than are their private sector counterparts. Their legal duties highlight the essentially different character of corporate boards and their regulation within the private sector. Directors in this context owe their legal duties specifically to the corporate body — note the public duty of the chief executive under s 44 of the FMA Act to make 'efficient, effective and ethical use' of Commonwealth resources. Accordingly, their duties, as stated in the CAC Act, stand to be judged by reference to their corporate (as distinct from their governmental) responsibilities. Other potentially difficult legal questions may also arise in the future as to the applicability of directors' defences that are generally available in private corporate law — such as defences of due diligence and business judgment — in the foreign context of the public sector.

Difficulties in coordination and collaboration within and external to government

A further difficulty that continues to arise is that of coordinating collaboration across agencies and portfolios within the public sector and externally. This tension arises partly because of the need to coordinate policy formation and implementation vertically through the Commonwealth and state governments as well as horizontally, across the institutional 'silos' of each level of government. Effective policy implementation and service delivery across the whole of the public sector may sit uneasily with the formation of policy within government departments that are adhering to principles of individual responsibility, line accountability and the ultimate authority of parliament within the Westminster system. Chapter 5 outlines the formal mechanisms for collaboration between departments, which include interdepartmental committees and task forces.

An important consideration in advancing cross-government approaches is the recognition that the key foundations for cross-governmental coordination are often the 'softer' associations of an informal and unstructured character, which supplement more formal processes such as interdepartmental committees. Senior executives interviewed for this project generally felt that the contact they undertook with others to maintain whole-of-government approaches, although informal, was extensive, relevant and effective. One rationale given for the effectiveness of this contact (that seemed to sum up the general sentiment) was that 'the public sector works for the public good while the private sector has the profit principle as its bottom line'. Participants were generally happy to maintain informal relationships across departments, which they believed to be effective. One CEO said of the exchange of information: 'In terms of policy — none of these forums provides an opportunity. I don't think that there is a need to set up something formal but we do our policy work better when we are talking to other people about it. We try hard to have open lines of communication with other departments but I'd be hesitant to say that it could not be improved.'

Managing government 'as a whole' represents a distinct element in the conception of governance within the public sector literature. It addresses a practical and conceptual difficulty in the public sector that is quite distinct from the conceptual problems addressed in private corporate governance.[2] The most significant issue, and the most significant source of tension within the public sector, however, remains one of horizontal coordination in practice within a traditional system that is built upon individual and agency accountability.

Reflections of difficulties in practice

Reflecting the tensions between vertical and horizontal government identified above, interviewees in the mid 2000s, who were required to report under the FMA Act, tended to acknowledge the continuing difficulties in realising the concept of whole-of-government. They noted that the FMA Act did not encourage whole-of-government approaches — rather, it simply made the chief executive separately accountable. Mindful of the responsibility of the chief executive for the efficient, effective and ethical use of resources under the FMA Act, one chief executive said: 'The FMA Act focuses on the individual responsibility of the CEO. I like the concept of separating decision making from the minister (e.g. through a board), but I also like the concept of me being personally responsible. Requiring the co-signature of the CFO was a good move'.

It was also said that some CAC bodies, which had been set up for program delivery, were assuming a policy-making role. This perception emerged in interviews with some CAC body interviewees whose bodies operated within small portfolios, and was significant in the case of Centrelink, an FMA agency that is discussed in chapter 5.

FMA agency respondents remarked upon the increasing accountability requirements, both in CAC bodies reporting to central agencies and in the ANAO's performance audits. One interviewee observed that 'the layers are building up'. Thus, the effective integration of agencies and authorities within the whole-of-government remains a significant difficulty. With an eye to improving this, one option considered by FMA agency participants was to make portfolio bodies accountable to the minister. They saw a 'fragmentation' of the bureaucracy at

---

2 At times, there appear to be analogies with the broader concerns of private corporate governance — for example, the improvement of corporate social responsibility and corporate ethics may appear to have similar ultimate objectives to some whole-of-government objectives.

the very time when service delivery and national security demanded greater coordination within government. They thought, for example, that the delivery of extended entitlement programs now presented difficulties, as did achieving broad political agreement among commissions. They commented on the difficulties now associated with performance management and understanding the risk profiles of quite different organisations across the public sector.

Some more specific structural and procedural issues, which have tended to highlight this fragmentation, were also referred to. These included the fundamental difficulty perceived in the minister delegating power to a board and the difficulties involved in strengthening the relationship between minister and chair (a suggestion made by the Uhrig review) when the chief executive remained the full-time employee. Another related issue was a clear concern among many FMA agency interviewees for the difficulties and ultimate value in maintaining stakeholder representation. There appeared a weakening faith in the value of the 'representative' board — the only possible exception to this being the value seen by many interviewees in maintaining jurisdictional representation in regulatory commissions.

Finally, senior executives saw a significant gap between the concept of 'governance', considered as a universal code of good practice within the public sector, and the need for more active public engagement with (and access to), the public sector in practice. A few interviewees felt that the 'governance' era had been less successful in publicising and addressing its 'sins of omission' as distinct from highlighting its achievements. They questioned their true capacity to control what was actually happening in the field.

Cross-portfolio board representation

In chapter 9 it is noted that, for some secretaries, departmental representation on CAC bodies is considered a part of their role. The explanation given by those reporting under the FMA Act for not undertaking such representation was their concern for 'ending up in a position of political vulnerability with the minister — since the minister is ultimately accountable'. This group also provided plausible explanations for their view that representation by CAC body representatives on departmental executive boards would not be a good idea. They emphasised the need to preserve the confidentiality of agency decisions and their concern for the lack of public CAC Act responsibility within the sector. FMA agency participants were also equivocal about the value of the chief executive sitting on the boards of CAC bodies. Other difficulties in secretarial representation on boards are canvassed in chapter 9.

Further, FMA agency participants commonly saw other more effective and less risky ways for departments to obtain input from CAC bodies (e.g. through portfolio chief executives' meetings, representation of CAC bodies on policy committees and other specific departmental subcommittees). As noted earlier, some FMA agency participants expressed their concern for 'external' (i.e. outside the portfolio) representatives on executive boards. For example: 'I wouldn't want it. Perhaps on subcommittees yes, for technical expertise. But not on the executive board because some of the business is highly confidential and what does a non-executive director become — a conscience?'

Coordination with CAC bodies

Departmental perspectives on their relations with CAC bodies and other portfolio agencies were also addressed during interviews. Within state-centric public governance, the effective coordination of department and agencies within the portfolio is a key indicator of the successful melding of horizontal and vertical governance. For their part, CAC bodies often held a firm view that departments could do more to keep them informed of policy directions and suggested that more representation by departments upon their boards might be helpful (chapter 6). As noted above, however, some agency heads saw difficulties in their being represented on the boards of CAC bodies. These difficulties emerged in this comment: 'I would never come between a chair and the minister, but they (i.e. CAC bodies) do need to understand that the minister will ask advice of the secretary. It's the secretary's responsibility to report to the minister on the whole portfolio'. This divergence in the views of those reporting under the FMA and CAC acts identifies a potential difficulty for integrated government and whole-of-government objectives.

Tensions in accommodating concepts and language of governance

The difficulties of absorbing corporate entities within the framework of central government are relatively apparent in the previous consideration of the statutory framework. Possibly less well understood, however, has been the extent to which private corporate law and governance has tended to import to the public sector new concepts and measures of corporate regulation and performance monitoring (chapter 2). As mentioned earlier in this chapter, the passage of the CAC Act served to highlight once again the different and distinctive aspects of the public/private divide that are associated with corporatisation and the privatisation of public enterprises (Farrar 2005: 445; Bottomley 1994: 530). One ongoing difficulty for the governance of the public sector in the future will be the need to sustain the variety of accountability regimes that are best suited to bodies of varying public and private character.

The very language of accountability in the public sector echoes the vertical responsibilities of those deriving their power and authority from the constitutional power and authority of parliament and cabinet. By contrast, the corporate board enjoys relative constitutional autonomy and its members are subject only to external regulation by ASIC, an independent corporate regulator. For this reason, difficulties may be expected to arise in considering whether ASIC or the Finance Minister should assume responsibility for bringing legal action against the directors of such bodies (DFD 2012b). Corporate governance in the private sector can only be understood by reference to market expectations and monitoring. Questions therefore arise as to the way in which the multiple concepts of accountability within government might be reconciled with the regulation and market monitoring of private corporations and corporate entities. In the authors' empirical study, questions of accountability were raised in three areas in particular, namely interviewees' recognition of structural (or 'hard') elements in regulation and accountability, their recognition of 'soft' elements of accountability, and their measuring and promoting of superior performance.

'Hard' and 'soft' elements in accountability and governance

As noted in chapter 1, the distinction drawn between 'hard' and 'soft' elements in governance recognises differences between the formal and structural (hard) elements and the behavioural and relational (soft) elements (Edwards and Clough 2005). In practice, many in the public sector identify three 'hard' elements of accountability within the Commonwealth public sector. These are first, the system of arrangements, organisational structures and processes that are employed to ensure accountability and responsibility in policy/service design and delivery; secondly, the multifaceted elements of public accountability, compliance, and performance (chapter 1); and thirdly, the demands of essential governmental functions which include service delivery, policy outcomes, legislative administration, statutory responsibilities, reporting lines and financial management.

In interviews with the authors, there remained a primary emphasis upon 'hard' rather than 'soft' governance, with relatively fewer references to 'soft' governance elements. Nevertheless, interviewees appeared aware of the importance of both hard and soft elements in measuring 'good governance' and monitoring performance within the sector. A typical 'hard' governance orientation was: 'Governance is primarily about the compliance environment in which we operate. It's about ensuring that we implement the systems, processes and safeguards so that we are operating legally and appropriately within our remit.' In considering this environment, FMA agency interviewees commonly referred to parliamentary accountability (senate estimates), accountability to ministers and accountability through 'informative and comprehensive' annual reporting (chapter 5).

Some FMA agency interviewees distinguished between 'accountability' in a strict sense and other, more informal, monitoring mechanisms such as stakeholder surveys, meeting performance measures or adopting risk management techniques, such as 'traffic lights' warning systems. Others were reluctant to accept the views of outside stakeholders as a measure of accountability. One interviewee put it this way:

> I don't find our constituencies all that helpful. If you look at the mission statements of some of them it's the 'take no prisoners' approach — protecting the environment at all costs. They don't take account of economic factors and so on ... there is no one style of leadership that is necessarily right. I've seen secretaries at extremes — highly directive or a kibbutz-style management. Neither is right — I want to hear people's views, but then I take action.

The responses of interviewees demonstrate that, while both hard and soft factors are considered relevant at different times, there is a wide range of different approaches adopted and no particular method is favoured. This range of different approaches tends to reflect interviewees' recognition and management of multiple accountabilities and their underlying public values, as detailed in chapter 1.

While most interviewees emphasised hard elements of governance, there was nevertheless a clear appreciation (especially at departmental level) that governance is not limited to 'hard' elements alone (i.e. structures and processes). A number of 'softer' elements were also identified as very significant, including transparency, trust, behaviour and ethics. These elements reflected the norms and values of public sector governance that were outlined in chapter 1. One atypical 'soft' governance approach that appeared more conducive to integrated governance was: 'to start with a couple of softer concepts ... and then, given the establishment of the sum of that, we set out the systems and the structures that go together to make up the governance arrangements'.

Measuring and promoting superior performance

At the time the CAC Act was passed in 1997, many of the accepted elements of good corporate governance in the private sector appeared to have possible application in the public sector as well. In the private sector, a positive correlation had been found between good corporate governance and improved efficiency (Millstein and MacAvoy 1998), although the link proved difficult to establish satisfactorily until more complex composite measures of both hard and soft factors in corporate governance were utilised (Larcker, Richardson and Tuna 2004; Edwards and Clough 2005).

Although good corporate governance (measured across a range of hard and soft variables) has been acknowledged to improve corporate performance in the private sector, those reporting under the FMA Act seem less convinced of its relevance to improved performance in the public sector. Individual and organisation performance management had been well established in the public sector since the 1980s (Bouckaert and Halligan 2006; Mackay 2004).

As might have been expected, participants reporting under the FMA Act, in particular, tended to see issues of accountability and performance in terms of their accountability to the minister and parliament. There seemed a less technical approach generally to assessing and measuring performance, suggesting that this driving force for good corporate governance practice in the private sector might be one area deserving of closer consideration in its application in the public sector. One interviewee said, for example: 'There's a performance assessment with the secretary to individual executive members. There isn't a formal process. However, I monitor it closely in my head and am very conscious of it all the time'.

Further comments, which served to reinforce the impression that improved performance may not have been among the primary considerations for interviewees, were these: 'We focus on behaviours, rather than measuring performance assessment against outcomes. But I guess it's hard to assess behaviours without having some link to outcomes,' and 'We don't have an instrument for measuring and assessing the decision-making success of the board — and perhaps we could have'. A number of interviewees referred to the excessive focus they saw upon individual performance agreements and assessments rather than upon the collective performance of the board.

Conclusion

This chapter has highlighted several tensions that are associated with the state-centric and society-centric elements of public governance; these are explored further in subsequent chapters of the book. Some tensions within the vertical lines of traditional departmental authority have acquired new dimensions. The relationship between ministers and the senior public service, for example, has been complicated by the interposition of ministerial advisers. Less prominent aspects of departmental authority may also have been brought into sharper relief following the passage of the CAC Act, the implementation of the recommended Uhrig review board templates and the subsequent classification of public sector bodies by Finance. The advisory and executive management status of departmental committees remains clearly established within government, although, the status of certain 'decision-making' bodies, such as joint Commonwealth–state bodies, regulatory bodies, international bodies and ministerial councils raise interesting questions.

Part II. Rise of Corporate and Public Governance

4. System Governance

System governance refers to public sector governance that is focused on the centre of government and takes that perspective in viewing departmental governance (chapter 5) and authority governance (chapter 6). This typically involves cross-public service (or public sector) activity, which has significant implications for the specialised line agencies that make up the bulk of the machinery of government. There is a pervasive vertical basis to the public sector that reflects hierarchical relationships, but also a strong horizontal quality in the sense that agencies are required to comply and respond to standards across the sector and increasingly expected to collaborate (chapter 1). These horizontal and vertical dimensions become more complicated where they are extended to other sectors and levels of government. How these relationships work out vary with the governing styles of the political executive and the demands from and responses to the changing environment.

In addressing the dimensions of system governance, this chapter first seeks to clarify administrative and political machinery and dimensions of system governance and central steering. It then addresses changing approaches to governance and strategies for coping with complex and intractable problems. The chapter concludes with a consideration of challenges and governance styles, the limitations that arise in practice and the implications for the effectiveness of public governance.

Overview of system governance

The governance of the public sector system is focused on the central agencies and, of course, the political executive. The domain may be either the public service as a whole (centred on departments of state and their associated portfolios and agencies) or the non-departmental public sector (centred on the bodies that feature boards and come under the *Commonwealth Authorities and Companies Act 1997* (CAC Act)). For many purposes it will be both. This is a perspective of frameworks, principles and practices that apply across the public service or sector.

Governance elements at the system level are in many respects a more complex variant of those at the agency and public body level, and they are the subjects, respectively, of the next two chapters. The system level, however, is invariably more complicated because of horizontal and vertical questions about *span* (across the public sector) and *depth* (encompassing macro as well as meso and micro levels) with regard to questions about policy development, program management and implementation and system maintenance. The political and administrative components need to be based on effective working relationships. The configuration of departments, agencies and authorities in the core public service and the broader public sector, and how their relations are defined, allow for different approaches. Questions of system capacity and capability, the values appropriate for public servants, compliance and performance, and how the public service is envisioned, are important.

The main instruments of system governance have long been part of the machinery of government (Weller 2007). The political executive encompasses: the prime minister and the PM's private office; an active cabinet and cabinet committee system; and ministers and their political advisers. For the public service, the core organisations are the central agencies and the departments of state. Rounding out the system as a whole is the spectrum of other agencies and authorities that are located in departmental portfolios, plus interdepartmental committees (IDCs) and task forces. In addition, there is a long tradition of providing advice to government on the management of the public service by way of a collective mechanism that brings together the expertise of departmental secretaries. Originally known as the Management Advisory Board, its most recent incarnation is the Management Advisory Committee. The latest version for providing a forum for discussing Australian Public Service (APS) issues is the Secretaries Board. At the level of intergovernmental relationships, there are the ministerial and official meetings of the Council of Australian Governments (COAG).

As the key organisations in this public sector, the central agencies have as their mandate whole-of-government and systemic responsibilities that cross the public service: the Department of the Prime Minister and Cabinet (PM&C) for policy, The Treasury for economic policy, the Department of Finance and Deregulation (Finance) for financial management, and the Australian Public Service Commission (APSC) on human capital (table 4.1). Each organisation has distinctive and complementary roles and is presided over by the ultimate source of power and policy direction in the machinery of government, PM&C.

Table 4.1: Roles of central agencies

Agency	Roles
Department of the Prime Minister and Cabinet	Policy advice to the prime minister and the cabinet; and driving policy development and innovation and ensuring delivery of high-priority initiatives across the APS, in pursuit of the government's objectives.
Treasury	Economic policy; effective government spending and taxation arrangements: advice on budget policy issues, trends in Commonwealth revenue and major fiscal and financial aggregates, major expenditure programs, taxation policy, retirement income, Commonwealth–state financial policy; the central policy agency with a whole-of-economy perspective addresses issues ranging from macroeconomic policy settings to microeconomic reform, climate change to social policy, tax policy and international agreements and forums; program delivery role supporting markets and business; and providing commonwealth payments to state and territory governments.
Department of Finance and Deregulation	Assisting government across a range of policy areas to ensure its outcomes are met, particularly expenditure and financial management, deregulation reform and government operations; supporting delivery of government Budget; management of domestic property portfolio and key asset sales; and implementation of deregulation agenda and financial framework for government agencies.
Australian Public Service Commission	Promotes good practice in strengthening the capability of the APS workforce to meet the evolving needs of citizens and the government; supports leadership and learning and development in the APS; and fosters ethical behaviour and workplaces that value diversity.

Sources: <http://www.dpmc.gov.au/about_pmc/index.cfm>; <http://www.treasury.gov.au/About-Treasury/OurDepartment>; <http://www.finance.gov.au/about-the-department/index.html>; <http://www.apsc.gov.au/about/index.html>

The most important reorganisation of the machinery of government occurred in 1987, as a key element of the then Labor government's new micro-economic reform agenda. The restructuring focused on line departments that played an important economic role. The resulting mergers of these areas produced 'mega' departments that combined distinctive fields such as foreign affairs and trade, and education, employment and training. The overall departmental system was changed as 28 areas were reduced to 18 portfolio departments, which covered all areas of government and reflected the two-tiered ministry of portfolio ministers who form the cabinet and the outer ministry (in 2011, 22 and 8 respectively).

The basic structure that exists today dates from that time, although recent governments have modified the 1987 conception, and the current number of departments varies between 18–20 (Halligan 1987; Brooke 1993).

The relationship between the political executive and the public service

The significance of political control in the Australian approach to public management needs to be emphasised, even though much of the story about extending the political executive's influence predates this current period. The consistent pattern has been for the political executive, in the drive for a more responsive public service, to challenge elements of the traditional system. Three types of change have been important: the strengthening of ministerial influence and resources, particularly through the extensive use of ministerial advisors; the weakening of the public servant's position through the reduction in the breadth and exclusivity of the public service's senior roles; and, changes to the appointment and tenure of senior public servants who lead agencies (Halligan 2001).

The role and character of the public service was transformed as a result of change and reform during the last three decades (chapter 2). In the era of the 'mandarins', prior to the mid 1980s, the expanding bureaucracy occupied a strong position. Its position came to be questioned, which resulted in reforms being made to traditional features, under Labor governments (1983–96). This was followed, during the initial terms of John Howard's Coalition government (1996–2007), by a phase of diminishing influence within government, and of the bureaucracy becoming more subservient to the private sector. Under new public service leadership in the 2000s, a more reflective approach emerged — if one that was sometimes sidetracked by issues concerning the relationship between politicians and public servants. The Labor government of Kevin Rudd (2007–10) sought to address aspects of that relationship, while intensifying control over the bureaucracy and increasing demands for efficient performance.

Traditional values about the independence of the public service in providing advice to ministers prevailed until the notion of responsiveness made an appearance in the 1970s, and the position of public servants was challenged because politicians came to see permanent officials to be too influential. Responsiveness was eventually built into standard APS principles (MacDermott 2008). There was a succession of challenges to the relationship that focussed on the role of the public service on the one hand and the behaviour and resources of the political executive on the other. Over time, the trend has been towards strengthening the political executive. This has been punctuated, however, by debates about issues that slowed the rate of change, constrained political pressures on the public service, and produced clarifications of aspects of the relationship. These points of challenge have included debate about loss of permanency for departmental secretaries (1980s), the rise and roles of advisers (1980s–2000s), turnover of secretaries (1996), and the demands of a new government on public service (2009). The dynamics of change have progressively redefined the relationship, yet administrative tradition remains influential.

Senior appointments

The debate about the loss of tenure of heads of departments has been intense, with changes to the standing of departmental secretaries proceeding since the mid 1980s. These changes have caused an evolution from permanent positions, to ones that are governed by contracts and, more recently, to positions that are scrutinised by performance review and made competitive by pay scales.

The first formal change (1984) to tenure redesignated the permanent head as the departmental secretary on a fixed term. In 1994, the fixed-term statutory appointment of secretaries was introduced. The issue then centred on the effect on Westminster principles of applying contracts across the senior public service. This became a reality as senior executives were increasingly placed on individual employment agreements. In a further stage (since 1996), performance review was introduced for secretaries. This device in itself was unexceptional, although it could be employed (as it was, at times, under the Howard government) as a scrutiny device that reinforced the vulnerability of senior public servants.

The other aspect of continuity was the association of turnover with loss of tenure. Increasing turnover of secretaries in the 1990s assumed significance because loss of position now meant termination of employment. The turnover associated with changes of government was significant because it represented the ultimate departure from convention. The Coalition government disposed of six secretaries in 1996 without explanation. Even more telling was the readiness of successive governments to dispense with their chief adviser (e.g. the secretary of PM&C). Since 1993, three secretaries of PM&C have resigned with a change of prime minister, and it became accepted that the incumbent would not necessarily continue with a new government. A partial exception was Terry Moran in 2010, who remained at the behest of the new prime minister during the Labor government's first term, but only for a year.

The Rudd government promised to preserve the tradition of permanence, and was able to make changes at the top without incurring public debate about the process. Five new departmental secretaries were appointed 20 months after the 2007 election (in a process that involved shuffling 11 senior executives) as the government sought to place appropriate officials in significant positions. Performance bonuses were removed because they were thought to have a negative impact on performance.

While the occasional appointment has been challenged as having a political motivation, and other individuals can be argued to have arrived at their appointment on the basis of connections to, or experience of working with politicians, overall, professional public servants have dominated the bureaucracy, even if their domain has been eroded by the rising influence of political advisers. Yet, concerns about the short-term focus of politicians has produced a new formulation of the secretaries' role in terms of stewardship (discussed in chapter 5).

Political advisers

Political advisers have been a particular source of contention between the government and the bureaucracy. The Labor government of Bob Hawke (1983–1991) installed a new set of political mechanisms at the cabinet and ministerial levels (Campbell and Halligan 1993), strengthening political direction to give more prominence to collective responsibility and its priorities. It also proposed a political tier within the senior public service, but eventually compromised with a new position, the ministerial consultant. The minister's office was expanded as an alternative to overt politicisation, and political appointments were increasingly interposed between the bureaucracy and politicians. Ministerial staff took over roles that were previously undertaken by public servants, and could be routinely involved in departmental processes. The ministerial adviser became an established part of government (Halligan and Power 1992; Dunn 1997).

Questions about political–bureaucratic relationships followed on from earlier debates about the role of ministerial advisers, particularly in the aftermath of the 'children overboard' affair (Weller 2002; Maley 2000, 2010).[1] The Senate Finance and Public Administration References Committee (2003) inquiry into the conduct, management and accountability of ministerial staff received evidence about difficulties in relationships between advisers and public servants, the need to clarify roles and responsibilities and the dangers of politicisation. The extensive contact between public servants and the political executive (ministers and their staff) was recorded by the APSC survey of APS staff, leading the public service commissioner to suggest the need to document the role of ministerial advisers through a code of conduct (APSC 2006).

---

1   The children overboard issue in 2001 centred on whether asylum seekers had thrown children overboard, as alleged by government ministers in the context of an imminent federal election.

With the growing influence of ministerial advisers, the nexus between the political executive and senior officials became frayed, and public debate continued about the character of the relationship. The press accepted some degree of 'politicisation' as a given, one focus being the impact of ministerial advisers on public servants (Barker 2007), and other observers noted the lack of accountability attributable to advisers when they became involved in major public policy issues (Walter 2006). The lack of a governance framework under which advisers could be directed to operate was also noted (Tiernan 2007). At the same time, the role and contribution of advisers in augmenting the resources of the minister and dealing with partisan questions has long been recognised.

As part of its accountability and integrity agenda, the Rudd government recognised the effect of the increasing numbers and roles of ministerial staff on the relationship between ministers and public servants, and the lack of consideration that had been given to formalising their responsibilities. A code of conduct for ministerial staff, introduced in 2008, stipulated that ministerial staff were not empowered to direct APS employees who were not subject to them. Political advisers were now expected to be accountable where they had a policy role, although doubts remained about their conduct (e.g. Moran 2011).

Central steering and coordination

As governing has become more complex, challenging (Head 2010) and subject to multiple influences, central steering and coordination have taken precedence. Central steering covers several functions and mechanisms, the choice of roles being shaped by context (e.g. system of government and administrative tradition), leadership style and environmental challenges (Halligan 2011c). As governments, both in Australia and internationally, have moved away from disaggregated public sectors and have sought to reassert central control in order to improve performance, coordination has returned to prominence. The tension between the de-centering and re-centering of governance is a perennial issue (chapter 3), but what emerges from the changing dynamics at the centre depends on the mix and the country context.

Of the Anglo-Saxon countries, Australia has placed emphasis on maintaining a strong prime minister's department and enhancing the resources of the political executive. While several models have been evident during the reform era (table 4.2), which correspond in part to the reform stages that were outlined in chapter 2, the long-term trend has been towards strengthening central steering, and that system has been pushed to new levels when political leadership has been more strategic, intergovernmental or performance focused.

The main dimensions of central coordination are generally strategic direction, priority setting, coordination and driving the implementation of change and policy although, in practice, those dimensions are not all significant at the one time. Steering within a governance perspective may be primarily one of 'setting priorities and defining goals' whereas, under new public management (NPM) it may mainly be 'an interorganisational strategy aimed at unleashing productive elements of the public service' (Peters and Pierre 1998: 231). A broader view is that the state is both less in charge and more focused on being a societal player within a governance framework (a society-centric view), but a state-centric position continues to be relevant to national government like that prevailing in Australia (chapter 1).

Coordination falls within steering (Dahlström, Peters and Pierre 2011). Following one scheme for analysing levels of 'coordination' generically (Metcalfe 1994), steering might cover activities such as government strategy and establishing central priorities, whereas coordination within steering would include the search for agreement and avoidance of divergences among departments.

Although a perennial consideration in system design, as the vacuum at the centre widened, coordination has featured more in reform agendas (Peters 2006; Bouckaert, Peters and Verhoest 2010) and, some would argue, has acquired fresh characteristics. A traditional conception of coordination envisages parties taking each other into account in a process of harmoniously or reciprocally linking activities and decisions (Kernaghan and Siegel 1987). Coordination may once have been regarded as more remedial and reactive, such as responding to disasters and communications problems, but traditional approaches were not solely retrospective, even though there is more emphasis now on the prospective. Another conception addresses procedural and policy/functional coordination that is centred on central agencies (Painter 1987).

Horizontal government approaches, which have been developed in the last decade in order to promote interagency collaboration and cooperation, reflect both old and new forms of organising for connecting distinct parts of the public sector. Such approaches represent a break with conventional notions for dealing with complex policy problems in Anglophone countries. Within these concepts and applications, there are a range of meanings that vary between managing horizontal relationships (operating more at the interagency level) to broader formulations that envisage integration of government operations (Verhoest and Bouckaert 2005).

Models of coordination

The several approaches to studying the centre have different emphases. An executive leadership or core executive emphasises the role of the political executive (e.g. Campbell and Halligan 1993). The literature on the 'steering state' covers a range of positions that share a division between steering functions and implementation, although how this separation occurs varies widely in practice. A variation on this theme is the hollowing out of the state (Frederickson and Frederickson 2006), which focuses on delivery beyond the centre. Moving closer to the core, the question of the state's capacity has received attention, including the relationship with coordination (Painter and Pierre 2005; Verhoest and Bouckaert 2005). The specialised field of central agencies is under-researched, but Lindquist (2001) has distinguished the strong centre in Anglo-Saxon countries, based on central institutions and high capacity for coordination, from the smaller and less influential centres that exist within European systems.

Five models are differentiated (Halligan 2006) for considering central coordinating strategies that are based on (1) whether relationships are concentrated in the core of central government or encompass third parties (such as state governments and non-government providers); and (2) the mix of political and administrative machinery that is used. Each coordinating strategy has different implications for the effectiveness of governance (table 4.2, compare table 2.2), and various instruments are relevant to specific relationships, such as conditional grants and performance management, and more generally the use of political levers for directing the public service.

Table 4.2: Coordinating strategies

Characterisation	Central agencies	Political executive
Integrated hierarchical	Transactional control	Traditional relationships, reliance on public service
Prototype 'steering' and 'rowing'	Strategic and selective steering	Assertion of political executive, cabinet and committees, ministerial discretion
Devolved (weak centre)	Downgraded steering role, departments and agents prominent	Accountability management
Integrated governance	Rebalancing steering at levels of political executive, central agencies and departments	Prime ministerial control, political and performance management and control
Strategic governance	Strategic assertion horizontally and vertically	Strategic priorities and planning prime minister. COAG mechanisms

The *integrated hierarchical* model is grounded in traditional public administration that steered through laws and regulations, hierarchy, and control over the details of financial and personnel transactions. The *prototype steering model* departs from this transactional basis by differentiating strategic policy from operational and delivery matters. The emphasis is on the redefinition of the centre to enhance directive capacity and political focusing, with decentralisation being a secondary consideration. A balanced steering and rowing arrangement is one possible outcome, but it may also be a stepping-stone to a stronger 'steering state' conception, as discussed next.

The *devolved model* is assumed to be a product of reform design, either management and/or market driven, and represents a strong commitment to decentralisation and selective steering at best. It needs to be distinguished from systems internationally that lack a strong centre; weak centres appear to either reflect state traditions, divided central agencies or cultural and political factors that are less determinate (e.g. Lindquist 2004 on Canada). The dominant principle is competition, whereas, the more integrated conception discussed below features collaboration. The main mode of control is 'hands off' under NPM that is reliant on contracts, and 'hands on' where performance is central (Newman 2002).

The fourth model, *integrated governance*, combines the attributes of a strategic centre with active line departments. In terms of governance, it unites elements of modern governance and state-centric approaches (Richards and Smith 2006). This is a demanding option that benefits from the directive role of the political executive and relies on a system of performance management. The final model, *strategic governance*, emphasises strategic planning and priority setting at the centre and is likely to be driven by the prime minister and his or her department and by incorporating capable ministers in key areas. Intergovernmental relations have centrality for driving major policy agenda collaboratively but subject to performance requirements. Compared to the previous model this one ratchets up the intensity of the pursuit of strategically defined priorities. The 'steering state' dimension may still be present but the 'rowers' need to be knitted in to the centre more directly.

These models have been tried successively over recent decades. A combination of internal and external sources of change facilitated the emergence of new approaches, which was first apparent with major reform in the 1980s (Campbell and Halligan 1993). The intensity of the Australian shift to devolution and the subsequent reassertion of the centre resulted from both system shortcomings and environmental uncertainty.

The general pathway for central steering, over 20 years, has displayed features of each of the models. The *integrated hierarchical*, the dominant approach of the post-war years, relied on the archetypal mechanisms of traditional coordination — the interdepartmental committee and central agency control of transactions. It was succeeded by the *prototype steering* model, under which an explicit solution was prescribed by the managerial culture of the 1980s. Central agency intervention was to be minimised, which meant that traditional controls over line departments were relinquished: 'They were to assume strategic directions allowing line departments to make specific resource decisions. The central agency stance should be more that of catalyst and intermittent coordinator' (Campbell and Halligan 1993: 43).

This was followed by an exploration of the *devolved* model (Zifcak 1994) that increasingly assumed NPM features. A strong commitment to market principles was associated with the neoliberal policies of the Coalition government in the 1990s. Within a philosophy that emphasised the private sector, choice for consumers and purchasers, and the use of market mechanisms, action was taken to transfer responsibilities, to privatise, and to conceptualise the public service as a business operating in a competitive environment that was to be judged by its performance. Departmental activities were reviewed using an approach that incorporated competitive tendering and contracting, purchaser-provider arrangements, and business process re-engineering. Market testing of agencies sought to improve internal capacity by benchmarking and outsourcing aspects of corporate services. The resulting disestablishment of monolithic multifunctional departments, and reliance on third parties for service provision, produced increasingly siloed agencies and a fragmented system. Under this devolved public management model, the agency was the focus, individual contracts provided the basis for employing senior public servants, and a disaggregated public service was the result.

The impact on central agencies of the application of management and market principles was resounding. The old Public Service Board was supplanted by a modest commission (Campbell and Halligan 1993). Finance acquired a 'strategic' role (Wanna and Bartos 2003), but its diminished role in the second wave of market reform (the second half of the 1990s) meant that debate centred on whether it would survive organisationally (one option being to re-integrate it with Treasury). PM&C confined active intervention to where it was required, and was no longer providing leadership for the public service. In Lindquist's (2001) terms, Australia moved from a strong centre to a smaller centre, with a corresponding reduction in capacity, coherence and control of coordination. At this stage it had moved to the devolved end of the spectrum that was comparable in some respects with the system operating in New Zealand, which was generally regarded as the outlier in terms of central steering.

Steering through integrated and strategic governance

There was movement again within the public management reform cycle in the 2000s: from an intense neoliberal reform agenda in the first five years of the Coalition government, reflection on the results of that agenda and a changing international environment produced shifts, refinements and revaluation of the worth of the public service functioning under new central agency leadership that suited different agendas. The *integrated governance* model emerged as a more comprehensive approach that displayed features of the earlier models.

Several themes were recurrent: delivery and implementation, performance, coherence and whole-of-government, and responsiveness to government policy. This model shifted the focus to some extent from the vertical towards the horizontal and a greater concern with cross-agency programs and relationships within central government. At the same time, there was a reinforcement of and extension to vertical relationships. The whole-of-government agenda also had a centralising element, in that central agencies were driving policy directions or principles, either systemically or across several agencies. The result was the tempering of devolution through strategic steering and management from the centre and a rebalancing of the positions of centre and line agencies.

The Howard government tightened its control of the centre through management of the appointment processes within the public service, public boards and parliamentary positions (e.g. a political appointee headed the cabinet secretariat). The political control aspect also underlay each dimension of change: improved financial information on a program basis for ministers, strategic coordination under cabinet, controlling major policy agendas, organisational integration through abolition of bodies and features of autonomy, and monitoring the implementation of government policy down to the delivery level. The rebalancing produced, according to Hamburger (2007: 210):

> a network of central coordinating mechanisms in place of the direct central control and institutionally based central agencies [and a system] in which political control of administration is coordinated by a Prime Minister whose head-of-government role exists within a strong culture of collective involvement of other ministers through the Cabinet.

The overall result was significant potential for policy and program control and integration using the conventional machinery of cabinet, central agencies and departments.

There were five dimensions to the integrated governance strategy, which operated at several levels, as discussed below.

Central steering of departments through the resurrected central agency

The overriding trend in the 1990s — to devolve responsibilities to agencies — remained a feature, but it was modified in two respects involving central agencies. This occurred first through the enlarged role of PM&C because of its revitalised role in policy coordination and other major agenda in the early 2000s, as discussed below.

Secondly, there were more prominent roles for the other central agencies in espousing and enforcing principles, and monitoring and guiding in the areas of budgeting, performance, human resources and values. Finance's role and capacity to oversee financial management and information was enhanced, with a greater focus on departmental programs, a renewed emphasis on cash accounting and an expansion of staff capacity, in a shrunken department, to provide the necessary advice for government. The APSC invested in improvements to its capacity for monitoring and evaluation, particularly through an annual report, 'State of the Service', that surveyed employees and agencies and scrutinised public service human resources, values and practice.

Central steering of performance through monitoring down to program delivery

A core principle of the 1980s was to require departments to manage as well as to provide policy advice. Under the market agenda of NPM, outsourcing, agents and specialised agencies were favoured for service delivery (e.g. Centrelink). The language of the mid 2000s was refined to enforce effective delivery as well as policy advice, with the latter defined in terms of outcomes.

Implementation had often been the neglected end of the policy spectrum. Under the market agenda, outsourcing, agents and specialised agencies were favoured for service delivery. The internal constraints on implementation were reviewed by the government as a result of public perceptions of the performance of delivery agencies, particularly those where ministers had direct responsibility. In late 2003, PM&C was responsible for an Australian Cabinet Implementation Unit, which was established to seek effectiveness in program delivery by ensuring government policies and services were delivered in a timely fashion and on a responsive basis. It was depicted as a partnership with agencies in producing systematic reform to the implementation of government policies, and ensuring effective delivery.

The authority of cabinet was drawn on as a 'gateway' and a 'checkpoint'. New proposals required appropriate details regarding implementation and cabinet submissions that were seen to have a risk element in their delivery were required to address a delivery framework including milestones, impacts and governance.

Policy proposals that were adopted required formal implementation plans with progress reported to the prime minister and cabinet against milestones that were set out in 'traffic light' format. Around 200 policy implementations were monitored under the Howard government. The 'traffic light' report to the prime minister and cabinet was regarded as a powerful incentive for organisational learning for public servants. Cultural change was promoted around a project management approach that employed a methodology designed to codify and think through the connections between policy objectives, inputs, outputs and outcomes (Shergold 2004b; Wanna 2006).

Ministerial departments and portfolios

The third important dimension of the model involved the swing back to a more comprehensive ministerial department and ministerial steering of portfolios. The targeting of the broader public sector was derived from election agenda and led to the review of corporate governance of statutory authorities and office-holders. An agenda was developed, because of the extent of non-departmental organisations, for ministerial departments to have tighter and more direct control over public agencies, and their governance (see discussion of *Review of the Corporate Governance of Statutory Authorities and Office Holders* (Uhrig review) in chapters 5 and 8).

The language of the mid 2000s enforced effective delivery as well as policy advice with the latter defined in terms of outcomes (Shergold 2004b). Departmentalisation was expressed through absorbing statutory authorities and reclaiming control of agencies with hybrid boards that did not accord with a particular corporate (and therefore private sector) governance prescription, as expressed by the Uhrig review (2003) (chapter 2, this volume). The medium term result was a reduction in the number of agencies in the outer public sector (114 to 84 between 2003 and 2012) and an expansion in the number of agencies that were placed within the core public service (84 to 111). The key example of agencification, Centrelink, was also affected. Established in 1997 as an independent statutory authority that was responsible for delivering welfare benefits, Centrelink accounted for about 30 per cent of Commonwealth expenditure. This position, however, changed from 2004 under the integrating governance agenda and Centrelink came to be increasingly integrated within the Human Services Department (chapter 5 and Halligan 2008b).

Steering across the public service: Whole-of-government and horizontal management

Australia was slower to adopt a systematic approach to whole-of-government issues than the other Anglophone countries of Canada and the United Kingdom, which pursued these issues in the 1990s while Australia was focused on management reform. The environment created by these reforms emphasised devolution of responsibility to agency heads and each agency pursuing its own business and policy agenda. The need to temper devolution with a broader, whole-of-government perspective came to permeate much government activity (cf Verhoest and Bouckaert 2005 for how such a trajectory was worked through elsewhere). The shift was expressed in three ways.

At the political level, the prime minister committed to a series of whole-of-government priorities for new policy-making that included national security, defence and counter-terrorism and other generally defined priorities such as sustainable environment, rural and regional affairs and work and family life (Howard 2002; Shergold 2004a). These priorities were pursued through a range of traditional coordinating and new whole-of-government processes including changes to cabinet processes that were aimed at strengthening its strategic leadership role.

The priorities were also followed through a range of coordinating or whole-of-government processes, including: cabinet and ministerial processes (e.g. Ministerial Oversight Committee on Energy); COAG and other Commonwealth–state arrangements (e.g. sustainable water management); interdepartmental taskforces, as discussed above (e.g. work and family life); integrated service delivery (e.g. stronger regions); and lead agency approaches. An example was the COAG agreement to develop a National Water Initiative to increase the productivity and efficiency of water use, sustain rural and urban communities, and to ensure the health of river and groundwater systems.

The organisational response to the external environment that was experienced by Australia in the 2000s was to build coordinating units within current structures centred on PM&C. The whole-of-government approach to national coordination covered strategic and operational levels: a National Security Committee of Cabinet, a National Counter-Terrorism Committee (for intergovernmental coordination), and a National Security Division for coordinating and applying whole-of-government principles to border protection, counter-terrorism, defence, intelligence, law enforcement and security.

Thirdly, the agenda was given impetus through a report, *Connecting Government: Whole of Government Responses to Australia's Priority Challenges*, by the Management Advisory Committee (comprising departmental secretaries, the primary vehicle at that time for examining and setting reform agenda: MAC 2004), which indicated how to address issues about whole-of-government processes and structures, cultures, managing information, budgetary frameworks. Whole-of-government was defined as denoting 'agencies working across portfolio boundaries to achieve a shared goal and an integrated government response to particular issues' (MAC 2004: 1). Despite this specific definition, the boundaries were not readily drawn for coordination was also viewed in terms of coordinating departments (i.e. central agencies), integration (reducing the number of departments) and cooperative federalism (MAC 2004: 6–7). Approaches to coordination could operate formally and informally, ranging from policy development through program management to service delivery. There was an underlying rationalist conception suggesting that difficult policy problems and management questions could be laid out, solutions designed and challenges managed leading to improved problem solving, service delivery and performance.

The medium term impact of horizontal coordination in Australia was mixed. The level of horizontal management activity expanded within the public service through a mixture of central agency push and shove using task forces, a reliance on traditional IDCs for some purposes, and some new interactive mechanisms. An official verdict reported some success but 'overall implementation of the Connecting Government report has been disappointing and the report does not appear to have had a fundamental impact on the approach that the APS takes to its work' (APSC 2007d: 247; Halligan, Buick and O'Flynn 2011; O'Flynn et al 2011). However, whole-of-government continues to be an imperative (Sedgwick 2010b; Metcalfe 2011), and is reflected in the aspirations for shared outcomes that were outlined in *Ahead of the Game: Blueprint for the Reform of Australian Government Administration* (AGRAGA 2010).

Performance management systems

The fifth dimension addresses the role of performance, which had become a central and constant theme for Australian leaders. The former head of the public service, Peter Shergold, declared that 'The next challenge is to ensure that the performance of the APS — as a coherent whole — is lifted', and used the concept of the 'performing state' for a system 'that is continuously open to, and reading its environment, and learning and changing in response: a state "inherently in transition"' (Shergold 2004b: 6). A consistent theme of Prime Minister Rudd was for improving performance (e.g. Rudd 2009b), and the Advisory Group on the Reform of Australian Government Administration regarded high performance as a criterion for the agendas in *Ahead of the Game*. These ideals and aspirations remain to be realised.

Australia's performance management has moved through stages (Halligan 2003b; McKay 2003), and continues to evolve hesitantly. In the first stage, the elements of performance management were developed within a centralised approach featuring Finance. The strengths of this process were institutionalised performance management elements and the requirement for formal evaluations. The weaknesses were the reliance on evaluations that were mandatory (and imposed top-down by a central agency) and the quality of program objectives and performance information. There were questions, also, about what program budgeting represented (Wanna, Kelly and Forster 2000), because a program framework was used as an instrument for managing and reporting on programs, but this did not lead to budgeting by programs that were linked to appropriations.

The second stage was based on the outcomes/output framework, devolution to agencies, principles instead of formal requirements, and an emphasis on performance information. The strengths of this approach lay in systemic review by central agencies, departments' ownership of outcomes, and management being modified by the influence of explicit results achieved. The weaknesses included insufficient information for parliamentary needs and for sound management, inconsistent departmental support for good evaluation, and the subjectivity of performance assessment. These limitations produced continuing reassessment of aspects of performance management practices such as the types of information provided.

The budget framework that was introduced in 1999 changed financial management and reporting by applying budgeting on a full accrual basis; implementation of outputs and outcomes reporting; and extended agency devolution to inter alia budget estimates and financial management. Departments and agencies were now expected to identify their outcomes and outputs and be held accountable for them. Agency heads were clearly assigned responsibility and accountability for performance. Agencies were required to identify explicit outcomes, outputs and performance measures. Reporting now occurred through budget plans (portfolio budget statements) and financial year results (annual reports). Major benefits of the new framework were to be an improved information base, better incentives to be efficient, greater precision about public value and, for the first time, the linking of outputs to outcomes.

However, the limitations of the framework in practice — the need for information on implementation and operations as well as results — produced reincorporation of departmental programs, a renewed emphasis on cash accounting, the Cabinet Implementation Unit and other changes including improvements to cash management, budgeting and program reporting and financial information systems. This meant, of course, enhancing Finance's role and capacity to oversee financial management and information, and provide the necessary advice for government.

The question of engaging ministers in the new system proved to be problematic as performance judgments ultimately involved them and there had been considerable investment in seeking improvements to the information provided through performance management. A number of the expected benefits did not accrue from the combination of a highly centralised budgetary process and highly devolved agencies. Most importantly ministers experienced difficulties with the lack of information on programs, the level at which they made decisions, which had been dropped under the new framework. At that time, however, Finance no longer collected program data on a systematic basis (Watt 2003), and what was available was not published. There was also parliamentary criticism of the lack of information available about the Commonwealth's position. This paucity of information was regarded as a result of financial management information systems that were accrual based, in contrast to those of traditional cash transactions.

Finance's Budget Estimates and Framework Review, to evaluate system effectiveness and responsiveness in meeting government needs, reported on the scope for streamlining the financial framework, improving information management systems, and enhancing the quality of financial information that was being provided to the government and its central agency. These measures enhanced Finance's role and capacity to oversee financial management and information, and a greater focus was placed on departmental programs, a renewed emphasis on cash accounting and an expansion of staff capacity, in a shrunken department, to provide the necessary advice for government. The reported changes included improvements to budgeting and program reporting and financial information systems (Watt 2003; DFA 2004). Program information was reintroduced surreptitiously (in so far as the details of its reintroduction were not public) by 2003.

A change of government produced an agenda to improve budget transparency, termed Operation Sunlight (Tanner 2008; Hawke and Wanna 2010). The diagnosis of the existing outcomes and outputs framework was savage. The government's response to the limitations of its performance management framework has been to seek improvements to it. Rather than discard outcomes as a focus, they remain, with augmented features, to several dimensions of the framework. Programs have been revived for portfolio budget statements and, along with outcomes, form the basis for reporting. Performance was reinforced and extended by this initiative, and there was greater interest in targets and league tables, and service delivery focused on outcomes. Yet, a series of studies, mainly by the ANAO, have raised questions about the efficacy of aspects of the existing performance management system and the need for significant renewal (Bouckaert and Halligan 2008; ANAO 2011; Hawke 2012).

The Commonwealth Financial Accountability Review (CFAR) has provided an authoritative diagnosis of the position that includes insufficient integration of the components of the resource management cycle, lack of coherence in the performance management process, the role of outcomes in appropriations, and weaknesses in performance monitoring and evaluation (DFD 2012b).

Reformulating steering under Rudd through strategic governance

What differentiates strategic governance from integrated governance? Strategic governance places greater emphasis on strategy, targeted performance and the design of governance nationally and federally. This difference was indicated by the style and actions of Rudd in the role of prime minister. Rudd's leadership approach was close to a 'priorities and planning style', which was defined by Campbell (1988: 59) as occurring when first ministers were 'in a strong political position and choose to pursue an ambitious, creative, and comprehensive legislative program'. This style favoured central agencies and their role in 'assembling coherent policies and programs'.

The government explored new ways for engaging the public (e.g. the Australia 2020 Summit of 1000 delegates, and community cabinets) and produced a five-point agenda (Australian Government 2008). A key aspect was the reform of governing through improved external engagement, building accountability and integrity, and modernising the federation. The focus on accountability and transparency addressed the question of respect for government institutions and 'public confidence in the integrity of ministers, their staff and senior officials' (Australian Government 2008: 73).

A new phase in intergovernmental relations was initiated in 2009 with the intention of strengthening vertical relationships within the federation. The COAG reform agenda was at the forefront of the government's modernisation and policy agenda. At the interface between levels, the Australian Intergovernmental Agreement on Federal Financial Relations was designed to improve the well being of Australians through collaborative working arrangements and enhanced public accountability covering outcomes achieved and outputs delivered. The arrangement provides for public accountability at the Commonwealth level with state-level flexibility regarding delivery and indicators (APSC 2010b).

Central steering was reformulated under Rudd through a strategic governance approach that placed greater emphasis on strategy, targeted performance and the design of governance nationally and federally. In his first two years, Rudd's 'priorities and planning style' reflected his political pre-eminence and the pursuit of an ambitious reform program that was centred on central agencies' roles in developing policies and programs. A major organisational audit of PM&C indicated that it was 'heavily focused on the day-to-day activities of government, and that [its] capacity to provide strategic policy advice could be improved' (PM&C 2008a: 3). A Strategy and Delivery Division was established to advance administrative priorities that were more strategic, long term and proactive. The overall objective was a strong department for supporting the prime minister's reform agenda for the nation with monitoring of progress assuming significance. The emphasis under Rudd has not been maintained by Prime Minister Julia Gillard.

Governance styles and issues

Challenges to governance

How the centre perceives governance challenges depends in part on governing style and whether governments are either seeking to anticipate problems before they become full-fledged issues or are merely responding as the need arises. While simultaneous invention is possible, the articulation of problems often reflects the general influence of both a global community and the specific circulation of ideas in the Anglophone realm (Halligan 2007a). In these days of assertive political executives, the definition of challenges is more often lead by the government, but the vagaries of public debate and the politics of governance mean that control of the agenda can be tenuous, particularly where clear direction and effective implementation are wanting. The political appetite for tackling different challenges is affected by a range of factors, including the source and nature of the challenges, the cross-jurisdictional and other complexities of the challenges, and the selection and coordination of different implementation strategies.

External challenges

External challenges have usually been fiscal in nature and economic factors (e.g. international competitiveness) have remained a driver, although nothing compares to the global financial crisis of 2008. Otherwise, the most important external threat during the 2000s was the issue of security and terrorism, which dominated both the domestic and international landscape (apart from the long-term impact of 9/11, there were terrorist attacks in Bali and the commitment of forces to Iraq), and had lasting effects on public management and the community. The then secretary of PM&C observed that the threat of global terrorism and the emerging challenges of counter-terrorism, protection of borders and domestic security had transformed Australian life and identity. 'Those issues, typically "non-routine", will test bureaucratic structures. Ensuring effective coordination of intelligence, analysis and strategic policy responses will test public administration' (PM&C 2003). The security question was still resonating in late 2008 when Rudd (2008) presented the first national security report to parliament as a coherent statement of the challenges and a comprehensive approach to them. The impact of internationalisation was demonstrated most dramatically by how the issue of climate change helped to derail the Rudd government, and continues to challenge the Gillard government.

Complex policy problems that cross boundaries

A number of whole-of-government priorities for new policy-making were adopted by Howard (2002), which included national security, defence and counter terrorism and other generally defined priorities such as sustainable environment, rural and regional affairs and work and family life. The Rudd government maintained and extended this emphasis covering some similar ground (e.g. national security) and new and more specific fields (climate change and productivity). Yet the question of how to handle the contending interests in the Murray-Darling basin, which emerged under Howard, also confronts the Gillard government.

Implementing government policies and priorities

Implementation of government policy was an issue at the beginning of the reform era as a result of political concern with public service independence, which produced a sustained process of redistributing power between politicians and public servants (Halligan 2001). Despite the use of different instruments, political control and performance continued to be an issue for governments, with the concern in the 2000s being that political priorities were not being sufficiently reflected in policy directions, and were not being followed through in program implementation and delivery.

Juggling and balancing relationships across the reform era

There are indications that, over time, the processes of change in the reform era have produced a return to several traditional verities. There are several strands to this argument.

First, the policy role of the senior public service experienced progressive attrition from the traditional position of centrality. With the rise of managerialism there was a reaction against the emphasis on policy work and the lack of management skills. At the same time, ministers increasingly relied on alternative sources of advice and their staff both advised and provided conduits for extra-government proposals. Over time, the policy capacity of the ministerial office was strengthened and the public servant's role became more limited. As well, external advice was routinely relied on and an atmosphere that encouraged contestable advice meant more competition than before. The overall effect was to transform the public service's policy role from a near monopoly to a competitor for government's attention.

Secondly, the traditional public service's identity derived from being clearly demarcated from its environment, particularly the private and political spheres, and being relatively closed. From the 1980s, these boundaries were systematically eroded. The assault on the senior public service was directed at the traditional career system. The political executive's influence could be expanded by transforming the officials' position through abolition of permanency and the introduction of a senior executive service that offered management flexibility and external entry. The shift of the public sector towards private sector practice, which had been apparent for over a decade, acquired centrality under Howard's first conservative government of the reform era. Agencies were required to identify contestable functions that could be transferred to the private sector, unless the public sector added greater value.

A further dimension was the coherence and identity of the public service. On the one hand management devolution and then the workplace agenda required agencies to be responsible for employment and other matters. The balkanisation of the public service was recognised as one possible consequence of a strong agency focus. On the other hand, there was a lack of countervailing mechanisms for fostering public service integration and identity.

At the same time, the concept of an apolitical public service was maintained throughout the reform era by successive governments. Even the leader of a government at times unsympathetic to the public service declared commitment to a 'non-partisan and professional public service' (Howard 1998b). If the rhetoric was consistent, the parallel language and action provided the guide to changing government thinking about the bureaucracy. While requiring this highly responsive system, governments continued to assert the integrity and apolitical character of the public service, and the *Public Service Act 1999 (Cth)* enshrined this central value.

Although overt political appointments were not much used in Australia, the Hawke government's desire for greater control was substantially realised. The combination of strong political direction and changes to the employment basis and insularity of the senior public service redistributed power between ministers and public servants and produced greater responsiveness. Careers at the most senior levels were no longer guaranteed. The promotion of a climate of insecurity for senior officials during the Howard government's first two terms moved beyond 'new government' behaviour. One diagnosis was 'personalisation' based on a narrow conception of politicisation — one linking appointments and use of the public service for party ends (Weller and Young 2001). In a broader sense that includes other dimensions of politicisation, the system might be pronounced as politicised (Mulgan 1998).

The weakened relationship between politicians and public servants surfaced as the 2007 election approached. There was private discussion among senior officials about the short-term focus of politicians, and eventually strident public comment about ad-hoc decision-making by the government in an election year. The press continued to accept some degree of 'politicisation' as a given (e.g. Grattan 2007 on how public servants have been constrained under the Howard government), and the debate surfaced again in the exchange that followed the then public service commissioner, Andrew Podger's (2007) reflections on the handling of senior appointments, which produced a defence of the record from Shergold (2007b).

A telling public disclosure was the declaration of a key central agency, Treasury, that it was ignored by the government in key policy fields. The secretary of the Treasury, Ken Henry (2007: 13–14), observed that the election year would 'test our mettle as apolitical public servants … Our capacity to ensure that our work is "responsible", and not just "responsive", will be put to the test. How successful we are will impact on our integrity as public servants and our long-term effectiveness'.

The strength of an administrative tradition grounded in Westminster has been apparent where governments have overstepped the limits of acceptability (Labor's back peddling on political appointees in 1983–84, the backlash to the purge of secretaries by the Coalition in 1996, and the response to the role of political advisers in the mid-2000s). System correction was again apparent with Rudd's current and evolving agenda (Halligan 2010b), but the effect of the Rudd agenda was a double-edged sword. It reinforced traditional values, a professional public service and accountability and transparency; while cutting the size of the service and making heavy demands on public servants, including a renewal of the emphasis on performance. The trade-off then was that the consolidation of the public service and reaffirmation of Westminster principles meant higher expectations for a modernised public service.

Four dimensions of the Labor government's agenda can be noted (Halligan 2010b). First, integrity and accountability comprised two elements: the government's view of the future public service and reinvigorating the Westminster tradition (independent and professional public service, merit-based selection, continuity of employment, and removal of performance pay). The Office of the Special Minister of State was used to pull together and strengthen a range of integrity and governance responsibilities under one minister: the public service, codes of conduct, privacy and various procedures for handling transparency and accountability.

Secondly, there was the interest in 'One APS'. A lament across the service has been the limitations of a devolved agency structure for conditions of employment. The public service head, Terry Moran (2009), asserted that 'the APS is not a collection of separate institutions. It is a mutually reinforcing and cohesive whole'. The prime minister echoed these themes by arguing for a stronger collective identity, a greater sense of cohesion and esprit de corps, and the need to address constraints on mobility and the disincentives public servants encounter in moves between departments (Rudd 2009a; AGRAGA 2010).

Thirdly, the public service was being consolidated in conjunction with the demise of outsourcing. The Rudd Government sought to reduce dependence on external consultancies although the pattern has been variable. Legal services were being brought more in house, and the government was reversing a reliance on outsourcing of information communications technology to 'correct imbalances'.

Finally, although the institution of the public service has potentially been strengthened by attention to political and private sector relationships and traditions, there were elevated expectations for performance and for improved innovative policy capacity. The perceived deficit in capacity was a factor leading to the review headed by the secretary of PM&C, and *Ahead of the Game* (AGRAGA 2009, 2010; see also chapter 2).

Governance failures and solutions

Governance issues have arisen from the fallout from aspects of new public management, weaknesses with corporate governance and strategic focus, and public crises over oversight and implementation. Features of new public management — such as disaggregation, devolution, outsourcing, and multiple services providers — supported specialisation but also encouraged fragmentation and reinforced vertical structures. There was also official concern with opaque governance. 'Good governance depends upon transparency of authority, accountability and disclosure' (Shergold 2004b).

Nevertheless, two extraordinary cases that occurred during the Howard government's fourth term revealed fundamental weaknesses in the internal operations of a major department and lack of oversight of a privatised body with public policy roles. The first case was one of internal governance failure involving the Department of Immigration and Multicultural Affairs (DIMA), and is discussed in the next chapter.

The second case concerned oversight of privatised public policy, and several governance issues that arose. The Australian Wheat Board (AWB) paid kickbacks to the Iraqi government in the form of a transport surcharge. The Department of Foreign Affairs and Trade (DFAT) claimed to have been unaware of the nature of the AWBs actions. Both DFAT and the Wheat Export Authority (WEA), a statutory body responsible for monitoring AWB, were unable to demand documents from the AWB, inhibiting their capacity to confirm or certify the AWB's claims. The AWB was found to have faked several of the documents that it had provided to DFAT (which were then forwarded to the United Nations (UN)) (Cole 2006). Two governance issues stood out: the unwillingness of senior officials and ministers to acknowledge awareness or responsibility (including the prime minister's failure to require ministers to accept ministerial responsibility); and the limited capacity of DFAT and the WEA to oversee the actions of the AWB (chapter 6). Neither could demand documents from AWB nor could they force it to cooperate with the UN investigation. Given AWB's role in representing Australian farmers there appeared to be serious gaps in the regulatory framework (see also the discussion in chapter 6 and Botterill and McNaughton 2008), and the corporate governance issues that arose from making payments in breach of United Nations sanctions (Cole 2006: liii, lix).

A deterioration in governance relationships occurred in the fourth term of the Howard government. Tensions between politicians and their public service advisers increased as party government became disengaged from the public service and pragmatic decision-making became a feature of an election year. Howard's mode of governing registered discontent at senior levels within the public service with private discussion among senior officials about the policy process (Henry 2007) and the lack of strategic focus of politicians. The head of the Treasury observed that the government bypassed his key agency even though it had developed frameworks for considering climate change and water reform. 'All of us would wish that we had been listened to more attentively over the past several years in both of these areas. There is no doubt that policy outcomes would have been far superior had our views been more influential. That is not just my view; I know that it is increasingly widely shared around this town' (Henry 2007: 6). More generally within the nation, the government was widely castigated for decision-making that was capricious, populist, short-term and ad hoc (Halligan 2008a).

Equally disturbing for public governance was the apparent loss of impetus as the first-term Rudd Government similarly experienced an annus horribilis as it compromised its agenda in the run up to the 2010 election, and the prime minister forsook policy and planning for short-term pragmatism. The turning point was provided by the very public implementation failure with two programs: the Home Insulation Program and the Building the Education Revolution Scheme (chapter 5).

Conclusion

System governance raises several sets of questions that go to the heart of government. Several different models for coordinating the system have been outlined. However, the effectiveness of central systems ultimately depends on both the political leadership and the capacity of the system to respond. If leaders' aspirations exceed the capacity of the system — apparent under the heightened demands of Rudd — this will invariably lead to shortfalls in capacity and associated dysfunctions. In contrast, Prime Minister Gillard's leadership in response to the demands of system governance remain elusive.

The art of system governance requires the mastery of complex vertical interrelationships at several levels within central government and nationally, the growing horizontal dimensions, and the reconciling of pressures from politicians and the environment. If modernisation of the system is undervalued and capability development miscalculated, a mismatch is also the result.

5. Departmental Governance

The department of state forms the core unit of the machinery of government at Commonwealth and state government levels. As ministerial departments, they play a central role in supporting the minister and communicating, directing and coordinating within a functional sphere of activity. For this reason, governance in and around the department has several dimensions. Departmental governance addresses how they handle their internal operations and external relationships.

The roles and operations of departments of state were historically derived from the notion of the ministerial department and government machinery that was good at forming and communicating policy advice; providing a range of administrative routines and activities such as program implementation; and which operated within understood boundaries with regard to hierarchy and standardisation. The parameters of the traditional model were relaxed, however, in the reform era and it became accepted that more flexible bureaucracy and adaptive solutions, and the use of third parties, were required within a public management focus (see chapter 2). With reform and the emergence of new ideas and challenges, including the more explicit engagement with corporate and public governance, departmental governance has been revisited over time and the core principles refined and mainstreamed.

This consideration of departmental governance examines both the place of the department and its internal and external dimensions. It draws on interviews with departmental secretaries (appendix 1), and case studies. The cases that are referred to reflect the cycle of governance issues that came to the fore over the last decade, including whole-of-government approaches (chapter 4), the evolving approaches to agency and portfolio relationships (Centrelink and the Department of Human Services), and outright governance failure that was revealed through public inquiries (e.g. the then Department of Immigration and Multicultural Affairs (DIMA)).

Governance of the department of state

Departmental governance is shaped by legislative requirements as to the roles and responsibilities of agency heads and other matters, such as reporting. Such governance depends also on the nature of the department and its responsibilities; a secretary's leadership style will play a role in the development of this culture. The immediate public service environment, as discussed in the previous chapter, is highly significant for the role of the department. The priorities of government, the political salience of issues and the propensity of ministers to intervene are relevant in the short term, but good departmental leadership and governance, supported by the emerging significance of stewardship, is expected to carry the agency through changing times.

There are both mandatory requirements and permissive expectations that shape departmental governance. The first are contained in various legislation, regulations and conventions. The second cover guidelines for good governance that may have general application, but which are likely to require adaptation to different agency contexts. These include internal structures, accountability instruments and various systems for handling risk and performance (e.g. APSC 2007c).

The general meaning, and several official conceptions, of governance have been raised in chapters 1 and 2. Here, the emphasis is on the departmental relevance of those meanings and conceptions. The Australian National Audit Office (ANAO) and Department of Prime Minister and Cabinet (PM&C) (2006: 13) prefer *governance* to be defined as 'the set of responsibilities and practices, policies and procedures, exercised by an agency's executive'. At the same time, PM&C also employs the term *corporate governance* in the *Requirements for Annual Reports for Departments, Executive Agencies and FMA Act Bodies* (2011: 17) to mean 'the process by which agencies are directed and controlled. It is generally understood to encompass authority, accountability, stewardship, leadership, direction and control'. Further, three of the corporate governance items specified are derived from an indicative list that the Australian Securities Exchange (ASX) uses for reporting. A 'Statement of main corporate governance practices in place' is a mandatory requirement for a departmental annual report, although the specified structures and processes are merely suggested.[1] Similarly, the auditor-general and the Australian Public Service Commission (APSC) appear to be comfortable using the terms governance, corporate governance and good governance interchangeably (McPhee 2008a: 4; APSC 2010a: 102–03).

It is not surprising, therefore, that those secretaries who were interviewed for this project (see chapter 3) did not adopt a uniform view of corporate governance reporting. While these official views exist, it is clear that (Tucker 2010: 124–25):

> No approach to corporate governance in the public sector is mandated. Rather a system has been allowed to develop without central prescription … [S]ecretaries have been left to their own devices as to how to develop and apply corporate governance in their departments. As a result no centrally sanctioned view of corporate governance has emerged, and no uniform departmental reporting regime has been applied.

---

1   The traditional country model for Australia, and the United Kingdom, also accords centrality to the term as in the code of practice, *Corporate Governance in Central Government Departments* (Her Majesty's Treasury 2005).

Because many secretaries had been accustomed to operating under the devolved departmental system, they did not necessarily support central responsibility for directing corporate governance.

Department of state

The department of state is recognised in the Australian Constitution, and forms the core of the machinery of government and the basis of portfolio governance. The current 19 departments of state (a 20th department, Veteran's Affairs, is located within the Department of Defence portfolio) are also the centrepiece of portfolio governance.

Departments vary in functions, size and complexity. Two main organising features are whether a department's functions are primarily cross-agency or not; and whether the department specialises in one role or combines several (policy, program delivery, regulation). In the first case, it is either a line department or central agency, although several combine features of both. Departments normally have a significant policy focus, but they may not have notable service delivery responsibilities. The complications in the mix of features are illustrated by one secretary's observation that his department, and its corporate governance requirements, differed from others because it was an old-fashioned corporate organisation and lacked a big administrative program. It was complex rather than large, the majority of its work being about policy with only an element of service delivery.

The departmental secretary

The secretary holds a key position as head of the department of state,[2] which is the cornerstone of Westminster bureaucratic systems (see also chapter 1). Extensive delegations to the secretary strengthen the position and organisation. The secretary's role is quite explicit under the *Public Service Act 1999 (Cth)* (PS Act), the *Financial Management and Accountability Act 1997 (Cth)* (FMA Act) and other legislation. The secretary administers the department under the minister and is responsible for its management. The main roles of secretaries are (AGRAGA 2010: 47):

- principal official policy advisor to the minister;
- manager, ensuring delivery of government programs and collaboration to achieve whole-of-government outcomes within their portfolio;
- leader with a stewardship role within their department; and
- Australian Public Service (APS)-wide stewardship, discharged in partnership with other secretaries and the APS Commissioner.

---

2   In some departments, the position of secretary is referred to as the chief executive officer.

The responsibilities of departmental secretaries include complying with the FMA Act, the PS Act and portfolio-specific directions and legislation (which includes 'efficient, effective and ethical use' of resources under the FMA Act (section 44). Secretaries are expected to maintain clear intra-portfolio communication, the method of which should be negotiated with heads of agencies, and to engage with stakeholders, particularly regarding departmental core activities. There is also an expectation of familiarity with key project management, human capital and information and communication technology (ICT) systems, and a commitment to the appropriate implementation and maintenance of systems (AGRAGA 2010: 47; see also the *Public Service Amendment Bill 2012*).

Secretaries may be specialists who head a single department (such as Attorney-General's or Treasury) or generalists who head several departments over the course of their career (Smith 2010). In late 2011, only four women held the position of secretary.

Governance conceptions of secretaries

Corporate governance has at least two dimensions, one addressing performance of the organisation, the other conformance to legal requirements and accountability (Edwards and Clough 2005). As indicated below, in interviews, secretaries adopted different starting points in response to questions regarding their understanding of corporate governance: compliance, responsiveness/instrumentalist, and cultural. There were also internal and external dimensions. Overall, compliance was more salient than performance in conceptions of governance.

In interviews that were conducted during the period of John Howard's Coalition government (1996–2007), secretaries focused on compliance and custodianship as being central to corporate governance. This was variously expressed as:

- the combination of structures and processes to ensure appropriate custodianship and advice within the context of an organisation;
- implementing a process that protects public money and makes heads of departments accountable for advice and decision making; and
- governance as a system and framework of controls and measures that provides a true and fair reflection in the financial statement. In signing off the annual report to the minister and parliament there is need for confidence in the accuracy and fairness of the outcomes described and the range of indicators and ethical details provided about departmental operations.

The notion of a governance as a framework that focused on internal governance of organisations was expressed as important:

- governance as the framework for establishing various mechanisms for decision making, including the Audit Committee. This goes beyond having mechanisms in place to answer questions on issues such as membership and timing; and

- a framework to guide activities. It is a set of arrangements to shape what the department and its officers do in carrying out government policy. Relevant to this is the Finance Governance Arrangements document that was written in terms of the outcomes of good governance that were proposed by the *Review of the Corporate Governance of Statutory Authorities and Office Holders* (Uhrig review).

Accountability roles were seen to be most apparent in arrangements for defining specific accountabilities and responsibilities for implementing government policy and administering legislation. These cover public accountability, lines of reporting, and responsibilities for financial management and staff management.

In interviews, two secretaries adopted distinctive positions, taking culture and responsiveness as their respective starting points. Corporate governance was acknowledged as being about 'the systems and the structure and the culture, which you establish in a deliberate way to discharge your responsibilities including your accountability but also your responsibilities to administer and to deliver'. Governance, however, 'obviously forms around structures but I generally don't like to start with structures'. Corporate governance starts with: 'softer concepts, including the culture of the place and the ethics and proprieties … about how things should be done'. This is followed by the systems and the structures that comprise governance in the development of a collegiate culture.

The starting point of the second position was as the government's instrument: 'Corporate governance is 1) being responsive to the objectives of the government of the day, and 2) having systems and processes in place to meet those objectives. Part of that is the APS Values and appropriate ethics, and part of it is meeting cost-effectiveness and productivity objectives'.

In secretaries' formulations of corporate governance, then, there were both common elements and also distinctive variations that suggested differences in leadership styles. This partly centred on how they viewed compliance — as a foremost consideration or not — and also their framing of governance in terms of both hard and soft elements.

Internal management and governance

As mentioned above, structures and processes are suggested, but not specifically prescribed, in *Requirements for Annual Reports* (PM&C 2011). Departments normally have between three and six committees that have some relevance to corporate governance, although departmental practices vary widely.

All departments have some variation on an executive management committee, board or group (see also the discussion in chapter 3). These are invariably advisory committees, although a secretary may give them more latitude to contribute to departmental processes. There appear to be two models, at least on paper. A decision-making conception was present with a small number of departments: for example, 'to provide key policy and management decision making'; 'the executive committee made decisions on departmental policy, financial and operational issues'; and 'the senior decision-making body in the department is the executive committee'. In line with the provisions of the FMA Act, advising the secretary is, however, the dominant approach. Examples of this approach include:

- advice to the secretary on overall direction, priorities, management and performance;
- oversight of corporate governance, accountability, operational effectiveness and monitoring of the financial performance of the department and its programs;
- provision of corporate leadership and strategic direction, setting of goals for the department and management of its overall performance; and
- a system that devolves ultimately to the secretary's accountability with some structures that advise and assist with decision making.

A secretary's explanation of how an intermediate structure worked was:

> The executive board here is a creation of mine — there isn't a legal requirement to have one. It's something I've decided to have to help the chances that the decisions I make have some buy-in. It's an opportunity for me to get counsel from senior people. At the end of the day I'm accountable. Formally it's advisory but I don't really run it that way — it's a collegial practice. But I don't think they [the board members] are under any illusion — they are helping me to discharge my accountabilities. But I do like to have full support.

Similarly, all departments have an audit committee, sometimes with the term 'risk' included in the title. It is now well-established practice to make external appointments to these committees. Beyond these committees, however, there is no consistency in the number or type of committees a department engages, including the secretary's leadership group, departmental operations executive, audit, and ICT committees. In addition to the core executive committee, a broader advisory group may be used.

There is evidence from State of Service reports for APS agencies (a term that is broader than departments) that communication was ineffective between senior leaders and other employees (only 35 per cent agreed it was effective) (APSC 2008: 208, also 2007d). The APSC expressed concern about the lack of improvement because the area had been cited in recent reports as requiring attention whereas, for 2008, there were 'continuing lower levels of dissatisfaction being recorded in the area of senior leaders, and in some instances higher levels of dissatisfaction' (2008: 110). Although agencies reported that policies and procedures existed for ensuring information was available, many staff disagreed that was the case. With the exception of meetings, 'departments relied on passive mechanisms to distribute their corporate governance information. This typically consisted of placing the information, along with large amounts of other administrative information, on a departmental Intranet site' (Tucker 2010: 141). Although communication on corporate governance occurred below the secretary, this was mixed and focused on senior executives. 'Staff below SES are largely left to their own devices to find information and while this is for the most part readily available and accessible, staff do not afford this activity a high priority because they perceive it less important than dealing with what they believe to be more pressing tasks' (Tucker 2010: 142).

Governance was more problematic in dispersed and large departments. One secretary posed the challenge of developing a good governance culture and the acceptance of governance down and through a large organisation of 2000–3000 staff across a dozen or more locations. The secretary of a large and amorphous agency perceived it to contain several governance systems over which it had not been possible to establish firm direction.

Portfolio governance

Portfolio organisation and management has developed following the 1987 changes to cabinet and the departmental structure (Brooke 1993; Podger 2009: 90). A distinction was drawn between cabinet ministers and junior ministers in the overall ministry, and was reflected in each portfolio (i.e. each had a portfolio minister and one or more junior ministers). The department provided the centrepiece of the portfolio that comprised other authorities and agencies. Budgeting and prioritising were now more clearly focused at the portfolio level, however, the level of coordination and integration varies between portfolios (Podger 2009).

Portfolios come in different configurations and sizes. Some have significant authorities under the *Commonwealth Authorities and Companies Act 1997 (Cth)* (CAC Act) (e.g. Broadband, Communication and the Digital Economy holds authority for the Australian Broadcasting Commission, Australia Post and Special Broadcasting Service), while others have responsibility for major agencies that are subject to the FMA Act (e.g. Human Services is responsible for Centrelink and Medicare; the Treasury portfolio contains 15 agencies including the Australian Bureau of Statistics, Australian Competition and Consumer Commission, Australian Securities and Investments Commission, Australian Taxation Office, Commonwealth Grants Commission and the Productivity Commission). Several others, however, have relatively few portfolio demands.

Figure 5.1: Configuration of the departmental portfolio

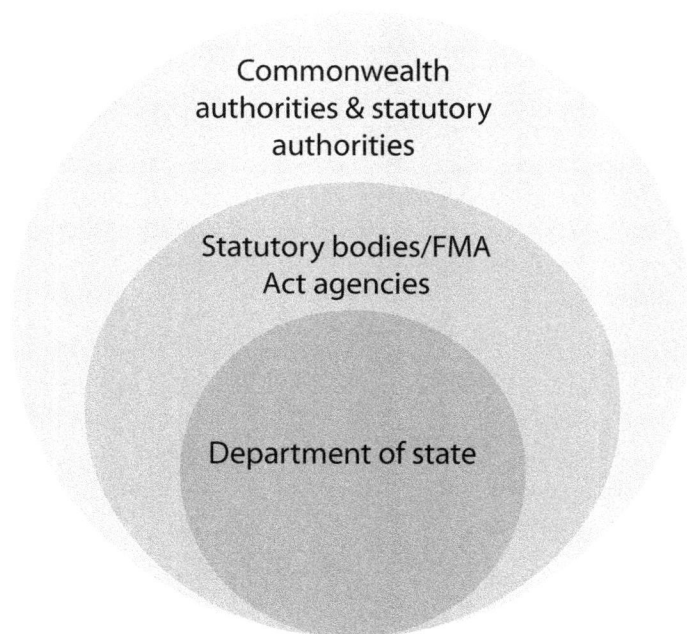

Source: Based on Finance categories: DFD 2009.

The resurrection of a more comprehensive ministerial department and the core public service followed the Uhrig review (2003, and discussed in chapter 2) into the corporate governance of statutory authorities and office-holders. The post-Uhrig review agenda was, in response to the proliferation of non-departmental organisations and questions about their governance, for ministerial departments to have tighter and more direct control over public agencies (chapter 9). The array of Commonwealth public bodies had been comprehensively mapped and typed by the Department of Finance and Administration (DFA 2005d). With departments of state employing only 22 per cent of public sector staff, most worked in approximately 180 agencies, many with statutory independence. The official concern was with different legislative bases, constitutions (boards or not) and opaque governance. For effective implementation, it was evident that there needed to be clarity of purpose, powers and relationships between ministers, public servants and boards. 'Good governance depends upon transparency of authority, accountability and disclosure. There should be no doubts, no ambiguities' (Shergold 2004b).

One means of achieving the recommended control was to revert to departmentalisation. This was expressed through absorbing statutory authorities and reclaiming control of agencies with hybrid boards that did not accord with a particular corporate (and therefore private sector) governance prescription.[3]

Centrelink and portfolio change

The case of Centrelink covers questions about the advantages of departmental versus agency delivery, how to handle relationships between departments and agencies, and levels of autonomy and integration. All three are susceptible to changing fashions and agenda. The original concept for Centrelink was of an agency that would merge two networks for social security and unemployment that were acquired from the departments that went on to become the agency's two major clients.[4] The mandate became that of a one-stop-shop delivery agency designed to provide services to purchasing departments, but with the potential to serve other departments as well (Halligan 2008b).

The agency was located within the core public service and within the Family and Community Services (FaCS) portfolio, but was a separate entity from the FaCS Department with its own legislation, accounting and reporting requirements. In contrast to the standard departmental model, Centrelink was responsible to the Minister for Family and Community Services through an appointed board of directors, which gave strategic direction and set the overall objectives and business rules. The client departments were the purchasers of services that were detailed in negotiated agreements with the agency. Each client — usually a policy department — negotiated a purchase price for specified services that Centrelink agreed to undertake. From the point of view of the primary purchaser,

---

3   Similar agendas for rationalising non-departmental organisations have been apparent in other Anglo-Saxon systems (Christensen and Laegreid 2006).

4   Centrelink was formally established in mid 1997. The agency acquired from the Department of Social Security the delivery of government services to recipients of social welfare benefits and services. The Department of Social Security's other responsibilities were transferred to a new Department of Family and Community Services. By 2005–06, Centrelink accounted for $63.5 billion, or about 31 per cent of total Commonwealth expenditure, and employed close to 27,000 staff who were spread across over 1000 service delivery points throughout Australia.

FaCS, the only direct formal relationship with Centrelink was established by the agreement, which detailed the services, funding arrangements, performance outcomes and reporting mechanisms.

The broader reform agenda of integrated governance that came into play in the 2000s, as a result of the Uhrig review into the corporate governance of statutory authorities and office-holders (see chapter 4, this volume), included resurrecting a more comprehensive ministerial department through absorbing bodies or extending controls. The review included two delivery agencies: the Health Insurance Commission and Centrelink. The Uhrig review's (2003) prescriptions of either a Board template or an executive management template had direct implications for boards that fitted neither.

The impact of the integrated governance agenda on Centrelink was comprehensive, as all dimensions were impacted: the relationship to ministerial direction, stronger ministerial departments in relation to policy leadership and control over public bodies, enhanced central agency capacity for monitoring service delivery and implementation, and the clarification of what constituted appropriate corporate governance for agencies like Centrelink with an advisory board. Two agendas were operating: one addressed agency governance and ministerial accountability and tempering the high levels of devolution in the public service. There were also Centrelink-specific matters that addressed governance issues, such as the operation of a purchaser–provider relationship within the same portfolio; governance by board and minister; and interdepartmental tensions (Halligan 2008b).

The position of Centrelink changed from 2004 when it was subsumed within a new parent department, and its board was disbanded. The creation of the Department of Human Services within the Finance portfolio was the most significant post-Uhrig review structural change. As a small agency, Human Services was structured to have responsibility for strategically directing, coordinating and brokering improvements to service delivery for six agencies operating under direct ministerial control and one advisory board.[5] The rationale was to improve the delivery of services within a whole-of-government approach that involved better collaboration and performance, and to strengthen the vertical (ministerial and departmental control) and horizontal dimensions (delivery network across agencies). The CEO of Centrelink, and five other agencies retained responsibility for day-to-day operations, but Human Services now provided 'assurance to the minister on cross-agency issues, the quality of outcomes, and the achievements of the government's objectives' (Department of Human Services 2005: 13).

---

5   Six agencies delivered services and payments that accounted for over $90 billion and also included the Child Support Agency, Health Services Australia and Medicare Australia.

Centrelink (along with Medicare Australia) was subsequently moved towards formal integration in the Department of Human Services. Centrelink retained its identity (as expressed through the brand and business lines) and a distinct role as expressed through the chief executive. The back-office functions of Centrelink and Medicare were combined: finance, human resources, ICT platforms, procurement and property management. The rationale was both efficiency and seamless service delivery, facilitating co-location of offices and one entry point. The official position on the integration, according to the minister (Plibersek 2011) is that it forms: 'part of the Government's Service Delivery Reform agenda to make it easier for Australians to get the services they need in a way that suits their circumstances. Service Delivery Reform will see … more one-stop-shops, more self service options for customers and more intensive support for the people who need it most'. The official position echoed that for Centrelink in its heyday as a somewhat autonomous delivery agency.

Looking at the longer term, the tendency of the Commonwealth to prefer the ministerial department is apparent. Accordingly, the cycle over 15 years has moved from integrated department to multi-purpose delivery agency to an integrated department. The circular process was complete in mid 2011 when Centrelink became integrated within the Department of Human Services.

External accountability and relationships

The main external relationships of departments are depicted in Figure 5.2. A distinction needs to be drawn between those departments that are part of government, those that are based in the broader machinery (oversight agencies) and those that are located outside (citizens and groups in society). The relationships with the political executive and parliament (under oversight agencies) are of particular importance for formal reporting and accountability. Central agencies were discussed in chapter 4. Relationships with other APS agencies are covered under collaborative governance, below.

Accountability relationships

The public service environment has altered in distinctive ways across the last three decades, with major implications for departmental accountability. It has changed first from the traditional focus on inputs and process to a management environment that emphasises outputs and results, and then to a market environment emphasising competitive elements (e.g. contestability), choice, outsourcing and contracts. This produced the greater emphasis on outcomes as well as outputs. Associated with each major change in the environment has been an extension of accountability responsibilities from the traditional core (i.e. ministerial responsibility and the departmental hierarchy) that featured ministerial responsibility to cover successively new modes of external scrutiny (e.g. through new administrative law), accountability management, and more recently market accountability, performance accountability and shared accountability within governance and collaborative contexts (chapter 1).

Figure 5.2: Key external relationships of the department of state

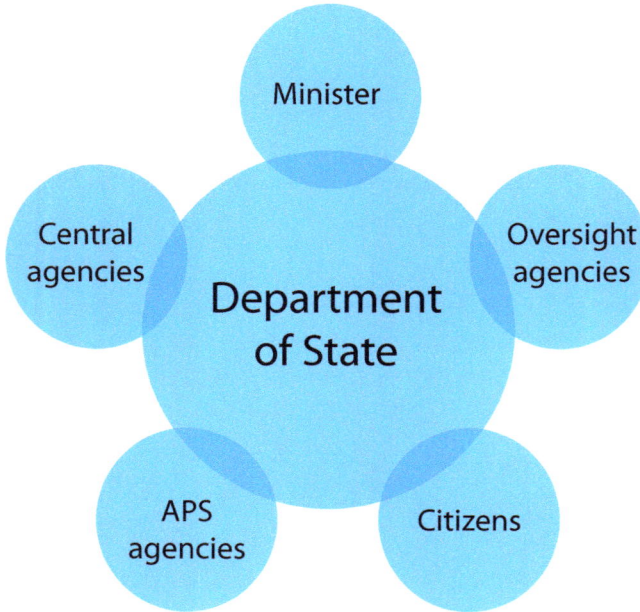

A further dynamic in the different accountability relationships is the tension between the internal and external domains that are defined in terms of different accountability mechanisms (Campbell and Halligan 1993). Accountability that is internal and formal is the immediate environment of the public agency, and has both managerial and political dimensions that are hierarchical in character. External mechanisms have the capacity to operate independently of the government — parliament, the audit office, the appeals tribunal and the court — and press for more exacting public reporting and accountability. Much of the activity around public accountability issues reflects containment and control within the political/ bureaucratic hierarchy up to the accountable minister, or tensions between internal and external agenda and pressures. Over time, the layers of accountability have multiplied (Halligan and Sadleir 2011; Mulgan 2003).

Departmental secretaries report to their minister on a regular basis and annually, as per their performance agreement. For parliament (and the public) Portfolio Budget Statements (PBS) provide details of the proposed allocation of resources to government outcomes. They are an important means by which the political executive and its departments and agencies are held accountable to parliament. The departmental annual report informs parliament and the public about performance against the outcomes and programs.

A secretary may take the demands of the role in his or her stride, but three factors may, at times, weigh heavily on individual performance. The first is the tradition of rigorous accountability with the heavy demands of reporting and the high level of scrutiny. The second is the interface with the centre where ambiguity in the relationship with the prime minister's office and PM&C can produce disputes because of different perspectives and ways in which individuals serve the same prime minister. The third derives from the pressures that may arise in a relationship with a minister where different conceptions emerge about the location of boundary between their roles and the extent to which it is reasonable to exercise political influence (see cases in Tiernan and Weller 2010: 146–47).

Accountability in the Department of Defence

The case of Defence brings into relief central questions of accountability. The department is large, with multifarious components, but it also has the complexity of the diarchy, consisting of the department secretary and the chief of the defence force reporting to the Minister of Defence, superimposed. The seemingly intractable governance problems of a conglomerate department like Defence have been left unresolved for years, but continue to become more pressing. The structure of the diarchy is cascaded down the organisation. Defence, however, has continued to be 'a single organisation of many parts. Each part has its own culture and history from which it draws capability … The continuing legacy of Defence's origins in five departments and separate services has left defence with complex accountability systems.' With the increasing demand for improved performance within tight budgetary conditions the accountability arrangements have come under greater stress (Department of Defence 2010: 11.1, 11.4).

Defence is candid about these failures damaging government and its performance, and the need therefore 'to redesign its accountability system to strengthen its capacity to drive better performance' (Department of Defence 2010: 11.5). The department has been the subject of an unpublished report to the department about how to undertake improvements because it was unable to assure the minister that the condition of accountability was not having a deleterious effect on the organisation (Parnell and Dodd 2010: 9).

Collaboration across departments (and beyond)

Questions of accountability, responsibility and effectiveness also arise in the handling of new forms of collaboration. The whole-of-government movement, which is discussed in chapter 4, has evolved into the language of collaborative governance (O'Flynn and Wanna 2008; APSC 2009c; Blackman et al 2010). The spectrum of arrangements ranges from policy design through to the management and integration of service delivery (e.g. APSC 2009c: 119).

The effectiveness of different approaches to collaboration depends both on the complexity of the policy or program task and the way it can be configured. In practice, there has been a wide spectrum of experiments ranging from crisis management through to the challenges of coordinating the administration of Indigenous programs and services (chapter 6 and Gray and Sanders 2006). A number of critical enablers and major barriers to effective whole-of-government operationalisation have been identified. In practice, significant tensions and paradoxes can arise from attempts to work across boundaries (O'Flynn et al 2011).

Of the several mechanisms of collaboration, the interdepartmental committee (IDC) was a central component of traditional machinery, numbering as many as 180 IDCs in the 1970s, mainly between departments with responsibilities ranging from routine administration, adjudication to policy. The policy IDCs (normally between 30 and 50), displayed two significant characteristics: operating as a collection of delegates who defended the interests of their department and tended to search for a consensus outcome (Painter and Carey 1979). IDCs have retained a recognised presence in the 2000s, and their traditional roles are recognised, but they are no longer the only mode of cross-departmental coordination for program design, review and management; new structural innovations are emerging for strengthening collective and cross-portfolio coordination (MAC 2004).

Task forces originally rose to prominence as a means of avoiding the defects of IDCs and as short-term vehicles for giving focus to government agendas. The task force became 'semi-formalised as a device to develop new policy or to deal with significant, urgent issues' (MAC 2004: 29). Whereas, once, task forces were distinguished informally from other cross-agency structures, the understanding was entrenched of the task force as 'a discrete, time-and-purpose limited unit responsible for producing a result in its own right'. Their capacity for operating independently from policy departments was strengthened by PM&C being, in many cases, assigned administrative responsibility for them (Hamburger 2007).

The traditional mechanisms — the cabinet (of ministers) and the central agencies — are of course prominent in coordination. Task forces became relatively institutionalised and addressed significant issues but, according to APSC figures, they only involved a relatively small proportion of senior executive service/

executive level public servants (14 per cent). Joint teams (regarded as longer lasting structures that blend functions across portfolios) accounted for 16 per cent. Membership of interdepartmental committees continued to be the most significant activity (29 per cent) (APSC 2007d: 230).

There are important questions about accountability and effective reporting where a number of departments and agencies are collaborating under horizontal governance (chapter 1), and more so when third parties are involved. Tucker (2010) examines the case of illegal fishing in Australian waters, which involved 10 agencies with different roles and objectives, each of which was focused on reporting to their minister. The sharing of accountability is now on the reform agenda (AGRAGA 2010) (see chapter 10, this volume), and may redefine some relationships where the arrangement extends beyond devices for satisfying compliance.

External focus

Consultation with external stakeholders — participatory governance — is reported as increasing, with program delivery more often the subject of such consultation. Senior and mid-level executives had substantial interaction with industry and contractors/consultants, but modest experience of consultation with communities and citizens (APSC 2010a: 57). Major delivery agencies make extensive use of citizen feedback (i.e. satisfaction surveys) (APSC 2009c: 128–34). *Ahead of the Game: Blueprint for the Reform of Australian Government Administration* places great emphasis on relating to citizens and recommends a coordinated approach to surveying attitudes (AGRAGA 2010) (see chapter 6, this volume). The head of the public service has concluded that 'Many departments are currently not very outwardly focused' (Moran 2010a: 11).

Oversight agencies and parliament

The external bodies of oversight and review — parliament, ombudsman, audit and administrative appeals — operate outside the direct control of government, and therefore contribute important and often public judgments about departmental governance. The ANAO produces regular performance and financial statement audits and guidelines that shape directly and indirectly much of what departments do.

The Commonwealth parliament exercises its oversight role most explicitly through its committee system. Three basic types of committee — scrutiny, investigation and legislation — produced 3220 reports over three decades (Halligan, Miller and Power 2007). There are regular instances of parliamentary committees having some form of policy impact through the much more commonplace activities of scrutiny and review. Officials in the executive branch continuously adjust their plans when they know in advance that these plans and the proposals that derive from them are going to be subjected to close committee examination. These intra-governmental scrutiny mechanisms can be contrasted with scrutiny of business through the market and corporate regulators — thus reinforcing that accountability is important but manifestly different across the public and private sectors.

Issues in public governance

The main issues of public governance can be divided into those that derive from the conduct of relationships within organisations and those with external actors. Internal issues arise from communication and collaboration problems between parts of the organisation (e.g. divisions and branches; or up and down the hierarchy). The lack of attention to 'soft' questions as opposed to the 'hard' types is a source of weakness in corporate governance (chapter 1).

The external influence on issues commonly stems from poor relationships with the minister and/or the ministerial office. The neglect of other stakeholders is also a source of difficulties. According to the APS commissioner's interpretation (Sedgwick 2010a: xvi):

> History suggests that various components of the APS will experience stress for which they are unprepared at different times— either because the organisational culture has become too fixed (as was arguably the case earlier this decade in the then Department of Immigration and Multicultural and Indigenous Affairs ...), or because they were dealing with the unexpected (arguably the case in the more recent incidents of Motor Dealer Financing Arrangements — OzCar and the Home Insulation Program).

Issues with accountability and reporting arise quite often and may be addressed through rationalising the governance of different types of agency and authorities, as discussed in chapter 4, or as instanced by the cases of Defence and Centrelink, discussed above and, DIMA, discussed below.

A feature of issues with accountability, which frequently acquire public prominence and are then subject to an official review, is that they encompass a number of distinct elements that have the cumulative effect of producing a breakdown in governance (compare international corporate governance failures where multiple corporate governance issues were significant in cases such as the collapse of Enron Corporation: McPhee 2008: 16). The DIMA and procurement cases illustrate this complexity.

Internal governance failure in DIMA

The case of DIMA demonstrates a range of governance issues — in particular a focus on structure and legal compliance rather than the appropriateness of decisions — and the vulnerability of governance where a complex set of factors comes into play.

It is rare for departments of state to fail. Policy failure is depicted as ubiquitous (Bovens and 't Hart 1996) with a range of programs, projects and public works, and the odd systemic failure is evident in government departments (Gregory 1998), but more usually of a specialised nature. The DIMA experienced an internal breakdown of basic operating procedures, culture and leadership in the mid 2000s.[6] The department had acquired a high profile because of the government focus on keeping illegal immigrants out and locating and deporting those that were already in Australia. The failure of governance in DIMA was revealed through a succession of inquiries into the handling of the detention of citizens. The then head of the public service, Peter Shergold, is reported as describing 'the cases as the worse thing that has happened in the public service in recent years' and blaming the failures on public service deficiencies. He is quoted as saying that in addition to failures in ICT systems and record keeping: 'It was a failure of public administration … it was failure in some ways of executive leadership' (ABC 2006).

The first investigation was the *Inquiry into the Circumstances of the Immigration Detention of Cornelia Rau* (Palmer 2005), which arose out of the illegal detention and deportation of an Australian citizen. The second involved the unlawful detention and removal from Australia of another citizen, Vivian Alvarez (Commonwealth Ombudsman 2005). Palmer reported an astounding range of weaknesses, flaws, and disconnects within an overall managerial approach that emphasised process and had an 'assumptive culture' (2005: x, 164–68).

In light of the Rau and Alvarez affairs, the government referred 247 immigration matters to the Commonwealth Ombudsman for investigation. The ombudsman, in several individual and one synoptic reports (2007), examined how and where the department made mistakes, discussed 10 lessons of public administration, including maintaining quality records, adequate controls on exercise of coercive powers, active management of difficult cases, removing obstacles to inter-agency exchange of information, managing complexity in decision making, checking for warning signs of bigger problems and control of administrative drift.

In order to account for the layers of complexity in the DIMA case, an interpretative framework covers four perspectives that include corporate governance and

---

6   For a fuller treatment of the case, see Tony Tucker's (2010) analysis.

closely related dimensions: the rule of law, new public management (NPM), political management and public governance (Halligan and Tucker 2008). Only the governance aspects can be examined here.

DIMA's roles of simultaneously encouraging and discouraging the entry of people to Australia attracted diverse staff to the organisation. The gatekeeper role, especially in compliance areas, appealed to law-enforcement professionals who frequently held strong views about protecting Australia. They needed leadership that carefully balanced the gatekeeper role with the actual views of government. This required corporate governance arrangements that engaged the organisation's owners (i.e. the minister) to ensure that the correct outcomes were pursued. It was the corporate governance leadership arrangements that set the tone for the culture of the department (Halligan and Tucker 2008).

Corporate governance arrangements were designed inter alia to insulate public agencies from failure and, in DIMA's case, they might have worked if both structural (i.e. formal) and behavioural (or informal) elements had been taken into account. However, Palmer (2005: x) found that the department's approach to implementing complex detention policy was 'process rich' and 'outcomes poor'. In Tucker's interviews, it emerged that staff perceptions of corporate governance 'reflected the mechanistic, process-driven nature of its operations', and a focus on structural elements — e.g. compliance with law — rather than behavioural issues of 'correct' decision making (Tucker 2010: 170). The resulting culture in the compliance and detention areas produced decisions, according to Tucker, 'that were lawful, but not necessarily fair'. How lawfulness was defined was mainly up to the staff. However, Palmer (2005: ix), concluded that DIMA staff in these areas had the authority 'to exercise exceptional, even extraordinary, powers. That they should be permitted and expected to do so without adequate training, without proper management and oversight, with poor information systems, and with no genuine quality assurance and restraint on the exercise of these powers is of concern'. He was unable to comprehend how these arrangements were allowed to continue over several years.

Senior executives reflected DIMA ambivalence towards corporate governance. One viewed corporate governance as a process control, reinforcing the traditional public service structures and largely unchanged from what existed prior to NPM: 'The rhetoric is new but … we spend a lot more time talking about it than getting on and doing it'. Another, expressed a more rounded understanding of corporate governance, but thought that the arrangements needed improvement because they weren't 'visible enough … Why aren't issues on corporate governance being distributed to staff? There is no buy-in' (quoted in Tucker 2010: 174). Departmental attitudes suggested that corporate governance was considered a passing fad from which DIMA would take what it needed, and leave the rest. A senior respondent observed that he was not interested in public administration: '[I'm] interested in results for government, results for clients, improving the way we do our work. We are a bread and butter department. I'm not too fussed about APSC and ANAO models. They are useful to some if they have the time … We use it when appropriate' (quoted in Tucker 2010: 173).

Following government action to restructure the department, all senior staff were replaced. By 2007, the new secretary reported that the department was back on track under new leadership (Metcalfe 2007). The DIMA case had broader implications for other departments (see the APSC 2007a, 2007c response), and produced a major reform agenda to correct the litany of deficiencies in departmental governance.

Procurement and program governance

Among the numerous issues of public policy that were prominent in 2010, the Green Loans Program and the Home Insulation Program (HIP) were accorded extensive scrutiny through a series of inquiries that included commissioned reports, ANAO and parliamentary committee reviews, and a departmental response covering both programs.

The Green Loans Program derived from a Labor government election commitment and was launched with the purpose of assisting families with installing solar, water saving and energy efficient products. It entailed offering householders a free home sustainability assessment and, on the basis of an action plan for reducing energy and water use, an interest-free 'green loan' of up to $10,000. The then Department of the Environment, Water, Heritage and the Arts (DEWHA) was the responsible agency. A range of services was procured in designing and rolling out the program between 2008 and 2009 (Faulkner 2010).

By late 2009, concerns had arisen about the program, and four reviews were eventually conducted, including ones by the Senate's Environment, Communications and the Arts References Committee (yet to present its final report) and the ANAO (2010). The Faulkner inquiry (2010: 3) reported an extensive lack of compliance with procurement guidelines and regulations, weaknesses in the contracting process and shortcomings in program arrangements. The key factors that contributed to poor procurement practices and outcomes were multiple. The first was the absence of effective program leadership. This was attributed in part to high turnover at branch-head level (and, to a lesser extent, other executive positions), and the inadequate levels of monitoring, supervising and advising of program staff by senior managers and leaders in the department. Ultimate responsibility lay with senior leadership in the department.

Secondly, there was a failure to establish a 'Program Centred Governance Model'. Without such a governance model, insufficient attention was given to program management and, consequently, there was a lack of definition of accountability. There was also a lack of engagement with corporate functions in the department during design and implementation of the program. Other issues were insufficient resourcing and skills within the loans team and the appropriate use of expertise during the program design phase. The final issue was the inadequate communication between the program team, on the one hand, and the department's executive, central corporate services, and the ministers' office on the other (Faulkner 2010: 4, 34–42).

The ANAO (2010: 18) concluded that the primary reason for administration problems with the Green Loans Program was the:

> absence of effective governance by DEWHA during the program's design and early implementation. DEWHA had no previous experience in designing and delivering [such] a program ... As a multi-faceted 'greenfields' program with a fixed budget and variable (and untested) demand, the Green Loans program required greater oversight than the department's business-as-usual activities.

The Home Insulation Program (HIP) was designed to improve the energy efficiency of homes, to generate economic stimulus and to provide support for jobs and small business. It was part of an Energy Efficient Homes Package within the Nation Building and Jobs Plan, which was the Rudd government's response to the global financial crisis (Hawke 2010). It was the subject of a review by Allan Hawke, which included the provision of 'high level insights into the effectiveness of program governance', and covered responsibilities of relevant agencies and states and territories. The report commented that complex relationships existed, particularly between governments. 'Unlike other components of the Nation Building and Jobs Plan, the HIP had no established pathway for national delivery. Oversight and reporting arrangements were part of those designed for delivery of the Nation Building and Jobs Plan, which had some unique features' (Hawke 2010: 11).

The ANAO concluded its review with the factors affecting the success of program's implementation (ANAO 2010: 175):

> if it receives strong executive-level support, and there is a sound governance framework in place to oversight progress and respond ... to any unexpected variations in performance. Governance arrangements need to be tailored to the requirements of the program with clearly defined roles and responsibilities, including decision-making responsibilities. This is important for allowing appropriate mobilisation of resources and addressing emerging problems in a timely and effective manner.

It goes on to observe that 'effective governance arrangements will incorporate a clear reporting framework that provides for accurate, reliable and relevant information to key stakeholders to assist decision-making on strategic priorities'. The reporting requirements need to reflect the program risks in relation to the administrative demands from data collection and analysis, and the targeting of audit and compliance (ANAO 2010: 175).

Directions for departmental governance in the 2010s

Departmental governance post-*Ahead of the Game*

The broad significance for the public service of *Ahead of the Game* has been discussed in chapter 2. For departments also, there are indications that they may face a new environment comprising characteristics that are either emerging or increasingly prominent in ideas and practice internationally. They have in common both a more open system and greater, if selective, oversight. The overall impact of transparency, open government, partnering and citizen engagement and feedback means new dimensions of responsiveness and collaboration are required.

A second theme is the new forms of oversight that are apparent here and in other Anglophone countries: reviews of departments, the role of external appointments and incipient use of boards for agencies. *Ahead of the Game* has already committed to capability reviews based on, but different from, the approach adopted in the United Kingdom. They are expected to include external participants from outside the public service. There are, of course, precedents for drawing on external experts in corporate governance, such as their use on departmental audit committees and reviews of aspects of governance.

As yet, there has been no inclination to move down the UK path of corporate boards that include independent non-executive members. These boards have been mandatory since 2005, although the concept dates from the 1990s, and have variable performance and weakly defined roles, according to a recent survey by the Institute for Government (Wilks 2007, 2008; Parker et al 2010). Yet, more generally, the notion of boards including external members has been surfacing in Australia (e.g. that proposed for the Australian Taxation Office: AAP 2011).

Secretaries' and ministers' roles and the place of stewardship

The relationship between secretaries and ministers has at times been fraught with issues about boundaries. Ministerial styles vary widely. Under Westminster tenets, there has been a tendency for successive governments to claim ownership of the public service. This can have significant implications for transitions between government when tensions arise with a public service perceived by new political leadership to have been too close to its predecessors. A significant clarification of the secretary's role is the stewardship function that has been previously recognised (e.g. ANAO 2003c) but not accorded prominence. According to AGRAGA (2010), the APS-wide stewardship is a core role of the secretary, and one that is 'discharged in partnership with other secretaries and the APS Commissioner'.

Politicians' lack of strategic focus and 'short-termism', which was evident during the fourth term of the Howard government, indicated that an alternative was needed to relying heavily on political direction. The stewardship role is designed for the public service to have 'the capacity to serve successive governments. A stewardship capability must exist regardless of the style of any one minister or government'. Stewardship covers 'financial sustainability' and efficient resource management, as well as 'less tangible factors such as maintaining the trust placed in the APS and building a culture of innovation and integrity in policy advice' (AGRAGA 2010: 5).

The secretary's role has generally been regarded as having several well-understood components that cover policy advice to the minister, administration and/or management, and these have now been specified in legislation. The 'public interest' element has also been given explicit recognition (Halligan 2011a; PSAB 2012).

Conclusion

Departmental governance has been evolving and is now better understood by the senior public service. At the same time, the departmental environment is more demanding and policy complexity is greater. Different levels of governance also come into play. The trend towards horizontal governance (see chapters 1, 3 and 7) expands the number of actors that have to be factored in to departmental governance. The *Ahead of the Game* reform agenda also has extensive implications for departmental governance.

Important questions continue to exist about the relative autonomy of departments from central agencies, and of agencies from portfolio departments. There are continuing pressures from the centre for a better balancing of devolved department responsibilities and central agency influence (see chapter 4 for historical swings in relationships). While the central agencies have regained some of the roles that they lost in the 1990s, departments like Finance envisage that further redefinition is required, and the strengthened role of the APSC is also significant. These tendencies have implications for the interface between departmental and system governance (chapter 4).

Despite the close attention given to governance improvement during the last decade, significant cases of failure have continued to arise, particularly where several internal and external factors intersect. There are questions to be asked about how this occurs despite extensive governance learning and standard setting, and whether the challenges, complexities and risks of modern departmental governance make this inevitable. More generally, the ongoing cycle of renewal ensures that every decade or so there is a shift in governance approaches, and this can be of great significance for how departments operate.

The functional principle on which most departments are founded continues to provide the most effective basis for the delivery of government priorities and public services. Yet, much of the clamour for change involves opening up the departmental silo to new forms of engagement. How the different imperatives are reconciled will provide a continuing challenge for departmental governance.

6. Board Governance in Authorities and Companies

As seen in chapter 4, governance across the public sector 'system' as a whole encompasses both departmental governance (chapter 5) and the governance of authorities and companies. The governance of these authorities and companies is the subject of this chapter. Although Commonwealth authorities and companies are an important arm of central government, their governance is founded upon the *Commonwealth Authorities and Companies Act 1997 (Cth)* (CAC Act) rather than the *Financial Management and Accountability Act 1997 (Cth)* (FMA Act). As a result, they are more likely than other public sector bodies to be influenced by principles of corporate law and governance drawn from the private sector. Importantly, the CAC Act's treatment of directors is modelled on equivalent provisions of the *Corporations Act 2001*, transposed to the public sector context and modified accordingly. These foundations give rise to the unique features of public sector boards, and to some of the tensions that were considered in chapter 3.

Perhaps the most distinctive and significant feature of CAC bodies is the decision-making board that governs them. In terms of vertical positioning, within the horizontal and vertical planes considered in chapter 1, the ultimate responsibility of the body and its board to central government is established in several ways. Commonwealth authorities must be established for a 'public purpose' and companies are effectively 'owned' by government shareholders. Appointments to the board are generally made by responsible ministers, and the board is required to take account of government policy and meet a number of reporting requirements.

Despite these governmental controls however, CAC boards have been conceived as autonomous corporate boards, chiefly with a view to meeting government operational and commercial ends that might ultimately include privatisation through sale on the market. This gives rise to the idea that CAC bodies and their boards might also enjoy a degree of autonomy and independence from government that is absent in central and line agencies. The corporate features of CAC boards, particularly the potential to add external board members, also suggest that they have a valuable role in bridging the gap between government and outsiders to build important associations and partnerships. In addition, they suggest the importance of these bodies in fulfilling the key elements for a stronger Australian Public Service, which were foreseen in *Ahead of the Game: Blueprint for the Reform of Australian Government Administration* (AGRAGA 2010: 16; chapter 2, this volume).

As noted in chapter 3, providing 'strong leadership and strategic direction' (AGRAGA 2010: 20) will require continuing central control of authorities and companies while also building 'essential' horizontal strategic policy advice, which is founded upon collaboration between agencies and external groups such as academia, business and the broader community. Authorities and companies are likely to play a significant role in meeting and balancing these two objectives. Balancing vertical control and horizontal collaboration in these circumstances requires particular attention to the governance of CAC bodies and suggests the potential for developing a unique conception of corporate governance within the boards of these public sector bodies.

The roles of the board and management

Deep questions of political, economic and legal ideology inform assessments of appropriate corporate governance models for both the private and public sectors, especially in modelling from one sectoral context to the other (chapters 2 and 3). Accordingly, in the contemporary context of governmental policies of corporatisation and privatisation, there is an important question about 'whether the private sector company model, and its associated governance mechanisms, is a theoretically viable governance structure for the commercial activities of the executive government and whether this model is able to deliver the efficiency and accountability benefits its adoption assumed' (Grantham 2005: 181).

The importance of Grantham's question is highlighted in current debates in corporate law concerning the allocation of power within the corporation and the roles to be played by directors, particularly in guiding and monitoring management. The issue of what can reasonably be expected of the directors of a large public company, particularly the non-executive directors, has received consideration recently in a series of ASIC enforcement proceedings against the directors of the James Hardie, Centro, and Fortescue Metals companies. Expert commentary on these cases points to an emerging gap in Australian law between a conception of boardroom responsibility grounded in prudential oversight of management and one grounded in ultimate responsibility of the board, even for critical aspects of operational management (Austin 2010, 2011).

In addition, these cases reopen debates about the extent to which directors can lawfully delegate their responsibilities and rely upon the information and advice of others, including that provided by senior management. These issues are also live under the equivalent provisions of the CAC Act. Indeed, clarification of the responsibilities of boards within government departments is an issue that has been raised again in CFAR's Discussion Paper (DFD 2012b: 41). So, the impetus for reform of the legislative architecture for board governance can arise in both public and private sector contexts, with commonalities as well as contrasts in their underlying difficulties, as exemplified by the CFAR and these landmark ASIC cases respectively.

In the context of the consideration of public sector boards in this book, such cases and legislation remind us of the very different considerations that are applicable to the allocation of powers and responsibilities between the board and executive management in a private corporation, compared to those applicable in a public sector authority or company. In the private corporation, the potential liability of directors rests upon maintaining the clarity of their roles and interactions vis-à-vis management in particular. This remains a vital division of roles and responsibilities, despite the clearer recognition of the legal liabilities of senior executive management since the recommendations of HIH report (HIH Royal Commission 2003: Vol 1: 116; 130).

In Commonwealth authorities and companies, however, the allocation of power is greatly complicated by the role of the minister in appointing directors to the board and the unclear lines of communication that may subsist between the minister, the chief executive and the chair. It is also complicated by the overlay of public service values and standards that bear upon those who manage and staff organisations regulated by the CAC Act. Moreover, boards under the CAC Act are legally obliged to decide and act in the best interests of their organisation, but within a whole-of-government setting in which their organisation also plays a part in serving the broader public interest.

These complications obscure largely unresolved questions as to the roles and responsibilities of ministers and boards in the relationships between those exercising powers in public sector authorities and companies. They help to explain the real difficulties that are now likely to be encountered in attributing legal liabilities to each in appropriate cases, and they suggest the reasons why difficulties will be experienced in considering whether ASIC should bring legal action against the directors of such bodies, as distinct from the finance minister authorising them. CFAR's Discussion Paper raises the difficult question of maintaining enhanced portfolio arrangements and the control of the centre while also accommodating more flexible structures, (DFD 2012b: 32-36). These remain important considerations in the ongoing agenda for reform.

The legal framework for authorities and companies

As has been outlined in chapter 3, the CAC Act regulates the reporting requirements of Commonwealth authorities and the conduct of the directors and officers of such bodies. Significant authorities under the CAC Act include the Australian Broadcasting Corporation (ABC) and The Australian National University (Kalokerinos 2007: 14). An authority is a body corporate which has been incorporated for a public purpose (s 5 and subs 7(1)(a)) and is able to hold money on its own account. This public purpose sets the distinctive public sector context within which directors' duties in corporate law (such as the duty to act for 'proper' purposes) are now assessed under the CAC Act. In defining the legal duties of the directors of authorities and companies, the CAC Act adopts almost identical language to that adopted for private companies governed by the Corporations Act itself. It adopts, for example, the same key concepts of 'good faith' and 'care and diligence' in the assessment of directors' primary legal liabilities.

The reporting obligations of authorities are set out in Part 3 of the CAC Act. In this respect, the directors must prepare an annual report (s 9). The responsible minister is to be notified of significant events (s 15) and both the responsible minister and finance minister are to be kept informed of their progress (s 16). In the case of a government business enterprise (GBE), the body must also provide a corporate plan (s 17). It is the requirement that authorities report to ministers that emphasises their public responsibilities, as distinct from the responsibilities of a private company. It is this reporting requirement that also helps explain why the boards of such bodies will adopt government policy as their starting point in exercising their authority as a board.

By contrast with authorities, a Commonwealth company is a company incorporated under the Corporations Act in which the Australian government holds a controlling interest (other than through interposed Commonwealth entities). Since a Commonwealth company is incorporated under the Act, the legal responsibilities that are applicable to the directors and officers of all private corporations apply equally to the directors and officers of Commonwealth companies. Accordingly, the directors of Commonwealth companies, like the directors of authorities, owe equivalent legal duties of care and diligence, as well as duties of good faith. They also owe civil duties to the company not to misuse their position, or information obtained in the course of performing their duties. Directors who breach their duties of good faith, or misuse their position or information, can be seen to have breached civil obligations and committed criminal offences.

Although lying closer than authorities to privately incorporated companies in their form, the same influence of the government over Commonwealth companies remains evident. The CAC Act specifically requires such companies to comply with the general policies of government once the minister notifies the directors of such policies (s 43). As for authorities, the CAC Act provides the essential levers for governmental control. It imposes reporting obligations upon Commonwealth companies, which include the requirement of an annual report, and the same reporting obligations that apply to authorities.

The adoption of the same legal liabilities and responsibilities that are applicable to the board and individual directors of corporations governed by the Corporations Act, imports the essential features of private corporate law and practice into the governance of boards of CAC bodies. It has also imported elements of the codes of practice, performance indicators and market judgments, at work in the private sector, to corporate boards within the public sector. The process has been reinforced through directors sitting on boards in both sectors bringing their experience to new roles on public sector boards. At the same time, the statutory requirements that companies adopt government policy and report (like authorities) to responsible ministers continue to add a distinctive public sector dimension to the governance of these boards.

The distinctive features of the corporate CAC board are critical to understanding the governance of the board in practice and the importance of this to the conceptions of corporate, public and public sector governance that are outlined in chapter 1. These same features influence individual directors in balancing their public and private responsibilities and the dynamics of decision-making within the board. Individual directors may, for example, acquire power within the board through their appointment by the minister to whom their board is ultimately responsible. In chairing the meeting and reaching collective decisions, the chair may be constrained by an awareness of this (Edwards, Nicoll and Seth-Purdie 2003: 40). These considerations for the autonomy and governance of the board are unique to boards of public sector authorities and companies.

The use of corporate bodies in the public sector

The use of corporate bodies within the public sector has been associated with the growth of new public management and its accompanying phases of privatisation, commercialisation, the outsourcing of government operations and efficiency drives in the public sector. Along with these developments, such bodies have been seen as convenient vehicles for providing a degree of operational and commercial independence from central government.

Following the release of the *Review of the Corporate Governance of Statutory Authorities and Office Holders* (Uhrig review) in 2003, however, there has been some retreat from the utilisation of authorities and corporations in the public sector (chapter 2), with many essential governmental functions having been returned to departments and central agencies. Both the Uhrig review, and the governance arrangements that were subsequently published by the then Department of Finance and Administration (Finance) in 2005, suggest that there may be less reason today than in the past for establishing corporate entities under the CAC Act (DFA 2005b). The creation of new CAC bodies is considered separately in chapter 8.

The 2009 *List of Australian Government Bodies and Governance Relationships*, published by Finance, reflected a reduction of 17 Commonwealth authorities that were then reporting under the CAC Act, this number falling from 81 in 2004 to 64 in 2009 (DFD 2009: xxiv–v). By February 2012, the number of Commonwealth authorities reporting under the CAC Act had fallen further to 62 (DFD 2012a) while, between 2004 and 2012, there was a roughly corresponding increase in the number of prescribed agencies reporting under the FMA Act from 64 to 87 (DFD 2012a). Although Finance also reports a significant reduction in the number of departmental bodies such as joint Commonwealth–state bodies, international bodies and advisory bodies, the overall reduction in the number of authorities and departmental bodies appears consistent with the strengthening and streamlining of central government.

The two Uhrig review templates, which were considered in chapter 2 (i.e. the 'board' and 'executive management' templates) provided an important stimulus for the reduction in Commonwealth authorities. They continued, for some time, to influence the post-Uhrig review governance arrangements and policy guidelines that were formulated for the formation of CAC bodies, which were subsequently adopted and published by Finance (DFA 2005b). The board template reflects an independent board, more akin to that of the board of a private sector company. This template also reflected the government's view at the time that a statutory authority ought to be one in which it was appropriate for the board to have the necessary authority and power to appoint and remove the chief executive, to determine strategic direction and set corporate plans, to supervise management and hold management accountable for performance (Uhrig 2003: 27).

As a test of the independence of a public sector body, this formulation largely duplicates the legal authority and autonomy that is enjoyed by the board of a private corporation. It re-states an underlying assumption of board independence in both the Corporations Act and the CAC Act that may have been obscured in the widespread adoption of boards within FMA Act-reporting bodies as well as CAC bodies.

In their application to public sector boards, the Uhrig review templates emphasise the authority of the corporate-style board and its constitution operating in a setting quite removed from its origins in private corporate law. In the longer term, the Uhrig review templates may be seen to have begun shaping boards with a distinctive public sector character. This distinctive character derives primarily from the clearly defined governmental purpose of the body and an emphasis upon the particular skills, expertise and experience that is needed to fulfil that purpose. At the same time, even the Uhrig review templates are not immune from subsequent review and reform of governance architecture, as exemplified by the Commonwealth Financial Accountability Review (CFAR).

Finance's governance arrangements

Following the Uhrig review, Finance published its *Governance Arrangements for Australian Government Bodies* (DFA 2005b). These arrangements greatly extended the earlier Australian National Audit Office guidelines which had set stronger policy foundations for the governance of CAC bodies by way of an advisory or governance board. The arrangements that were proposed by Finance generally favoured departmental control and FMA Act supervision rather than the establishment of a corporation or independent entity with a governance board. Given the corporate features of authorities and companies, the arrangements proposed by Finance and the requirements of the Uhrig review board template encounter difficulties in their application in practice.

Finance's governance arrangements help to clarify the policy to be applied in establishing and regulating the creation of corporate bodies in the future. Their importance in this regard is considered in chapter 8. For the purposes of this chapter, however, the governance arrangements also suggest the factors that influence the governance of a body and whether a body should operate under the FMA Act or the CAC Act. These factors are said to be the purposes and functions of the body, its financial sector classification, whether a governing board would be effective, the appropriate employee coverage and the level of independence of the body (DFA 2005b: 32).

The Finance arrangements tend to identify the circumstances in which the board template should not be applicable, rather than those in which it should. One reflection of this, for example, is said to be that a governing board is 'not an appropriate governance structure for an FMA Act agency' (DFA 2005b: 38). To some extent, this leaning may reflect the concerns of John Howard's Coalition government (1996–2007) when commissioning the Uhrig review for clarifying the role of those business regulatory authorities, which was the foundation subject of the review. Continuing to identify the essential features of the board template in the public sector, however, remains an important task in distinguishing these boards from the advisory and management boards that are used widely in FMA Act-reporting bodies.

While the governance arrangements favour a CAC body for undertaking a commercial enterprise, the CAC body is not otherwise generally favoured. The arrangements consider the independence of a body to be more the product of the terms of the enabling act, reflecting its essential purpose, than a question of its regulation under the FMA or CAC acts. They also tend to favour the use of a statutory authority under the CAC Act, rather than a company although, overall, the most significant reduction between 2004 and 2009 recorded in Finance's *List of Government Bodies*, occurred in statutory authorities, with many of these being converted to statutory agencies (DFA 2005d; DFD 2009).

Those departments which appear most inclined to utilise the legal form of the company are the Department of Broadband, Communications and the Digital Economy (DBCDE), the Department of Immigration and Citizenship (DIAC), and Finance itself. The reasons for these departments utilising companies appear to be predominantly the extent of their commercial operations. Unsurprisingly, for example, the many CAC companies established within the portfolio of DBCDE are commercial subsidiaries of Australia Post and the ABC. The reasons for utilising such companies rest largely upon their commercial and administrative suitability and their 'fitness for form' (rather than their need for independence). In this respect, the Uhrig review board template has focused attention upon the critical decisions to be made by the board of particular bodies and the essential governance required of such a board.

For a time, in its application of the Uhrig review in practice, Finance appeared to consider the 'interaction' of a new body with existing bodies and the 'synergies between bodies' in assessing suitable governance structures for bodies (DFA 2005b: 33). This suggested the importance of administrative suitability and convenience as distinct from departmental control and 'fitness for form' as governance indicators. Upon this measure, important elements were the status of other bodies with which the subject body interacted closely and the cost of maintaining an independent body and a governing board. Such an approach echoed the early Organisation for Economic Co-operation and Development *Principles of Corporate Governance*, which emphasised the 'relations' between different decision-making groups as well as the structures and processes for decision-making (OECD 1999; 2004a). Indeed, the title of Finance's *List of Government Bodies and Governance Relationships* now suggests the importance of relationships in determining the features of a body's governance.

The relationships between bodies do provide a helpful administrative guide within government. They also represent, however, a shift in focus from the Uhrig review board template, which focuses more upon the essential purposes of the body, as expressed in the enabling act, when seeking to articulate the essential features of the governance board.

GBEs: CAC bodies with corporate autonomy

At one end of the spectrum of CAC bodies lie government business enterprises (GBEs), which in some instances are earmarked by the government for later privatisation. In this context, a GBE is a Commonwealth authority or Commonwealth company as defined by the CAC Act and prescribed as a GBE under the CAC Act regulations. Finance's 2011 *Commonwealth Government Business Enterprise Governance and Oversight Guidelines* (DFD 2011b) provide guidance for the governance of GBEs. They are particularly instructive as to the essentially different perspectives that prevail in the public and private sectors, even in the case of those CAC bodies that are designated as GBEs.

A consideration of the governance of GBEs provides valuable insights into the different factors involved in the governance of CAC bodies more generally. In the first place, the conduct of the directors of wholly owned company GBEs is governed by the Corporations Act, while the conduct of the directors of authority GBEs is governed by the CAC Act (DFD 2011: 10). Secondly, in the case of GBEs that are not wholly owned Commonwealth companies, the GBE guidelines are to apply 'to the maximum extent possible, consistent with minimising the risk of a potential oppression action by minority shareholders under s 232 of the Corporations Act'.

The ultimate control by ministerial shareholders of the strategic direction of both company and authority GBEs, (and the accountability of both to the minister shareholders) is achieved through an agreed statement of corporate intent that is reached with the directors, and statutory reporting requirements. The hallmarks of the public sector also remain evident in the three key interests of the minister shareholders, as stated in the GBE guidelines, namely: the performance and financial returns of the GBE, the reporting and accountability arrangements necessary to facilitate the active oversight of the GBE by the Commonwealth and the Commonwealth action needed to provide the strategic direction of its GBEs, in cases where it prefers a different direction from the one proposed.

For many years, successive Australian governments have been able to rely upon the privatisation of large public sector enterprises to relieve budget pressures. The most recent of such privatisations has been the sale of telecommunications organisation Telstra by the Howard government. Such GBEs represent the end result of years of investment and subsidisation by governments and taxpayers. They are CAC bodies that have reached the highest state of corporate development, enabling privatisation where appropriate through sale on the market. Presently, there are seven prescribed GBEs namely: ASC Pty Ltd; the Australian Government Solicitor; the Australian Postal Corporation; the Australian Rail Track Corporation Ltd; Defence Housing Australia; Medibank Private Limited and, the latest addition, the NBN Limited. There are also a further five entities which, although not prescribed, receive advice from the Government Businesses Advice Branch.

Upon their sale and privatisation, GBEs become corporations much like any other public corporations listed on the market. As such, they are equally subject to the general law, as nearly as is possible, as are individual citizens. Their officers are subject to the legal duties imposed upon all directors under the Corporations Act, to regulation by the Australian Securities and Investments Commission (ASIC), and to regulation by the Australian Securities Exchange listing rules and *Principles of Good Corporate Governance and Best Practice Recommendations* (ASX Corporate Governance Council 2010). In addition, they are subject to the judgments of the market itself. Painting this picture of the post-privatisation world of the GBE serves to remind us of the very substantial differences that exist in reality between corporate governance as conceived in the public and private sectors.

One difficult question Australia may need to consider more closely in the future is whether fattening the public sector calf for sale on the private market will always be possible. This is because GBEs have often evolved from the need for government to provide essential services and infrastructure — communications, transport and postal services being the obvious examples. Often, the high establishment and maintenance costs, and the national significance of these services, have earmarked them for provision by government rather than the private sector. However, partnerships between governments and the private providers of infrastructure and essential services (or the investment managers who now finance these services) have grown more sophisticated and the government is assuming a more direct role in establishing the investment funds (such as the Future Fund and nation-building funds) that are now required to finance major public developments. In these circumstances, the need for fully government-financed enterprises may be reduced over time.

There are also dangers in government embracing a closer relationship with private providers and financiers. As governments become more reliant upon large private corporations and financial investors to provide infrastructure and major services, departmental control of essential infrastructure becomes more problematic. In 2006, for example, the different expectations of the government and the market were clearly revealed during the highly political process for the privatisation of Telstra and the Telstra 3 sale. At this time, both the board of Telstra and the market supported Sol Trujillo, the then chief executive of Telstra, in rejecting government-nominated members on the Telstra board. The government, on the other hand, saw such nominations as vital to the representation on the board of regional users of Telstra facilities. These users of Telstra's services were, at the time, publicly and politically important, although economically insignificant. In the final result, the government used its power of appointment to appoint Geoff Cousins — a director who the government felt would represent these interests — to the Telstra board.

Another supervening danger that looms in government–private sector relationships is the more active role now required of government in responding to the threats of transnational business. In an era of global markets, governmental control and sovereignty will increasingly rest upon difficult questions of corporate ownership and control associated with international competition and investment flows. In the 2006 bid for Qantas by Airline Partners Australia (APA), for example, the interests and motives of the private equity partners and hedge funds, upon which the success of the bid ultimately depended, remained unclear. Several of the private equity partners in the proposed bid have since collapsed. The temporary grounding of the entire Qantas fleet both domestically and internationally in late 2011 in the wake of industrial action by Qantas management and unions illustrates, in part, a corporate response to the pressures of global competitiveness.

Although Qantas is a private corporation, cases such as this suggest the problems that may be encountered in ensuring the continuity of core Australian industry and services, in the face of uncertain private foreign ownership of major public corporations, post-privatisation. Cases such as this also have implications for governments seeking to maintain a guiding hand in the governance of the boards of GBEs, post-privatisation.

The governance of CAC bodies in practice

At the other end of the spectrum, lie a number of important authorities and companies, governed by the CAC Act, which are utilised for service delivery and other government purposes. For these bodies, the emphasis may now be less upon their commercial and corporate independence, and more upon their capacity to integrate the vertical and horizontal elements that are inherent in providing both 'strong leadership and strategic direction' (AGRAGA 2010: 20). The corporate form of these bodies and their boards equips them particularly well within government for enhancing collaboration between agencies and with external groups, but renders them more difficult to control and direct within central government. This illustrates some of the institutional tensions that were canvassed in chapter 3.

The role of the board

At the time of the Uhrig review, and in its aftermath, those officials who were interviewed by the authors in 2005–07, whose agencies reported under the CAC Act, were often clearly conscious of where their board might ultimately be placed for the purposes of applying the Uhrig review board templates and regulation by the CAC Act or the FMA Act. In the governance arrangements published subsequently by Finance, one indicator of the governance arrangements most suitable for a body was the level of independence of the body (DFA 2005b: 32). In formulating the principles to apply in governing the boards of authorities and companies as independent commercial entities in the public sector, both the CAC Act and the Uhrig review drew heavily upon principles of private corporate law.

Furthermore, those reporting under the CAC Act at this time expressed some sense of disillusionment, reflecting their belief that there was no longer quite the same rationale, as once there may have been, for establishing CAC bodies as a business or commercial 'arm' of government. They referred to the 'great' boards they had established and to the care they had taken in finding members with the skills required to set up such boards. They often expressed 'disappointment' that these boards seemed to have made a less significant contribution in practice than they might have expected, rather than concern for uncertainty in their relationship with relevant portfolio departments and core agencies.

Many interviewees referred to the poor representation of core government agencies on the boards of CAC bodies, and to their lack of access to relevant governmental and policy information. As to departmental representation on CAC bodies, the evidence referred to in chapter 9 suggests that, while some secretaries consider representation on CAC bodies a part of their role, others reporting under the FMA Act held concerns for this. Senior public service representation on bodies outside their departmental structure can raise additional concerns about membership of the body, independence and conflict of interest (chapter 3).

The Uhrig review saw the legal status of a body established as a CAC body in terms of the authority, autonomy and capacity of its board. This test tends to emphasise the rationale of the enabling legislation in establishing the body and the essential purpose of the body. At the time of the Uhrig review, the 'independence' of the board was not seen to establish a particularly strong rationale for establishing or maintaining CAC bodies in the Commonwealth public sector. Rather, the independence of the board from government was seen to be achieved in other ways by experienced people, without the need for an independent body and decision-making board.

The board's level of independence

The reporting and other requirements that are imposed on authorities and companies in the CAC Act suggest that the independence of the board proves difficult to achieve in practice. At the time of the Uhrig review, three elements were commonly seen to undermine the independence and capacity of the board in CAC bodies. These were the minister's appointment of the chair and board members, the minister's dealing directly in practice with the chief executive as well as the chair, and the appointment and consultation processes generally, all of which tend to ensure that the influence and expectations of the minister condition the judgments of the board.

One telling feature was the ready acknowledgment of participants in the authors' research that in even the most 'independent' of CAC bodies the 'business judgment' exercised by the board is significantly circumscribed by the demands of government policy. Both the autonomy of the board, and the dynamics of board decision-making, are potentially undermined by this supervening influence and unwarranted ministerial intervention. While the process for the appointment of board members (chapter 9) may involve the relevant minister, the prime minister, the governor-general and the Commonwealth Executive Council (with assistance provided by cabinet, the Department of Prime Minister and Cabinet and other relevant departments), the relevant ministers are expected to make appointments on the basis of merit, and to take into account the skills, qualifications and experience of prospective directors (PM&C 2009a).

Although boards may or may not be involved in identifying the skills and experience required when vacancies arise, the boards of some CAC bodies do, in practice, present the minister with clear indications of the skills and experience needed on their board and potential candidates. Such an approach appears more likely to meet with a closer consideration by the minister of the needs of the board, and better outcomes, than an approach in which candidates were simply proposed to the minister.

At the time of the Uhrig review, directors of authorities and companies were generally keen to assert their independence of government. Directors rated their independence somewhere between 'totally' independent to 'mainly' independent or 'heading towards' independence. For example, one chair stated: 'We are totally independent. This is because we have built in representation from both sides of politics. We can't be a rubber stamp for the minister without the other side of government knowing all about it'.

Significant factors mentioned, or implicit in, responses at the time suggested that the board may be less independent in reality. The fact that board independence does not extend to the board's independence of the minister and government was often taken for granted. For example, a CAC chairman said: 'We are totally independent … absolutely independent. This is despite the fact that the board members are all mates with the PM'. This conclusion is reinforced by chief executives, who tend to be more equivocal about any perceived independence of the board.

For many of the same reasons that the board of a CAC body in the public sector lacks the authority and independence of a board in a private corporation, it also tends to lack many of the dynamics of collective decision-making that are apparent in a private corporate board. These dynamics are significantly influenced by the minister's general hand in the appointment of board members and by the fact that the discharge of the functions and roles expected of the chair, the chief executive and other independent board members are likely to be fundamentally different in the public sector.

Business judgment in the public sector board

In Australia, the concept of a 'business judgment rule' was borrowed from American corporate law and redeveloped throughout the 1990s to provide a clearer defence for the directors of private corporations in seeking to discharge their legal duty to act with care and diligence. So long as the director makes a genuine and rational business judgment in the interests of the corporation, the defence may be open to them. However, the concept of 'business judgment' and the availability of the same defence to the officers of authorities and companies under the CAC Act invite closer consideration of precisely what the directors' business judgment might mean in the public sector context.

The overarching public purpose of the board and the board's adherence to relevant government policy are both taken for granted in practice. Directors believe that they must manage the affairs of the company only within the relatively narrow scope for their judgment that these policy constraints permit. This fact reminds us of the significant difficulties that arise in practice in transferring the statutory duties of the directors of a private company to the directors of a public sector body. The boards of Commonwealth companies are not responsible to shareholders in a general meeting, despite the fact that they are incorporated under the Corporations Act. The authority of the board of a private corporation is much wider and is constrained only by the relatively limited powers of the shareholders in general meeting, by any limitations expressed in the company's constitution and by the law itself.

These constraints upon the exercise of their power are clearly understood by the directors of authorities and companies. Some evidence of this was seen in the authors' interviews with CAC body representatives. For example, the chair of one authority commented: 'It's how we do business. Our board sees its independent business judgment as its expertise on the organisation's business. The government director often remains silent on the actual business. But, of course, the board is incredibly sensitive to the government's requirements/ policy'. Similarly, the chair of a GBE put it this way: 'We are totally independent, very independent. We are at arms-length from government. We are also sensitive to government's wishes however. Our corporate plan specifies what we do and it wouldn't cross our mind to buck government policies'.

One important gloss upon the influence of government, as it is exerted on the boards of CAC bodies, is found in the rare occasions on which the CAC body might assist the minister in the formation of policy (see also Edwards, Nicoll and Seth-Purdie 2003). The chair of one CAC body in this position said: 'We develop a policy for the institution and give this to the minister. There are no government guidelines as to the sorts of things we can do. The government can set policy and direction within a framework of serving the people. A good chair and board can lead the government'.

Board concern for government acting as shareholder and customer

Another difficulty for the boards of CAC bodies arises when they must deal with government acting in different roles and capacities — particularly as shareholder, regulator and customer. In these circumstances, a charter setting out the expectations of both the government and CAC body was seen to be useful. Different examples of the importance attached to clarifying the body's relationship with government arose in the course of the authors' interviews.

For example, one representative of an authority said: 'There is an issue with government sometimes being a shareholder and sometimes a customer. So, I've changed my view a bit from simply referring people to the Act. I agree that a charter that spells out roles etc. could be useful, particularly in the face of possible ministerial change'. Another said: 'We have a reasonably formal approach. The government is a customer, so we need a customer service strategy as well as a strategic plan and corporate plan. This is what we'll do in the future. Government policy is reflected in the corporate plan and the 5-year strategic plan, which are given to the minister'.

Although tending to require several different contractual foundations for the relationship between government and CAC bodies, these statements do reflect the various relationships that are now arising in practice and the need to clarify the different roles required of both government and CAC bodies when acting in different capacities.

Directors' views of corporate and board performance

The responses of participants reflected different approaches in their assessment of board performance. In their approaches, participants often referred to their 'informal' and 'subjective' assessments of performance, as well as self-assessment mechanisms. Greater effort appeared to be being made to align performance more with corporate and strategic plans. For example, the chief executive of one CAC body said: 'In future, we will align corporate strategy and corporate performance'. The director of another body said: 'We have a complete performance management framework. This is tied to our business plan and ultimately to our strategic plan'. Finally, the chair of a CAC body stated: 'We have started a process of self-assessment of the board as a whole. This has been instituted to line up the organisation's performance with board performance'.

As might be expected, these responses indicate that assessments of corporate and board performance in CAC bodies are tied closely to the business and strategic plans of the body, rather than to metric market measures (as in the private sector), and that performance assessments are supported by the self-assessments of board members.

A focus on skills and experience rather than 'independence'

Several developments, which are associated with the need for greater collaboration between the public and private sectors, suggest the potential value in the augmented capacity of boards within departments and agencies. These developments invite consideration of the difficult conceptual question of whether it may be possible in the future to design a board within FMA Act-reporting bodies which brings together very senior and diverse people from the private sector to provide collaborative and collective expert advice to the chief executive. As boards become more specialised, it may be found difficult to maintain the authority of the chief executive and central governmental control. The board of Infrastructure Australia, for example, was established in 2008, following the election of the Kevin Rudd's Labor government (2007–10), in order to coordinate and prioritise various strands of private expertise and experience for the benefit of public capital expenditure. In this exercise, overall control and responsibility for the public interest resides with the chief executive and the minister, although the equal representation of very senior public and private interests on the advisory board appears to herald new dimensions of the public–private partnership within government. For these reasons, the board of Infrastructure Australia is considered in greater detail below.

The Uhrig review suggested that establishing clear purposes and clear individual authority will be essential to the success of organisations. Of course, the challenge in establishing boards for a particular purpose and their role lies in defining what that purpose and role should be. The more that governments attempt to define the purpose and authority of these bodies and their boards, the less scope there may be for genuine 'decision-making' by the board. Board members sitting on CAC bodies are arguably constrained in this way already, by their need to consider government policy at every point in their decision-making. Nevertheless, there is a sense in which an approach seeking to maintain governmental control also denies the potential value of a more broadly constituted decision-making board. The more the role and authority of the board is limited and refined, the more this potential may be denied. Some of these questions appear to have been raised from time to time in making appointments to certain boards such as, for example, in making appointments to the board of the Reserve Bank of Australia (chapter 8).

Improving the capacity of the public sector board

It has been suggested in this chapter that, of all the reasons for establishing a CAC board, perhaps the most compelling are that the board potentially offers a greater real capacity than individual departmental secretaries or chief executives in complex decision-making, a greater capacity to serve the public sector in vertical and horizontal integration, and a greater capacity to build partnerships and collaboration between government and outsiders.

This augmented capacity in decision-making appears to have been suggested in *Ahead of the Game*, which proposes maintaining 'strong leadership and strategic direction' as a key objective (AGRAGA 2010: 20). Achieving this objective will require not only maintaining central control but also building 'essential' horizontal strategic policy advice, founded upon collaboration between agencies and external groups such as academia, business and the broader community. Authorities and companies are likely to play a significant role in meeting and balancing these two objectives. Situations may arise (for example, those in which boards are required to represent competing state interests) when board decisions must reflect the extended range of experience and expertise upon the board. In these circumstances there may need to be compromises made and the collective capacity and responsibility of the board provides significant additional capacity.

It also seems that the declining need for CAC Act-reporting bodies may be a product of the changing shape of the public–private relationship itself. Wettenhall and others have already noted at length the many and varied forms that the public–private partnership has taken, and the related difficulties that now arise in settling a typology for and protecting the public interest (Wettenhall 2003). Mention has already been made of Infrastructure Australia, a board considered in more detail below, which may hold significant decision-making power in practice, yet operates within the control of the chief executive of the Department of Infrastructure and Transport and its minister. Appointments to such a board by the minister might be used to establish a 'tailored' advisory or executive board in a way that is not generally possible in the private corporate board. In the authors' research, CAC body interviewees often considered the skills and qualifications of board appointees a more significant issue than their independence. If this is so, then the exercise may be one of building the board that is best tailored for the purposes of government.

Of course, it takes courage on the part of ministers in making the right appointments to boards, without merely representing sectional interests, and a sophisticated understanding of government policy on the part of appointees. One common view expressed to the authors by experienced CAC body representatives was that the set of skills required on the board might be routinely put to the minister (as it often was) with the strong request that appointments be made to provide those skills. In such an approach, the board remains responsible for setting the threshold criteria needed for board membership to achieve the body's overall purpose, while leaving it to the minister to appoint specific people. The issue here is, however, the extent to which the minister considers and acts upon the board recommendation.

This rather ideal approach seems to acknowledge the reality of the minister's strong hand and active involvement in specific appointments, while also clarifying the responsibilities of the board and minister in the process. The board is required to consider (and decide upon) the skills it requires and the minister is required to consider more clearly the suitable candidates within the range of the stated criteria.

Infrastructure Australia and public-private partnerships

In January 2008, Rudd announced the establishment of Infrastructure Australia. The new statutory Government and Business Advisory Council constitutes 12 members who are drawn from industry and government. Five members come from the private sector, one of whom is the body's chair (Sir Rod Eddington's appointment as the chair of Infrastructure Australia was subsequently announced in February 2008). Three members are appointed by the Commonwealth, another three by the states and territories, and one by local government.

It is clear that the board of this advisory body represents a different focus from that in the past, by providing the active agent for public–private partnerships. The purpose of the board of Infrastructure Australia has been to identify a steady stream, or 'pipeline', of projects to encourage private sector investment. The Government and Business Advisory Council advises the Office of Infrastructure Co-ordination within the Department of Infrastructure and Transport. This office provides policy recommendations through the Council of Australian Governments. More particularly, Infrastructure Australia has three key objectives: first, to conduct audits of nationally significant infrastructure, in particular water, transport, communications and energy; secondly, to draw up an infrastructure priority list involving billions of dollars of planned projects; and thirdly, to advise government investor and infrastructure developers on regulatory reform that is aimed at increasing the speed of projects.

The government retains effective control of Infrastructure Australia and the new board is essentially advisory in its capacity. The scale and importance of the new board, however, mark it for closer consideration. The idea itself is not new and derives in part from the extensive use of the Future Fund (chapter 8). Ideas for use of the Future Fund have ranged from university infrastructure funding, under the Howard government, to new suggestions such as a future fund for the financing of issues related to Indigenous Australians, and a sustainable fund for the arts, which was proposed at the 2008 Australia 2020 Summit. What is new, however, is the significance of this board in its representation of public and private interests within a single board in a core government agency.

The informal and social association of private and public representatives upon the board replaces the contractual association that might in the past have been forged through negotiated agreement between government and a private provider. What is gained from this closer, more direct association within the board is greater flexibility. What may be lost is the clarity of legal responsibilities in a contractual relationship. It is true that the board remains advisory in function, but its size and significance are likely to mean that people of power and influence in the private sector will be appointed, and the line that is drawn between the board's advisory role and its de facto decision-making power blurred. The intermingling of public and private interests within a board such as this may also mean that real questions of conflict of interest for the board's members may arise.

While the purpose of the Infrastructure Australia board remains as presently stated, that is to undertake an infrastructure audit and identify infrastructure priorities, the advisory character of the board may be maintained. As serious financial decisions are made in the future, however, many critical questions as to how a decision-making board is to operate within core governmental agencies will be raised more pointedly. The issue has not really been addressed on this scale before within one single, government-controlled board.

It should be remembered that these plans for Infrastructure Australia may rest ultimately upon governments effectively harnessing for critical public purposes the estimated A\$1.1 trillion that is currently in Australian superannuation funds. The management and governance of these private funds is itself emerging as a significant and challenging issue. A critical issue for new bodies such as Infrastructure Australia will be satisfying the market for corporate capital and private sector fund-managers that investment in particular projects is worthwhile and profitable for private trustees and investors. Whether private companies and private financiers see the same benefits as governments in the projects prioritised by the Infrastructure Australia board may prove an interesting question.

Conclusion

Enthusiasm for independent corporate entities may be waning in the public sector. Nevertheless, a review of the experience of corporatisation in the Australian public sector suggests the need for greater integration of corporate and commercial activity in central government, as well as the need for greater collaboration between central government and the private sector. Together, these needs highlight the potential value of CAC boards participating in more complex advisory, representative and management functions. In this respect, the fading of 'corporate' governance as a conceptual underpinning of governance generally within the sector may be accompanied by the evolution of a unique form of public sector board — a board that is mindful of the needs of government and government policy in a rapidly changing environment for public sector governance.

Since the Uhrig review, there has been a retreat from the active use of Commonwealth authorities and corporations within the public sector, except in the case of the clearest commercial enterprises preparing for privatisation. The blurring of the line between governmental and commercial functions adds a further complexity. The legacy of the era of corporatisation and the adoption of corporate-style or 'governance' boards, however, has been to suggest the value of such boards within the public sector as a lynchpin for the vertical and horizontal integration of central and outer government. In so doing, it has also suggested the potential of such boards, in collaboration or partnership with outsiders, to enhance the capacity of decisions that are made by departmental secretaries and the chief executives.

At the same time, the use of boards in the management of CAC bodies continues to sit uneasily with the ultimate legal authority and accountability of the secretary or chief executive, so that balancing strong central leadership and external collaborations to enhance strategic direction remains a challenge. The choice between boards and other governing mechanisms in interjurisdictional and cross-sectoral contexts provides an interesting challenge in marrying organisational independence, governmental accountability and the public good, as signalled by the reforms flagged in *Ahead of the Game* and the CFAR. In the longer term, these more recent developments in the governance of boards in the public sector may be re-shaping the institutional relationship between government and the private sector as well as the character of public–private partnerships.

7. Participatory Governance

Previous chapters in this volume have dealt with horizontal aspects of governance but largely as they occur within government. As indicated in chapter 1, however, compared to 10 or 15 years ago, the move toward horizontal governance arrangements that involves non-government organisations and citizens has accelerated. Collaborative behaviours involving many more networked-type arrangements are increasingly observed in a post-new public management (NPM) environment (e.g. OECD 2009a); this was a major theme of the Advisory Group on the Reform of Australian Government Administration's (AGRAGA) review *Ahead of the Game: Blueprint for the Reform of Australian Government Administration* (AGRAGA 2010). The Advisory Group's foreword to *Ahead of the Game* stated as one of its reform priorities: 'forging a stronger relationship with citizens through better delivery of services and through greater involvement of citizens in their government' (2010: v).

For Jocelyne Bourgon, any new theory of public sector governance should start with the ideal of democratic citizenship (2007a). It follows, she says, that there is a need to: build collaborative relationships with citizens and groups of citizens, encourage shared responsibilities, disseminate information to better inform discussions, and seek opportunities to involve citizens in government activities. Included here would be allowing citizens to reframe issues that have been set for discussion (Lenihan 2009) and even the rather radical situation (for some within central government) of letting non-government players initiate agendas (Bond et al 2007; Lovan, Murray and Shaffer 2004). This point connects to the broader debate about deliberative democracy that is highlighted in chapter 1.

This chapter, therefore, focuses on governance in the public sector with a particular emphasis on the various arrangements under which citizens and organisations outside of government can be involved in public decision-making processes. It is confined to issues that are considered of relevance at the Commonwealth level of government, although a few state examples are included.

The first part of this chapter examines a framework, the aim of which is to identify the possible purposes and levels of participation, who should be involved, the methods of doing so and, at what stage in the policy cycle it can be done. Governments can involve citizens in a range of ways, from simply providing information to the public, through to delegated control to citizens (Arnstein 1969). As indicated below, the Organisation for Economic Co-operation and Development (OECD) has usefully identified three possible levels at which governments can involve citizens in the policy process: providing information, consulting and 'active participation' (OECD 2001a; OECD 2003a).

The second part of the chapter focuses more on circumstances where governments need to actively engage individuals and organisations in policy processes — 'active participation' in the OECD's terminology — and deals with some challenges and implementation hurdles that are faced by the public sector, if participatory governance is to be progressed effectively, in involving citizens and non-government organisations in the decision-making process. The final section offers some concluding observations and suggestions for change, which make use of the Council of Australian Governments (COAG) Trials — an attempt by COAG to engage Indigenous Australian citizens in the decision-making process for policy on issues related to their lives. This case study powerfully illustrates the critical challenges to effective participatory governance.

Participatory governance frameworks

Many elements need to be considered in involving non-government players, including citizens, in public sector decision-making. First, there are different *levels* of involvement — from simply providing information to citizens and relevant groups, to the other extreme of empowering them with actual control over the final decision. Second, there are many options about *who to involve*. Third, there are different *mechanisms* for involving stakeholders, which relate to the different levels of involvement. Finally, both the level of involvement and the method used can vary at different *stages in the policy cycle*. Many frameworks are to be found in the literature on some, if not all of these elements (e.g. Walters, Aydelotte and Miller 2000; Bishop and Davis 2002; Edwards 2003; Bryson, Crosby and Stone 2006; Fung 2006; IAPP 2007), however, there is no single approach. The level and method of involvement, who to involve, how to do that and when, depend critically on the purpose of the participation, where: 'Participation is shaped by the policy problem at hand, the techniques and resources available and, ultimately, a political judgment about the importance of the issue and the need for public involvement.' (Bishop and Davis 2002: 21).

Successful involvement, therefore, requires a good fit between the purpose, timing within the policy cycle, choice of stakeholders and mechanism (NIG 2004: 12). Fundamentally, whatever the purpose and therefore level of involvement chosen, successful involvement will require open and skilful relationships to build and maintain levels of trust (see below). Again, whatever the purpose, as is the case with involvement of non-government players generally, a risk-management approach is of value to assist in working out the consequences of involvement: not just the benefits, but also the costs in terms of time and resources and, ultimately, what impact can be expected on the desired outcome.

What is the purpose of involvement?

Using either a descriptive or normative perspective, various authors have addressed the purpose and levels of involvement in the policy process by governments with non-government players. The best known of these is Arnstein's 'ladder of participation' that has eight levels: manipulation, therapy, informing, consultation, placation, partnership, delegated power and citizen control (Arnstein 1969). More recent schemes have fewer levels, such as that of the International Association for Public Participation (IAPP), which presents five different purposes of citizen involvement with increasing levels of public impact, to: inform, consult, involve, collaborate and empower (IAPP 2007).

The OECD has a simpler framework for participation, which can be expanded as required. OECD publications (OECD 2001a: 23; OECD 2003a: 13–14) refer to three possible levels of participation of non-government players with government: through government providing information; government consulting; and government providing the means for 'active participation' (OECD 2003a:13):

- When *information* alone is provided, it is a one-way relationship, with the government effectively keeping the public or relevant stakeholders informed: 'It covers both "passive" access to information upon demand by citizens and "active" measures by government to disseminate information to citizens.'

- When it *consults*, it is a two-way relationship with the government that goes beyond the provision of information to listening to the public and gaining feedback from them on issues that are chosen by government and, hopefully, also providing feedback on how public input affects decisions.

- If *active participation* occurs, then it 'is a relationship based on partnership'. It would be expected that government would work with the public to not only provide feedback on how their input affected decisions, but also develop options reflecting their concerns. As the OECD states, this process 'acknowledges equal standing for citizens in setting the agenda, proposing policy options and shaping the policy dialogue' but adds that 'the responsibility for the final decision or policy formulation rests with government'.

The third category of active participation could include the option of government either delegating authority to others in decision-making, or actually handing over decision-making to give others joint decision-making powers or even 'control' (Bryson 2004). Active participation of outside players, therefore, means more than a process by which governments seek *to* engage the public or organisations on their terms; it is a process of engaging *with* stakeholders and citizens, which may include a player outside of government initiating the engagement.

The OECD reports that, while there has been an increased prevalence of both information provided by government to citizens and opportunities for feedback and consultation, initiatives involving active participation are rare 'and the few instances observed are restricted to a very few OECD member countries' (2003a: 15).

Who to include?

The options around who is to be involved with governments in the process of policy development range from the broadest, involving the public at large to the narrowest, where the policy process is confined to an elite group of senior bureaucrats, which is perhaps widened at times, to include experts. Fung provides many possible ways of selecting participants. The first is to permit self-selection from the general population, but this could lead to under-representation of key groups. A second method is to recruit participants selectively from subgroups who are less likely to otherwise be engaged (e.g. senior citizens). Other methods are to select randomly (e.g. citizen juries); engage 'lay stakeholders' (e.g. school councils); and involve professional stakeholders. Fung describes these five groups as 'mini-publics'. Other ways could be to involve professional politicians and expert administrators (Fung 2006: 66f).

How narrow or broad the involvement should be (as well as when and how it will take place) will depend on several factors, including a judgment about the likely value added (e.g. the participation of certain key stakeholders holding information that is not otherwise available) as well as the likely consequences if a group is not involved in relation to attaining desired objectives and successful implementation (Bryson 2004: 27). Greater involvement would be expected where it is important to get decisions accepted, than if it is the quality of the decision that is more important (Lovan, Murray and Shaffer 2004: 17).

The question of who to involve interrelates with the question of what mechanisms to use in participatory processes — different groups of citizens will prefer different forms of involvement, as the next section shows.

What mechanisms to use?

Using the OECD categorisation, Table 7.1 provides examples of appropriate consultation instruments for the information, consultation and active participation levels of involvement. So for example, if the purpose of involvement of citizens or stakeholders were to provide information to the public, then online websites or an education program would be appropriate. If the desire were to have active participation by those affected by a decision, a policy action team or a citizen's jury would be more appropriate. In the relatively rare cases where a government hands over a decision to a group of citizens, then deliberative polling or some form of delegation of decision-making would be appropriate.

The mechanisms of involvement not only need to be related to the purpose of involvement but also aligned with the capacities and interests of particular groups — for example, the young and the old or minority cultural groups may have very different preferences about how to input into government decision-making processes, than say, business or environmental groups. Remote Indigenous communities can be expected to prefer face-to-face meetings rather than use information and communication technology (ICT) in a consultation process.

Table 7.1: Purpose of involvement and appropriate instrument

Information	Consultation	Active participation
Online websites	Web-based	Open-space technology
Education and awareness programs	Discussion groups	Advisory committees
Newsletters	Public hearings	Negotiation tables
Telephone hotline	Polls	Policy action teams
Community meetings	Survey research	Citizen panels/juries
Shop fronts	One-to-one interviews	Deliberative polling
Media stories	Road shows	Delegation

Source: Various, including Queensland Government (2010).

An issue that is hardly covered in relevant literature is what is the appropriate reaction from government when citizens wish to *initiate* a participatory process? If a group of citizens/experts or others wants to initiate a policy dialogue with government representatives, what should be the role of the public servant in this dialogue? Obviously, guidelines would be needed, particularly to manage a situation in which active citizen participation cannot be avoided in order to resolve complex policy issues.

Of increasing importance over the last few years has been the use of online channels of involvement of citizens. This technology has added considerably to the possibilities of tailoring methods of participation to the needs of those intended to be involved (OECD 2001a; OECD 2003b: 50; Chen 2007; AGRAGA 2010: 17). Governments, therefore, are commonly favouring providing information to citizens online and increasingly using the internet as a mechanism for consultation. Active participation online, however, is not yet common and is complex for governments to manage: 'e-participation' creates a real challenge technologically if governments want to retain ultimate control (UN 2003: 85ff; OECD 2009a: 70). As already mentioned, online dialogue between public servants and the public is an example of a difficult issue for governments to confront in creating opportunities for participation.

Ahead of the Game recognises that Australians increasingly prefer the internet to other methods of contacting government. In discussing 'engagement with citizens', however, the review confusingly conflates consultation with citizens with engaging citizens online, which also unduly emphasises involving citizens in design and delivery through the use of ICT over other forms of engagement (AGRAGA 2010:17). There is no doubt that, unlike 10 or so years ago, current governments have no choice but to consider how best to use online mechanisms, and for whom, when pursuing 'active participation' with its citizens. As the OECD has stated, decisions about whether or not to use ICT mechanisms and how, need to be integrated into the broader decision processes around the purpose, the particular needs of those to be involved and the time when it is to occur in the policy process (OECD 2003b: 85f).

The first significant step has been taken in the direction of 'e-participation' with the Australian Government agreeing with its Government 2.0 Taskforce, which expects 'technology to increase citizen engagement and collaboration in making policy and providing service' and achieving 'a more consultative, participatory and transparent government' (Australian Government 2010: 3). It would be worthwhile assessing, in a year or so, the impact of the new technology on the extent of citizen collaboration.

When in the policy process?

The literature on participatory policy issues has tended to neglect the fact that the purpose and form of participation may vary according to the stage at which policy is being developed. This is particularly so when decisions are made as to who is to be involved, and how, at the early stage of defining the nature of the problem or setting the agenda: if the problem is misdiagnosed, time and resources can be wasted and ineffective outcomes could emerge (see Walters, Aydelotte and Miller 2000: 357). Bryson makes the interesting point about the relationship between the early stage at which the problem is defined and possible solutions: it may be hard to get relevant stakeholders to participate in assisting in problem definition if they do not also see a way to resolve it, and contribute to that process (2004: 25).

When it comes to making decisions, non-government organisations or groups of citizens can be dismissed as having no role — they can be regarded as non-representative and unqualified for a role in policy development at this stage. Those who advocate active citizenship, however, would dispute this: 'active citizenship can play a very important role in the decision-making phase: convincing people, channelling consensus, revealing the nature of general interest on an issue, and so on' (Moro 2003: 145). Decisions can be shared with citizens, even if they do not agree with them.

There can also be a role for citizens in the implementation stage: 'Their role in the planning phase can consist above all in taking into account obstacles that stand in the way of implementation and that are not visible to other agents'. They can also 'test' tools and parts of policies. When policies are to be implemented, citizens can be brought into a coordinated partnership with government to assist in ensuring success (e.g. collecting and sharing good practices) (Moro 2003:145). Finally, in the evaluation phase, citizens can provide valuable feedback about what works, for whom and why. Important accountability issues can arise at this point, as discussed below.

Active participation: Issues and challenges

So far, this chapter has identified various levels of citizen involvement in government decision-making processes, from simply receiving relevant information through to actively participating in those decisions. It has been argued that a risk management framework needs to be adopted to work out what type of involvement would best match the issue, who to involve, the mechanisms of involvement and when it should take place through the various stages of developing policies.

Involving citizens and non-government organisations more broadly in government decision-making is sometimes referred to as 'participatory governance' (Edwards 2002: 52; Lovan, Murray and Shaffer 2004; Bond et al 2007; Osmani 2007; Edwards 2008). The essence of participatory governance is to provide non-government actors, both individuals and organisations, with a means to genuinely and actively be part of the process of developing policy. In terms of Table 7.1, active participation would include both collaboration and empowerment. In an article on participatory governance, Osmani (2007:1), defines 'effective' participation as where:

> all the relevant stakeholders take part in decision-making processes and are also able to influence the decisions in the sense that at the end of the decision-making process all parties feel that their views and interests have been given due consideration even if they are not always able to have their way.

The term 'community engagement' is very similar, and commonly used to include active engagement around delivery issues on the ground.

The topic of participatory governance was not high on governments' agendas a decade ago. So, why has the subject generated interest now? There are four possible explanations for the emergence of a focus outside of government toward citizens (Edwards 2008: 8–9): declining trust of citizens in public sector organisations, along with rising expectations of being consulted; the emergence of many more complex policy problems that governments are unable to resolve on their own; the unintended consequences of 'managerial' type public sector reforms embedded in NPM (chapter 2) which downplayed the benefits of collaborative behaviour; and the rise in importance of ICT (see also Head 2007: 442–43).

Whatever mechanisms are used, more participatory or inclusive processes of governing appear to be inevitable now, if governments are to have an enhanced capacity to cope with the blurring of boundaries across the government and non-government sectors and to facilitate good policy making (Edwards 2002: 58). A move toward greater engagement with stakeholders and communities goes hand-in-hand with an enabling if not expanding role for government.

Despite what now appear to be strong imperatives, the OECD has found that, while providing information to citizens or consulting with them was quite common across its member countries, there was far less use of 'active participation' (OECD 2009a). Key questions, therefore, are addressed in this chapter in an attempt to elucidate the challenges faced and some possible ways forward in promoting levels of participation. It is these challenges that face those charged with implementing the relevant recommendations in contained in *Ahead of the Game*.

Three fundamental and interrelated challenges emerge from the relevant literature, which need to be tackled for successful active citizen and stakeholder engagement: strong leadership, building up and maintaining trusting relationships, and willingness to share decision-making power. These are discussed below. If these three fundamental factors are overcome, more practical implementation issues are surmountable, including reshaping accountability arrangements, aligning structures and processes to the issue and context, ensuring appropriate cultures and capabilities, and exploring effective ways of evaluating participatory strategies.

Case study: COAG trials

The above challenges are illustrated here by reference to experiences arising from Australian government efforts to engage Indigenous citizens in decision-making processes, with a particular focus on the COAG Trials. This is a useful case study of participatory governance on four levels. First, it illustrates many of the dimensions and elements of participatory governance that are outlined in this chapter. Secondly, it concerns an area of ongoing topicality and controversy (not least because of the Northern Territory intervention) as well as inherent suitability for participatory governance (given the relationships between Indigenous communities and their representative bodies, and different portfolio responsibilities and levels of government). Thirdly, it concerns a recent initiative that emanated from government (and from a cross-governmental perspective) about Australian communities, with direct and indirect relevance to their governance. Finally, it is an area of study that is documented by various official reports and other commentary of relevance from a governance perspective.

In 2000, COAG announced its vision for a closer relationship between governments and Indigenous communities, including a reconciliation framework to address the growing social and economic needs of Indigenous Australians. In 2002, the COAG Trials were initiated. Eight trial sites were chosen with one in each state and territory.

The main aim of the COAG Trials was 'to improve the way in which governments interact with each other and with communities to deliver more effective responses to the needs of indigenous Australians' (COAG 2002). Several objectives were set for the trials, including: to 'work with indigenous communities to build the capacity of people in those communities to negotiate as genuine partners with government', and to 'build the capacity of government employees to be able to meet the challenges of working in this new way with Indigenous communities' (Morgan Disney & Associates et al 2006: 4). The trials incorporated a shared-responsibility approach, which was intended to emphasise the concept of partnership between government and Indigenous communities.

In 2006, Morgan Disney & Associates conducted an official and independent evaluation of the trials for the Office of Indigenous Policy Coordination (2006: 5). The failures and challenges of the trials that emerged in this official evaluation varied across communities. Illustrated below, they are numerous, with the primary causes being a lack of coordination, communication, understanding of culture, trust, power sharing and appropriate governance arrangements.

Fundamental factors

Leadership

During the last 10 years, a new language has emerged from the public sector and its leadership about collaboration, cooperation, and collegiality and recently proposed citizen-centred policies. Leadership of this new agenda has been driven from the centre. In the context of the report *Connecting Government: Whole of Government Responses to Australia's Priority Challenges* (MAC 2004), a former head of the Department of Prime Minister and Cabinet (PM&C) said: 'There is increasing recognition by governments of the need to engage at the community level, whether community is defined as stakeholders with shared interests or residents who live in a particular location. There is also a growing awareness that interaction has to move from consultation to collaboration' (Shergold 2005a: 1).

In May 2008, the former prime minister Kevin Rudd progressed this agenda by talking of the need for an 'inclusive policy process that engages with average Australians' (Rudd: 2008). More recently, the previous head of PM&C, Terry Moran, made several statements along the same lines but using the current language in vogue of 'citizen-centred' policies and actions: 'We must work tirelessly to put the citizen at the centre of our programs and policies' (Moran 2009: 3). The *Ahead of the Game* report identified what needed to be done to engage citizens, including making government information more accessible, mainly through online sites (AGRAGA 2010: 19).

Even if there were serious commitment shown by Commonwealth public service leaders to this agenda, this does not necessarily mean it would be reflected further down the hierarchy. In recent surveys of public sector officials in Australia, the proportion of public servants consulting with stakeholders has shown an increase, although the most common forms of consultation were in relation to service delivery rather than policy development. Where consultation took place, it was more commonly undertaken with industry, rather than other non-government stakeholders (e.g. APSC 2009c: 123; APSC 2010a: 117). Whether this accurately reflects good judgment in terms of attaining desired outcomes, or whether it reflects fears that are associated with the difficulties of engaging with the public, is unknown. There can be little doubt, however, that attitudes of public officials need to be clarified and addressed if participatory governance is to be progressed toward reaching achievable outcomes. Apart from the fear of losing control by sharing decision-making power generally, the loss of control will be felt particularly acutely if power sharing involves dominant lobby groups who do not represent the community at large. There is also, as noted later, an inherent tension to be managed between the vertical accountability responsibilities of officials and the call by government for them to be more responsive to citizens' needs.

Unless there is committed government leadership in encouraging effective participation, it is unlikely that actively engaging citizens in decision-making is going to have the necessary bureaucratic support to make it work. There is a vicious circle here. On the one hand, non-government groups with little power can only function well if there are enabling conditions for them to operate; on the other hand, the centralised process of decision-making requires these groups to be able to apply pressure on government. Once a process of participation is set in motion, however, and there is committed leadership, the practice of participation should help remove some of the impediments to successful participation (Osmani 2007: 32).

In the context of the COAG Trials, there was much evidence of very strong leadership from the top and a real commitment to make these trials work, with secretaries of departments personally committing to having their performance measured in terms of results in the trial sites for which they were responsible (Morgan Disney & Associates et al 2006: 5). Particularly strong in his leadership was Peter Shergold, whose previous work experience had given him grounding in Indigenous issues. Attitudes at the top, however, did not translate well on the ground, where officials were too often seen to be unable to make a 'quick decision' and, where decisions were made elsewhere, there sometimes was not sufficient ownership of them (2006: 23).

Trusting relationships

Trusting relationships are the essence of any successful collaboration. They have been described as both the lubricant and the glue — that is, they facilitate the work of collaboration and they hold the collaboration together (Bryson, Crosby and Stone 2006: 47–8). Trust is a vague as well as complex concept, however, and it can have many meanings, depending on the context (Yang 2005: 275; Blind 2006). In the public sector context of engaging citizens, trust refers to interpersonal or inter-organisational behaviours where the expectations of each party are clear and confidence exists that what is committed to will be delivered. Trust exists where people have confidence in government, its individual agencies and its leaders (Yang 2005: 273; Blind 2006: 3).

Research indicates that citizens today have less trust in public sector organisations than they once did (World Economic Forum 2005; Blind 2006; Seldon 2009). Citizens are now not only more cynical about government but, also, generally better educated and able to articulate their perceptions, judgments and needs (Cavaye 2004: 87–8; Peters 2005: 85; Sankar 2005: 3; McCabe, Keast and Brown 2006: 5).

The World Values Survey has found that for 2005–08, Australia ranked below the OECD average of 38 per cent of individuals reporting high trust in parliament and also below the 23 per cent of individuals reporting high trust in their government (OECD 2009b: 16). As such, a 'democratic deficit' has been identified: voting every three or four years is no longer sufficient for citizens to adequately voice their views or, indeed, have a satisfactory way of achieving adequate engagement with government. Jim Cavaye (2004: 88) recalls the emergence of the One Nation Party in Australia, and its success in rallying the protest vote, as a wake-up call to government about the need to actively engage citizens. As indicated in chapter 1, it has become increasingly common for governments to accept that purely representative democratic processes are not enough and need to be supplemented with meaningful citizen engagement between elections within a more deliberative framework.[1]

There is a burgeoning literature on the concept of trust but it is only relatively recently that this concept has been brought into public policy dialogues. This has occurred as governments recognise that declining trust by citizens in government needs to be consciously acted upon, and that citizens may need to be actively included in the policy process if desired results are to be achieved (OECD 2009b: 28). Not all countries have observed a decline in trust in their institutions — some Scandinavian countries such as Norway and Sweden have not (Uslaner 2002) and it appears that one of the key factors is the degree to which citizens are participants in their democratic processes. A real challenge, therefore, is to foster a 'trust culture' (Blind 2006: 15) where citizens feel that they have a chance to make a difference in the process of making decisions.

There is a need to understand the causal links between trust, good governance and engaging citizens — a relationship which, as yet, is by no means clear (Braithwaite and Levi 2003; Wang and Van Wart 2007; Bourgon 2007b; Victorian Government 2007: 8). Good governance and trust may be related but 'there is something else at play, something really fundamental that goes to the core of the issue of trust, and relationship of trust between citizens and government that we have not yet either fully understood or tackled adequately' (Bourgon 2007b). Bourgon suggests that it may have to do with changing citizen expectations: 'Our citizens are losing some of the levers, which in the past gave meaning to the role of citizens, the ability to have the right to have a say, the right to vote, the right to hold officials to account' (2007b: 3). While the relationship between citizen engagement and trust is not clear, it is widely agreed that for governments 'there is no alternative to strengthening citizens' trust in government. If you do not do it, you drive up the cost of government for everyone and promote the disengagement of citizens' (OECD 2006: 2).

A recent survey by the OECD found that the main goal of governments in engaging citizens is to increase levels of trust (OECD 2009b: 28). A big gap was found, however, between the goal and the capabilities to achieve it: public officials are on a steep learning curve when it comes to building trust between governments and citizens (OECD 2003a). Even if the will is there, building conditions of trust, when the territory is new and the hurdles are great can be a significant barrier for public officials embarking on participatory governance processes (e.g. Alford 2002: 48–9). John Alford cites complexity of relationships

---

1   There is a growing trend toward citizen involvement, not only between elections in deliberative forums but also in other democratically innovative ways such as 'ongoing scrutiny and public control of decision-makers' — referred to as 'monitory democracy' (Keane 2009) and with connections to broader dimensions of deliberative democracy and societal governance (chapter 1).

— for instance, intergovernmental and broader accountability complexities, as well as the turbulence of the government environment — as potential obstacles to building trust in government collaboration (Alford 2002: 48–9). The path forward will not be through searching for some 'magic bullet' but from many small initiatives that are implemented over a lengthy period of time (Zussman 2007: 22).

In the evaluation of the COAG Trials, it was found that trust between government and community partners was higher when there was consistency between community committee membership and lead agency staff. Trust can take a long time to build up, and be quickly lost, as Diane Smith (2007: 3) relates following an incident that took place in West Arnhem Shire, after the Northern Territory Government released its media statement on taking over the administration of 60 or so Aboriginal communities under compulsory lease:

> To say that the Bininj members of the West Arnhem Committee were shell-shocked would be an understatement. In one day, without any consultation, their collaboration with the Australian Government had essentially been made null and void. Their role as the proposed local government for the entire region was thrown into question, their work over the last three years ignored, and their governance roles treated with disdain. A week after the media release, the army, police and Australian Government officials entered two communities in the region.

Sharing of power

A central challenge for governments in seeking to move toward citizen-centred governance in the decision-making process is the devolution or sharing of decision-making power.

While there is now much rhetoric around the need to increase stakeholder and citizen engagement in policy processes (e.g. MAC 2004), reluctance by officials to do so can commonly be observed (Allen 2006: 3). Lynelle Briggs and Roger Fisher (2006: 24) state that: 'Full participation with stakeholders in defining solutions to wicked problems, requires government to cede some formal control over the services that it provides, and reduces the direct accountability of government to citizens.' More recently, Briggs reiterated this point using citizen-centred language: 'it is important to recognise that a shift in power is at the heart of citizen centred thinking and, as we all know, a shift in power is not often willingly ceded or comfortably managed' (Briggs 2009: 4). She also admitted that the public service is 'fumbling around with citizen engagement models' (Briggs 2009: 6).

The actions of state governments often demonstrate a strong desire to at least acknowledge the importance of citizen engagement, if not to create a conducive environment for citizen-led or citizen-centred governance (e.g. Boxelaar, Paine and Beilin 2006; Blacher and Adams 2007). However, it still stands that the willingness to engage, and actual engagement, are more often than not conflated, resulting in an inadequate representation of what actual engagement should be and the necessary reshuffle of power structures and power sharing between the players.

The Senate Select Committee on the Administration of Indigenous Affairs raised questions about power relationships in the context of the government–Indigenous Shared Responsibility Agreements, which dealt with respective responsibilities of Indigenous communities and governments (Parliament of Australia 2005). Jon Altman explained to the committee that: 'If one party holds the purse strings and the other party has to sign off to get what would be regarded … as a fairly basic facility … then I can see the Commonwealth signing off on a fairly small cheque on their responsibilities (Parliament of Australia 2005: 101).

The basic issue here is one of sincerity, as well as the perception of sincerity, of the sharing of power between those who make decisions and those who have a reason to be involved in the decision-making process. This is so much easier said than done, especially for those within government who have been so used to taking responsibility for a consultation process. This process will become harder as the boundaries between government and other potential players, including citizens, become more permeable in the process of making public policy decisions.

Implementation challenges

So far, this chapter has dealt with the difficulties to be overcome in moving beyond the rhetoric to deal in practice with the fundamental challenges facing governments when they seek to actively involve citizens in decision-making. Even with strong leadership and commitment at the top, with trust having been built up and effective power-sharing occurring, some practical challenges remain to be overcome if effective partnering arrangements with non-government players in the context of citizen-centred governance are to be realised. It is no wonder that there is so often a gap between the rhetoric of citizen engagement that is used by governments and the reality witnessed on the ground.

Some of the more important implementation difficulties are:

- the need to *reshape accountabilities* where responsibilities are shared between government and other players;

- the *policy capability* of and *cultural environment* around public servants as well as the capacity of non-government groups to engage with government;
- *aligning governmental structures* to the issues and context at hand; and
- *evaluating what works* (see, for example, MAC 2004; Mandell 2006; APSC 2007a, b).

These are discussed in turn below.

Reshaping accountabilities

Earlier chapters have indicated that important and increasingly complex accountability issues are arising, either as part of the process of bringing more non-government players into the policy development process, or where there is a move from government-centred decision-making to wider involvement of non-government players in that process (e.g. Edwards 2002; Salamon 2002; Mulgan 2003; APSC 2007b).

Accountability in the public sector seeks to ensure that public sector agencies and their staff are responsible for collective and individual actions, and the decisions leading up to them (Barrett 2000: 7). This is in line with the Westminster concept of ministerial responsibility to parliament, which is discussed in chapter 1. Many other considerations arise once responsibility for decision-making is shared with non-government players: can the principles of individual and collective responsibility (if not accountability) to the taxpayer through parliament hold when the boundaries between and across the sectors are more blurred? As the boundaries across sectors blur, there is an inevitable tension between traditional vertical accountability mechanisms, which are inherent in the Westminster system, and horizontal accountability in terms of responsiveness to citizens. The challenge now is to reshape governance processes and practices so that this inevitable tension is minimised and managed (Lovan, Murray and Shaffer 2004: 2; APSC 2007b: 23; Bourgon 2007a: 11ff).

A key issue here, for both government and non-government organisations, in achieving good process in shared decision-making is to collaborate in clearly defining the respective roles and responsibilities and developing accountability systems which encapsulate the objectives of both vertical/hierarchical and horizontal dimensions (Edwards 2002: 2011). Essential ingredients include: agreement on the expectations of all parties; balancing expectations with respective capacities; credible reporting arrangements; and carefully designed and appropriate monitoring and evaluation mechanisms (Auditor General of Canada 1999; DFD 2012b).

The Australian Public Service Commission (APSC) has canvassed some questions 'about the compatibility of the existing accountability framework and the capacity of the APS agencies to effectively tackle wicked problems' (2007b: 23).

The report *Tackling Wicked Problems: A Public Policy Perspective* ponders the question of what type of accountability framework should be used to give enough flexibility for programs whose outcomes may take many years to realise. It takes the COAG Trials as an example, where the evaluations 'confirm that whole of government and partnership approaches aimed at changing the economic, health and social circumstances of disadvantaged communities, in particular Indigenous communities, require long-term commitments of 10 to 20 years in order to be realised' (2007b: 23). A disturbing but common complaint reported in an audit of the COAG Trials was that it was difficult to work out 'who was in charge' (ANAO 2007: 74) and the trial objectives were not clearly understood or necessarily shared by communities (Morgan Disney & Associates et al 2006: 6).

Alignment of organisational structures

Too often, where participatory governance mechanisms are put in place, they are observed to be operating in the context of traditional structures and processes which do not necessarily align with the purpose of participatory governance (e.g. Alford 2002: 52; Keast et al 2004; Boxelaar, Paine and Beilin 2006; Kettl 2009). A key implementation issue, therefore, is to redesign public sector institutions and practices to align more with the new participatory and interactive framework. Some suggestions about how this may be done are contained in recent Australian government reports (MAC 2004; APSC 2007b: 18). The APSC gives prominence to supportive structures and processes:

> There is a need for careful choice of the appropriate structures to support whole of government work. Structures and processes must be matched to the task — no 'one-size-fits-all'. If there is deep contention between portfolios or in the community, for example, and tight time frames are involved, a dedicated Taskforce under strong leadership and working directly to the Prime Minister, a senior Minister or a Cabinet committee may produce better outcomes than a more standard interdepartmental committee.

Again, it is not easy to turn this rhetoric into reality. There are Australian examples of where there is good intent and genuine engagement at the initial stages of the project, only for there to be a switch back to old patterns in the later stages of implementation. According to Lucia Boxelaar, Mark Paine and Ruth Beilin (2006: 120), during the course of one Victorian Government project, non-government participants in the team, who were initially referred to as 'actors', became known as 'community stakeholders' or 'customers' and marginalised from the change process. This case study points to existing practices (such as project management and evaluation) and structures of government as well as the culture that is embedded in them as factors that can obstruct participatory governance (Boxelaar, Paine and Beilin 2006: 122). Robyn Keast and Kerry Brown (2004) relate a similar Commonwealth–state experience in the case of the Queensland Goodna Service Integration Project.

A lesson that emerges here is not only the need, when engaging with communities, for conscious alignment of administrative practices and organisational culture but, also, a constant monitoring of what is happening in relation to the initial objectives.

A growing academic literature on Indigenous governance affairs, in Australia and elsewhere, points to the importance of 'cultural match' in ensuring successful policy implementation (Westbury and Dillon 2006: 8). In the COAG Trials, for example, attempts at a participatory approach were hindered by a divide between the types of processes and structures that were used by governments in an attempt to achieve results and ensure accountability, on the one hand, and traditional Indigenous governance arrangements on the other. If this disparity is not addressed early on in the process, with moves toward collaborative alignment, then all the commitment and rhetoric that can be brought to bear on the task will be insufficient to ensure the success of implementation.

Culture and capabilities

Closely related to the implementation challenges that are identified above is fostering an appropriate culture. This was found to be particularly relevant in the case studies analysed in the MAC *Connecting Government* report (2004). It was also emphasised more recently by the APSC (2007a: 20).

> In the APS context, high performing agencies also need to be characterised by a culture that encourages collaboration with other agencies and whole of government outcomes. Perceptions by stakeholders that an agency is insular and inwardly focused could be a sign of poor corporate health.

Writing about the Australian experience of community engagement, Cavaye has observed many cases of practices changing, but without any change in assumptions: 'There are examples of traditional thinking in community engagement approaches that amount to "we are from the government and we are going to engage you", rather than valuing and investing in relationships and building true partnerships' (2004: 94). Changing the culture within agencies towards valuing active participation with stakeholders and citizens will require strong leadership to influence the attitudes and behaviour of staff and the acquisition of relevant capabilities.

The extent to which there are both the relevant skills and capacity of public servants to engage with non-government players in the policy process is a real challenge and has been acknowledged by the APSC and by officials surveyed by it in the APSC State of the Service reports. The 2008–09 report found that: 'Sixty-two per cent of employees identified the ability to "nurture internal and external relationships, facilitating cooperation and partnerships" as the third most important capability they need to remain effective in the APS of the future' (2009c: 127).

One mechanism for building internal capability is to actively promote Better Practice Guides and related advice on the 'how to' of participatory governance. Heads of all Commonwealth departments have actually signed off on some principles and practices to guide whole-of-government initiatives, including increased engagement of non-government organisations in government policy and service delivery (MAC 2005). But more needs to be done to ensure participatory governance is engrained in public service culture and monitored to make certain it actually takes place. An audit by the ANAO of the COAG Trials identified the need for government staff to be trained in 'new ways of collaborative working' (2007: 74) including 'how to engage with respect for the protocols and processes in Indigenous communities' and relevant training for all staff engaged in whole-of-government and place-based initiatives (ANAO 2007: 87).

The officially commissioned evaluations of the COAG Trials raised a series of relationship issues in building partnerships, including Indigenous partners identifying a common set of required skills for government officers including: 'good listening; acting in good faith; high levels of good will; willingness to share power; recognising and acknowledging intra-community and familial relationships and how these impact on leaders; understanding the pressures on communities; being honest and open; and being human' (Morgan Disney & Associates et al 2006: 27). These are the skills that can be expected to be ones all public servants involved in 'engaging' activities will need to acquire.

An interesting question arises here in terms of the boundaries around the engaging activities of public officials. In answer to the question of how public officials should engage with citizens under an effective participatory regime, Lorne Sossin (2002: 89) considered that one approach was to view public officials as promoters of what has been termed 'deliberative democracy'. His view is that citizen empowerment cannot succeed without bureaucratic support and, in some cases, initiative. This is not to undermine existing bureaucratic channels but to transform them. This approach would require giving public officers: 'increased discretion to form ... relationships and re-conceiving the basic normative foundations of public administration to accommodate attachment rather than detachment. Under this view, values such as trust, engagement and self-disclosure would come to characterise bureaucratic behaviour' (Sossin 2002: 89–90).

Alongside the building of internal government capability is the equally important task of ensuring that those who governments engage have the necessary capacity to participate fully. 'There is a difference between participation which focuses on opening up opportunities for involvement and the capacity building/community development approaches traditionally used to empower disempowered people' (Involve 2005: 17). Non-government organisations also need to assure government that they have the capacity to be responsive to broad consumer and community needs (for an elaboration of this point, see Edwards 2002).

In the COAG Trials, some government officers lacked cultural awareness and a general understanding of Indigenous communities and culture, as well as lacking relevant skills to work in a whole-of-government environment. And some community leaders did not have enough understanding of government processes and culture or the skills needed: 'in relation to community governance, engagement and capacity building'. Morgan Disney & Associates et al (2006: 21) concluded that 'there was not enough attention given to conversations regarding working differently nor to cultural awareness training of the government agencies engaged in the Trials'.

Evaluating what works

To date, there has been little evidence of countries making progress in implementing, or even developing, appropriate evaluation frameworks of participatory governance (OECD 2009a). The OECD recently found that the 'evaluation gap identified in the 2001 report is alive and well' and that when standards have been developed, performance against those standards is not evaluated regularly (2009a: 58). Many reasons could be advanced for this, one being the lack of clarity that exists about the purpose of citizen participation (OECD 2005a:14). Another, and perhaps related, reason is that active citizen participation is required most on complex as well as sensitive policy issues which, so far, standard program evaluation methodologies have been unable to cope with. The OECD also suggests that there may be a fear that transparency will undermine support for engaging citizens (2009a: 59).

A starting point for any evaluation, however complex the issue at hand, is to ask its purpose before determining the next steps (Head 2007: 450). Some of the questions that need to be posed in the context of participatory initiatives are the following. Is the purpose to be about outcomes or only processes, and how well were relationships developed? Is the purpose to learn and/or to generalise from a particular instance? Is it about auditing and compliance, or is it about providing some encouragement to participants (Head 2006: 14)? Or is it some combination of these? The OECD survey of governments found that close to half saw a benefit in evaluation helping to improve the management of initiatives and, with most governments still at the early stages of 'embedding evaluation into their public engagement processes', they were focusing more on process than outcomes (OECD 2009a: 59, 62).

Another early question regards the perspective from which the evaluation is to occur. The government's alone? Or is it also that of non-government actors? If the perspective includes the latter, was the purpose of their participation and their respective roles, responsibilities and accountabilities understood and agreed? Or did they prefer a different place, method, timing etc.?

These and other questions are in a checklist that the OECD has developed on factors to take into account if evaluations of public participation in government decision-making are to be successful (2005a: 16–17). Critically, and as a prerequisite, the OECD stresses the need to encourage a culture of evaluation for this process to be successful and that much can be learnt from comparing progress across countries (2005a: 16–17). The Netherlands has a special 'centre of expertise' unit which evaluates better practice in participatory or interactive policy-making using a clear framework including measures of impact of citizen engagement (OECD 2009a: 181).

When launching the MAC *Connecting Government* report, Shergold saw issues relating to Indigenous Australians as 'the biggest test of whether the rhetoric of connectivity can be marshalled into effective action' (Gray and Sanders 2006: 6). Since then, each COAG Trial has been evaluated independently according to a standard set of issues. The purpose is as much about learning as the process continues, as it is about outcomes (Gray and Sanders 2006: 27).

A Canadian study assessing the impact of public participation has found that far more important than the technical challenges in evaluation is 'a low level of commitment to public participation within government policy departments (which) can contribute to ambivalence or even resistance toward its evaluation' (Abelson and Gauvin, 2006: 30). It is very likely that the same study in Australia would arrive at a similar conclusion, given the similarities between the two systems of government.

Conclusion

This chapter has explored the concepts of governance and partnership and what might be needed to make participatory governance work well. The chapter has examined the challenges and issues arising when governments decide that they need to involve stakeholders and citizens as active participants in the policy process. The challenges covered include both those that are preconditions for effective participatory governance to come into effect, and also those that are of a more practical kind.

Whatever level of involvement of non-government players that governments decide upon, it is of paramount importance that expectations on both sides are well understood and aligned. If, for example, the government wishes to provide information only, and not actively engage with citizens throughout the policy process, this needs to be stated at the outset. If the government has already made a decision which is irrevocable, but then wants to engage the community within that context (e.g. on delivery issues), that also needs to be clearly stated and understood before communities participate in discussions on any next steps. The Rudd Government's Australia 2020 Summit in 2008 is an example of active citizen engagement (and is used as such by the OECD (2009a: 27)) but, to the extent that the belated government response to the outcomes of the summit did not match public expectations, some trust in government would have been undermined despite the initial, positive steps towards engagement.

A related point is that clarity of language and intent and avoidance of rhetoric are of the essence in effective participatory governance. Angela McCabe, Robyn Keast and Kerry Brown (2006: 5), for example, have discovered how easy it is to use confusing language around community engagement. Incorrect and inappropriate use of the terminology can create inefficiencies within community engagement policies that may result in negative outcomes, a reduction of trust and/or failed community engagement potential.

At its heart, successful engagement requires that governments manage the fundamental tensions; this has been identified as a theme of this book. This chapter has highlighted several key tensions that need to be confronted by the Commonwealth government into the future. The most pressing appears to be that between the horizontal responsibilities of government out toward non-government organisations and citizens and the vertical accountabilities of the Westminster system (Briggs and Fisher 2006: 16; Fung 2009). What is to be the balance here? A related tension for officials is between serving democratically elected representatives of the people, on the one hand and, on the other, becoming involved in participatory democratic processes. A critical question for governments to confront in the twenty-first century is whether multiple accountabilities can be tolerated, and how far ambiguities in partnership arrangements will be acceptable? (Dobell and Bernier 1997: 258) How far can the nature of accountability arrangements change as a result of a convergence between public and private sectors? (Edwards and Langford 2002: 13–14; Barrett 2000: 62). These questions will need to be confronted by the Australian Government as the implementation of *Ahead of the Game* proceeds.

There are other tensions that need to be confronted. There is a tension between attempting to pursue the most efficient practices of citizen involvement with spending the required resources to gain trust and work collaboratively over what can be lengthy periods of time, with hopefully more effective outcomes achieved (OECD 2009b: 34). The role of government and its officials in being responsible for service delivery, and yet only being an 'enabler' of that process, also creates tensions. This is related to the frequently observed tension between the responsibilities of central agencies as enablers and line agencies, which are more involved in implementation, including attempts to work with communities. Different circumstances may require considerable flexibility, so no set of rules or even principles might apply, unless they can be implemented flexibly. On top of this, there is often the need to gain broad citizen involvement, but this has to be handled carefully without powerful lobby groups taking over the process of engagement. Finally, a real tension exists between needing professionals to build up policy capabilities on the one hand and, on the other, needing to rely on officials to engage outside of government to gain broader ownership of policy objectives (Brans and Vancoppenolle 2005: 164). How is the Australian public service going to pursue enhanced policy capabilities with the limited resources at its disposal?

Ahead of the Game emphasises the need for more citizen engagement, but how much of this is rhetoric (or 'cosmetic commitment' to use an OECD phrase (2009a: 33))? Will its implementation lead to 'active participation' by public sector players in relation to non-government players and citizens and, indeed, permit participation activities to be actually initiated by citizens? Or will 'citizen-centred' actions become stuck on meeting citizen expectations on quality of services rather than progress to their actual engagement in policy processes?

It is unlikely that the above tensions are able to be avoided, thus careful management is important; managing these tensions and dualities will require new structures and ways of working for government (Cavaye 2004: 98): new skills, new capacities, new and different types of relationships and interactions. This chapter has attempted to answer several questions to assist in managing these tensions better and highlighted some issues around the type of leadership needed by government, the need to build up and maintain citizen trust and how decision-making power needs to be shared. While recognising the difficulties that are faced by governments in consistently pursuing participatory governance, it is essential that answers be found for the questions that currently hamper effective implementation, including: whether to share accountability as well as responsibility for decisions, addressing structural barriers as well as the challenges of changing culture and enhancing staff engagement capabilities.

Part III. Key Issues

8. Creating and Regulating Public Sector Bodies

Many of the matters that are covered in the first two parts of this book become most significant when governance structures and other arrangements for public sector bodies are designed, implemented and reviewed. This occurs, for example, when new bodies are created, existing bodies are restructured, and new or revised governance regulatory requirements are introduced. Accordingly, the formulation of governance arrangements and key appointments for public sector bodies warrant attention from both central and organisational perspectives. These topics constitute the focus of chapters 8 and 9 respectively.

The conventional spectrum of bureaucratisation, commercialisation, corporatisation and privatisation of government entities still leaves much room for a multiplicity of governance arrangements at both sectoral and organisational levels. The adoption of particular approaches to designing, implementing and reviewing corporate governance arrangements at the federal level in successive Commonwealth government initiatives that have been undertaken this century, (e.g. Uhrig 2003; DFA 2005b; AGRAGA 2010; and DFD 2012b) marks a break from twentieth-century practice, and also reflects changes in priorities and trends in public administration from one government to another. The implications beyond the Commonwealth public sector of such developments in governance architecture are still a work-in-progress across the Australian states and territories (e.g. NSW PBRC 2006: 68–70).

Accordingly, this chapter concentrates upon the Commonwealth level of government, but with modelling implications for other levels of government in Australia and other countries in the Westminster tradition. It addresses issues affecting the design and regulation of governance arrangements in the public sector that stem from a range of sources. These include public sector trends, official reviews of governance arrangements, whole-of-government guidelines, and legislation for specific public sector bodies that regulates their governance. Two case studies are provided that cut across these different sources — the Reserve Bank of Australia (RBA) and the Future Fund.

The changing environment for governance design

The features of the governance and regulatory environment that surround an existing or proposed public sector body affect its design and reform. First, the selection of appropriate governance frameworks and arrangements is responsive to the cyclical and counter-responsive trends within the public sector itself (chapter 2), as well as the different governance orientations and models that are adopted by central government over time (chapter 4). In short, the phases of public sector reform and their influence upon systemic, central and organisational conceptions and forms of governance have flow-on effects for the governance of public sector bodies of all kinds, together with official policy and other guidance about their governance.

This connection between public sector reform and governance's own evolution is evidenced by the continuous attention that is given, in official reviews of Australian public administration both before and after landmarks such as the *Review of the Corporate Governance of Statutory Authorities and Office Holder* (Uhrig review) (see chapter 2, this volume), to the structures and forms of governance and their connection to governance performance and accountability. Indeed, the multiplicity of governance structures and forms across the Commonwealth public sector that existed before the Uhrig review stands in contrast to the rationalisation and recentralisation of public sector bodies in its aftermath.

Secondly, as governance becomes more integrated within and across societal sectors, levels of government, and geographical borders, the cyclical trends and counter-trends within the public sector become subject to a series of cross-cutting influences. This, too, has an influence upon governance structures and relationships. For example, *Ahead of the Game: Blueprint for the Reform of Australian Government Administration*, foreshadows a range of innovative governance structures for developing strategy and delivering outcomes across agency portfolios, societal sectors, and levels of government (AGRAGA 2010; see also chapters 2 and 10, this volume).

This sits well with an 'interconnected environment' that is witnessing 'a considerable expansion of government and some new approaches to government intervention', as well as 'some underlying changes in the means of delivering government programs and services' which, according to the Australian Auditor-General, include 'increasingly complex inter-relationships between: government agencies; different levels of government; and the private sector including not-for-profits' (McPhee 2008b: 3). The continuing attention to governance arrangements in subsequent official reviews (e.g. DFD 2012b) evidences the ongoing need for sophisticated matching of governance models to evolving governance needs, from a range of sectoral and other perspectives.

Finally, designing and implementing good governance arrangements presupposes that the governance architecture thereby established is used properly and neither circumvented nor undermined. Much of the potential for systemic breakdowns and dysfunctionalities, divergences of expectations, and conflicts of roles and interests amongst ministers, public servants, and other public officials, lies in situations in which the integrity of the governance architecture that safeguards the public trust is lacking, compromised, or bypassed altogether (Finn 1995). Examples of such fault lines from the literature include the use of informal ministerial influence to achieve what should properly be the subject of formal ministerial direction, the potentially conflicting obligations of allegiance for agency heads and board members in serving the twin masters of their organisation and the government of the day, and the over-identification of ministerial, governmental, and bureaucratic self-interest with the public interest.

All of these surrounding environmental features influence the creation and operation of governance structures and other arrangements for Commonwealth public sector bodies. In light of this, the next part of this chapter covers the aspects of governance design that have been embedded in governance architecture as a result of recent reviews, and which affect the choice of organisational form for a Commonwealth public sector body.

The impact of governance regulatory architecture upon governance arrangements

From Uhrig to *Ahead of the Game* and beyond

Whatever the shifts in governance priorities and trends from the standpoint of public administration that accompany the transition from one Commonwealth government to another, the governance regulatory architecture that is enshrined in the *Commonwealth Authorities and Companies Act 1997 (Cth)* (CAC Act) and the *Financial Management and Accountability Act 1997 (Cth)* (FMA Act), the Uhrig review templates, and other official guidance on governance arrangements (eg DFA 2005b, DFD 2011) have ongoing significance until superseded or replaced. Even subsequent reviews of governance models, such as those in *Ahead of the Game* and the Commonwealth Financial Accountability Review (CFAR), must take as their starting point for reform the interplay between such official sources of influence on governance design.

The Uhrig review and its general implications for governance are covered in chapter 2. This part of the chapter focuses more particularly upon the specific features of the Uhrig review-inspired agenda that have regulated the design and implementation of governance arrangements for Commonwealth public sector bodies, notwithstanding other ways in which public management and administration has moved on from that agenda. This understanding is essential for anyone involved in studying or critiquing governance arrangements, implementing or reviewing such arrangements, and reforming or modelling them. In addition, it is necessary to cover here at least those analyses and criticisms of the Uhrig review that highlight its benefits or, alternatively, relate to its gaps and weaknesses, from the standpoint of designing and implementing governance arrangements under prevailing official standards.

Against that necessary background, four scene-setting comments set up the analysis that follows. First, the Uhrig review does not cover (or purport to cover) all aspects of corporate governance in the Australian public sector. The brief in its terms of reference focused upon 'the *structures* and the *governance practices* of Commonwealth *statutory authorities* and office holders' — hence the primary emphasis upon 'governance arrangements', 'accountability frameworks', 'best practice corporate governance *structures*', '*formal* accountability and risk management requirement', 'relationship *structures*', 'accountability and reporting *mechanisms*', and 'a *template* of governance principles and policy options' (emphases added). These have intrinsic relevance for designing and restructuring Commonwealth government entities.

Secondly, while the Uhrig review certainly mentions a number of higher-order aspects of governance in passing — e.g. the Australian people's ownership of government, the constitutional system of government, the connection between parliament and statutory authorities, and organisational cultures and values — its main emphasis lies elsewhere. Reflecting and expanding upon the thrust of the Uhrig review, two years after the government received it from him, John Uhrig spoke revealingly about the report bearing his name. 'The more power you hand to somebody else, then the more you need governance to ensure that that power is not improperly used and is in fact used in a constructive way', he noted, adding that 'if you're going to reach the right conclusions about governance then you must see all of the issues *from the point of view of the owners*' (Uhrig 2005; emphasis added). This owner-centred priority has implications for how Commonwealth government entities are created and administered in ways that enhance those aspects of governance that relate most directly to their answerability to ministers and the government of the day.

Thirdly, the Uhrig review adopts a particular conception of corporate governance and its key elements. This is evident from the outset, in its conception of governance as encompassing 'the arrangements by which owners, or their representatives, delegate and limit power to enhance the entity's prospects for long-term success' (Uhrig 2003: 21). This particular conception and orientation permeate its underlying thrust, its detailed analysis, and its recommendations, organised around its professed governance framework of 'understanding success (*clarity of purpose*), organising for success (*structures, powers and relationships*) and ensuring success (*accountability and disclosure*)' (Uhrig 2003: 37; original emphasis).

As a result, some things that are critical to successful governance risk being under-emphasised or untouched, such as a balance between hard and soft dimensions of governance, and even the relationship between enhanced accountability to government and broader notions of governance, of which that relationship forms part (chapter 1). These emphases and limitations condition the use of the governance arrangements that flow from the Uhrig review and remain enshrined in the regulatory framework for public sector governance to this day.

Finally, at present, the governance regulatory framework for Commonwealth government entities contains a crucial alignment respectively between the choice of Uhrig review-based management templates, applicable governance legislation (i.e. CAC Act and FMA Act), and balance of regulatory and commercial functions. This also makes the Uhrig review and its implementation and criticism of ongoing significance, at least until a subsequent review unravels or reshapes those intertwined strands of the underlying governance architecture. At the same time, the CFAR review signals the ongoing need for review and possibly reform of this governance legislation, to improve its applicability to the multiplicity of Commonwealth public sector bodies, enhance their risk and performance management, facilitate better compliance and regulatory enforcement, and facilitate cross-governmental and cross-organisational outcomes.

Departing from the Uhrig templates in governance design and review

Importantly, from the standpoint of governance arrangements, the Uhrig review concluded that board structures are inappropriate for a number of statutory authorities, particularly those with mostly regulatory and not commercial functions (Uhrig 2003: 54). Together with another important finding 'that entities undertaking similar functions do not necessarily have comparable governance arrangements', especially in terms of the conditions under which Commonwealth public sector entities choose to have governing boards (chapters 2 and 6), these findings support the Uhrig review's overall recommendation for greater 'clarity', 'alignment', and other enhancement of governance structures and processes (Uhrig 2003: 7). These findings sit within the broader movement within government 'to revisit the independent operation of statutory authorities and agencies and to bring them closer to the centre of government' (Gath 2004: 3; and chapter 4, this volume).

Most importantly, the Uhrig review creates the management templates that are canvassed in chapters 2 and 6 — namely, a 'board' template and an 'executive management' template. These templates dovetail neatly with distinctions between board and non-board management structures, on one hand, and commercial and regulatory functions, on the other, as well as the conditions under which such things are regulated respectively by the CAC and FMA acts. In the Uhrig review's own words, use of the board template is confined to situations 'where government takes the decision to delegate full powers to act to a board, or where the Commonwealth itself does not fully own the assets or equity of a statutory authority (that is, there are multiple accountabilities)', with the executive management template applying in all other cases (Uhrig 2003: 10). This step also produces a greater alignment in Uhrig terms between organisational autonomy, independent legal status, and financial separation from the government for organisations with a commercial focus, which are best governed by a proper board under the management, financial and reporting accountability framework of the CAC Act.

Under Uhrig's rationale, this is distinct from the kind of governmental control and ownership, ministerial direction and decision-making, and financially responsible use of public funds for policy, regulatory, or essential service delivery purposes that is best suited to an agency chief executive (with or without an executive management or advisory group: see Uhrig 2003: 8), under the different accountability framework of the FMA Act. The central rationale and division of functions in play here is crystallised in the Uhrig review in the following terms (2003: 45):

> The freedom from general government policy associated with the use of resources, and accountability to the Minister for Finance and Administration for the use of those resources, is justified for those authorities competing with the private sector, or for those authorities not funded by the commonwealth [but not where] authorities perform functions on behalf of the Government and are funded by the commonwealth budget, and consequently should comply with general government policy in the use of resources.

However valuable the two management templates offered by the Uhrig review, the range and basis of justified exceptions to the templates are critical. The more that attention is focused on those bodies in the sector that are not simply engaged in service delivery, directed implementation of policy, and departmental advice and assistance to ministers, the more that anomalies and exceptions emerge that diverge from the two basic Uhrig templates. One Uhrig review-based response might be that, despite the wide range of different entities with different roles across the Commonwealth public sector, most will fit one of the two Uhrig review templates from both internal management and 'accountability to government' perspectives.

Another Uhrig review-based response might be that the two basic templates do not prevent or limit whatever internal governance arrangements might be necessary for essential organisational functioning. Still, the Department of Human Services, the auditor-general (and the Australian National Audit Office), and the Australian Research Council are different creatures from federal courts (including the High Court of Australia), the RBA, official regulators and commissions like the Australian Securities and Investments Commission (ASIC) and the Australian Competition and Consumer Commission (ACCC), and a federally created university like The Australian National University. Of course, none of this necessarily detracts from what might be one of the Uhrig review's ultimate benefits — namely, clarifying and addressing some of the problems and inconsistencies in how statutory authorities have been created and managed over time.

In any case, both the Uhrig review and the Howard government's formal response to it also accepted that the basic templates might need adjustment or modification for particular public sector bodies and circumstances. In words pregnant with possibilities that allow exception-arguing lawyers and policy advisers some room to move, the Howard government's published response to the Uhrig review accepted that 'in applying the templates, consideration will be given to any unique factors that may require an adaptation of the relevant template' (Minister for Finance and Administration 2004: 2).

The Commonwealth public sector has operated successfully since 1997 with a corresponding two-limbed legislative governance framework in the form of the CAC Act (i.e. for governmental entities pursuing commercial activities and appropriately managed by a corporate board) and the FMA Act (i.e. for other entities engaged in non-commercial activities and managed by an executive management group, headed by a departmental secretary in whom statutory responsibility resides). As others note, this also reflects a broad distinction between bodies that remain part of the Commonwealth government for the purposes of financial administration and accountability, and bodies that have a separate legal status and fund-holding capacity in their own right, but still fit broadly within the fold of executive government (Wettenhall 2004–05: 67). The CFAR review, however, raises questions about the viability of the basic models in the Uhrig templates and their corresponding governance legislation for governance design in the future (DFD 2012b: 32–3 and 87).

Formal governmental guidance on governance design arrangements

A number of policy and regulatory imperatives underpin the selection of appropriate governance structures and other arrangements for Commonwealth public sector bodies that operate under whole-of-government guidance provided by Finance. This guidance was developed in the post-Uhrig review phase in the form of *Governance Arrangements for Australian Government Bodies*, which was originally published in 2005. First, under a policy of reducing 'unnecessary proliferation of Government bodies', governmental functions and activities desirably should be allocated to and performed by an existing governmental entity, provided that a suitable governmental vehicle already exists for this purpose (DFA 2005b: x, 12–15). All things being equal, policy preferences also extend to creating new Commonwealth governmental authorities instead of new government-owned companies (DFA 2005b: 24–7) and to non-legislative structures for new bodies instead of additional legislation for them (DFA 2005b: 13–15).

Secondly, the policy decision to create a new Commonwealth governmental body must devote considerable attention to its overriding purpose, functions, and powers, on one hand, and, on the other, 'its financial, legal and staffing status' (DFA 2005b: x, 18–29). In making that decision, central agencies and other stakeholders within government must be consulted (DFA 2005b: x), from the standpoint of whole-of-government coordination in general and central agency oversight of Commonwealth public sector governance in particular.

Thirdly, in deciding appropriate governance structures and arrangements for a new governmental entity, attention should focus upon key matters such as its policy purpose and methods of interacting with governmental bodies, periodic review arrangements, financial relationship with governmental budgetary and appropriation matters, board or executive management structures, engagement of staff under or outside the *Public Service Act 1999 (Cth)* (PS Act), and appropriate balance of organisational independence and governmental control (DFA 2005b: xiv–xv, 32–42).

Fourthly, where the new governmental entity needs its own incorporating or governing legislation, that legislation must be attentive not only to the new entity's financial, legal and regulatory status, but also to the legislation's interaction with other public sector governance regulation, such as the CAC Act, FMA Act and PS Act. Beyond that set of regulation, it must also be sensitive to others laws and regulation with which an entity's incorporating or governing legislation might interact, in setting the boundaries of the entity's legal responsibilities, liabilities, and immunities (DFA 2005b: x–xi, xv, 42).

Amongst such sources of legal risk that are identified in the Finance's *Governance Arrangements for Australian Government Bodies* are laws concerning administrative and judicial review, taxation, governmental trade practices liability, copyright, and the shield of the Crown. The extent to which a statutory corporation or government business enterprise has the legal status and immunities of the Crown, and is subject to laws applicable to all, is an important question of governance design as well as legal responsibility. This affects the applicability of the *Corporations Act 2001 (Cth)* to the Future Fund board, for example.[1]

Such questions of legal risk allocation are important in contexts as varied as government contracting and outsourcing, public–private partnerships, establishment of statutory bodies and state-owned enterprises, and transformations of governmental status through corporatisation and privatisation. For such reasons, Finance's guidance in the *Governance Arrangements for Australian Government Bodies* includes advice to those creating and advising on governmental bodies to address the application of various laws to them, within a set of other factors affecting the choice of governance arrangements for these bodies (DFA 2005b: 42).

Fifthly, additional policy decisions about the new entity's regulatory or commercial focus, and its need for a governing board, as informed by consideration of the Uhrig review templates, determine its location primarily within the CAC Act or FMA Act management, reporting, and accountability frameworks (DFA 2005b: x–xi, 8). Under the influence of the Uhrig-based templates, corporate boards are reserved for commercially focused bodies that are legally and financially at arm's length from the government, with 'board-like' executive management structures being reserved for 'an advisory function to assist the Chief Executive' or 'where collective statutory decision-making requires a commission' (DFA 2005b: x, 35–8). The considerations that govern selection and use of public sector boards are covered in chapter 6.

Sixthly, given the connection between the FMA Act, the PS Act, and the core of executive government, a policy preference exists for new entities and their staff to be governed under this framework, unless there is a demonstrated need for the kind of commercial focus, governing board, and greater organisational independence that characterises the alternative CAC Act framework and Uhrig review-based board template (DFA 2005b: x). Seventhly, while departures from these Commonwealth public sector governance frameworks are undesirable for bodies located wholly within the Commonwealth government sector, the contemporary need for coordination, cooperation, and other regulatory action across levels of government and even societal sectors raises additional issues about governance structures and arrangements for such vehicles (DFA 2005b: x, 28–9). *Ahead of the Game* also addresses these issues (chapters 2 and 10, this volume).

---

1   *Future Fund Act 2006 (Cth)*, s. 39.

Finally, whatever governance framework applies, there are important aspects of departmental, ministerial and even parliamentary oversight of new governmental entities that also apply (DFA 2005b: x). This covers everything from minister–agency communication, departmental advice, and portfolio oversight (DFA 2005b: x) to a series of non-executive and even non-governmental accountability mechanisms that are evolving along with democracy itself (chapters 1 and 10).

In addition to official guidance from Finance, *Ahead of the Game* also contains analysis and recommendations that relate to matters of governance design. In terms of enhancing public sector efficiency and effectiveness, for example, it highlights a connection with governance design questions, as follows (AGRAGA 2010: 29):

> Agency efficiency can also depend on governance structures. For example larger agencies can achieve economies of scale that are not available to smaller agencies. In small agencies, different governance arrangements may have different costs. It is therefore important to consider what governance option will work best, particularly when establishing small agencies.

Most significantly, a number of its recommendations go directly to the public sector governance framework for designing and establishing new Commonwealth public sector bodies, as well as reviewing existing ones. In particular, Reform 8 (i.e. 'Ensuring agency agility, capability and effectiveness') and Reform 9 (i.e. 'Improving agency efficiency') suggest actions that relate to various aspects of governance arrangements, such as regular 'agency capability reviews', streamlined agency compliance, shared responsibility for cross-portfolio outcomes, alternative agency efficiency measures, and simplified and enhanced governance structures.

For example, Recommendation 9.2 ('Strengthen the Governance Framework') outlines the following brief for Finance, as the lead agency involved in developing and revising the *Governance Arrangements for Australian Government Bodies* (AGRAGA 2010: 69):

- Simplify governance structures for new and existing entities by consolidating the categories of entities that can be created.
- Amend the Governance Arrangements for Australian Government Bodies (Governance Guide) to ensure:
    - clear governance arrangements for inter-jurisdictional entities;
    - APS employees are clear about their responsibilities when appointed to company boards; and
    - all new and existing agencies are fit-for-purpose.

In outline form, some of these recommendations potentially cut across aspects of the Uhrig review implementation agenda, while others expand governance reform in new directions. Where the Uhrig review aligned each of its templates (i.e. board or executive management) with its corresponding function (i.e. commercial or regulatory) and correlative legislative framework (i.e. CAC Act or FMA Act) from both organisational and sectoral perspectives, *Ahead of the Game* more directly contemplates the need for innovative cross-portfolio and interjurisdictional governance models.[2]

Indeed, there is much in *Ahead of the Game* that reflects the virtues of a holistic system of public administration, with integration of whole-of-government, intergovernmental, and cross-sectoral elements, along with synchronisation of cross-agency coordination and shared best practices and outcomes. This alternative approach to governance framework-setting is underpinned by related themes of innovation (e.g. digitalisation), optimisation (e.g. regulatory deburdening), collaboration (e.g. cross-sectoral service delivery and shared expertise), participation (e.g. community-involved and business-engaged planning and delivery), empowerment (e.g. agency and community capacity building), and monitorability (e.g. regular agency reviews).

While reinforcing some of the themes and discussion of *Ahead of the Game*, the initial public discussion paper resulting from the CFAR, *Is Less More?: Towards Better Commonwealth Performance* (DFD 2012b), charts its own directions in outlining options that affect the design and implementation of governance arrangements. For example, it records that '(t)he issue of whether an entity is governed by a board or executive management is divisive under present legislative settings' and contemplates a possible reform agenda for 'revisiting the structure of financial framework legislation and considering whether the existing delineation of FMA Act and CAC Act entities is optimal' (DFD 2012b: 32 and 89).

The dynamic balance between central control and organisational autonomy means that '(i)t is therefore important to pay close attention to the design of the control arrangements for entities' (DFD 2012b: 31). Importantly, the CFAR discussion paper suggests refocusing attention on basic governance principles that apply to government bodies across the board, regardless of their organisational form and management structure, and signals the possibility of 'a single piece of legislation with templates that outline a set of core governance provisions covering financial and governance matters for new government bodies' (DFD 2012b: 32 and 42). Such legislation for 'fit-for-purpose governance arrangements' would complement moves towards 'more integrated portfolio governance', 'improved joint activities' and otherwise 'strengthening the whole-of-government performance framework' (DFD 2012b: 12, 33, 39 and 43).

---

2   Assuming that it becomes law in a form that does not differ too greatly or at all from the Bill introduced into the federal parliament in early 2012, the *Public Service Amendment Act 2012 (Cth)* facilitates these developments in its enhancement of the roles and responsibilities of departmental secretaries, along with the creation of the Secretaries Board.

From policy design to legislative implementation

In the discussion to this point, this chapter covers the key public sector sources that regulate official decisions to establish, review or restructure Commonwealth government bodies. The final part of this chapter covers the two cases studies and concluding observations and questions.

What makes the RBA and the Future Fund suitable case studies in designing and reviewing governance arrangements? The RBA is one of the regulators of relevance to business whose governance arrangements the Uhrig review was specifically tasked to examine, along with other key official business regulators such as the ACCC, ASIC, and the Australian Prudential Regulation Authority. It is not only an example of a major official regulator in its own right, but also one whose governance arrangements are left largely intact by the Uhrig review, whatever reforms might otherwise affect it. It is governed by legislation that is specific to the organisation, and therefore illustrates the important connection between governance requirements and legislation beyond the CAC Act and FMA Act. The RBA is also the subject of debate about matters of independence and allegiance that raise some of the governance issues canvassed in this and other chapters.

The Future Fund serves as a primary example of a major new entity whose regulatory design is informed, first, by what the Uhrig review set in train for governance arrangements and, secondly, by the choice between governance primarily under the CAC Act or FMA Act. It serves as an innovative illustration of how to combine aspects of both regulating acts and also provides an example of how the basic Uhrig review management templates are customised to particular needs in creating major new entities under legislation. Indeed, the statutory overlay for both the RBA and the Future Fund also serves to underline the importance of considering governance arrangements for statutory authorities and corporations through the prism of both executive and legislative domains of concern.

The Reserve Bank of Australia

The RBA is Australia's central bank. The *Reserve Bank Act 1959* establishes the following governance structure and arrangements for the RBA: it is a body corporate, can hold property, and is able to sue and be sued (*Reserve Bank Act 1959*, s. 7); it has wide general powers to fulfil its functions (s. 8); it is a CAC Act body, although it is statutorily exempted from some of the CAC Act's provisions (ss. 7 and 7A); its board is charged with ensuring 'that the monetary and banking policy of the Bank is directed to the greatest advantage of the people of Australia', and that its powers are directed towards best contributing to 'the stability of the currency in Australia', 'the maintenance of full employment in Australia', and 'the economic prosperity and welfare of the people of Australia' (s. 10).

The separation between the RBA's monetary and banking responsibility and its responsibility for payment systems is structurally built into the allocation of these two responsibilities; respectively to the Reserve Bank Board (RBB) and the Payments System Board (s. 8A). This example of aligning functional responsibilities with governance structures and other arrangements has modelling significance beyond the RBA to central banks in other countries (Caruana 2010: 60). These modelling implications go both ways, in light of the RBA's structural divergence from monetary and banking policy models in other countries (Uren 2011). For example, the 2007 'Statement on the Conduct of Monetary Policy' on behalf of the Australian government and the RBA has been criticised for introducing governance reforms that 'leave the RBA operating under an outdated and internationally anomalous governance structure that is incompatible with modern demands for central bank transparency and accountability' (Kirchner 2008: 18). In the wake of the global financial crisis (GFC), various issues concerning 'governance structures' arise for central banks across jurisdictions, and also for private sector participants in the market, as acknowledged in the RBA's 50th anniversary symposium (Caruana 2010: 54 and 60; and Kent and Robson 2010: 3).

For some time, successive Australian governments have publicly emphasised the independence of the RBB. At the same time, the Reserve Bank Act creates a number of important points of connection between the government and the board. The board must keep the government informed of the RBA's monetary and banking policy (s. 11(1)). If the government has 'a difference of opinion' with the board about how well its monetary and banking policy promotes 'the greatest advantage of the people of Australia', the federal treasurer and the board must strive to reach agreement. In the exceptional situation where they cannot reach agreement, the government has formal mechanisms available to ensure that its view prevails and that the board complies (s. 11(2)–(7)). The governor of the RBA and the secretary of Treasury are statutorily instructed to 'establish a close liaison with each other' and to 'keep each other fully informed on all matters which jointly concern the Bank and the Department of the Treasury' (s. 13).

Matters concerning different aspects of the RBA's governance regularly feature in both official and media scrutiny. Federal parliamentary committees scrutinise the RBA's annual reports, for example. In recent years, scrutiny of the RBA's governance in the financial press has ranged over a wide variety of issues. These include: broadening the RBA's network of overseas offices to provide on-the-ground assessments to inform monetary policy consideration (e.g. Freebairn 2011); institutional and personal conflicts of interest for RBB members (e.g. Uren 2011; and Kirchner 2011); governance structures and audits of RBA subsidiaries that have been targeted in official investigations (e.g. Maiden 2011; and McKenzie and Baker 2011); RBB composition and independence (e.g. Kerr

2011; and Kirchner 2011); and the impact of the Treasury secretary's board membership upon RBA decision-making and external perceptions (e.g. Uren 2011; Kirchner 2011; Kerr 2011; Hewson 2007; and Gath 2006).

The historical antecedents of the RBA's governance structures (e.g. Cornish 2010) and the Australian Government's satisfaction with the RBA's performance in the aftermath of the GFC (Uren 2011) stand apart from these concerns. Although not completely separate from each other, assessment of the RBA's economic impact is distinct from assessment of the RBA's governance performance against world-class benchmarks for institutional independence from governmental interference, board structures and representation, balance and appointment of internal and external members, public communication and transparency, and separation of monetary, governance, and statutory roles (Kirchner 2008).

Most significantly for the question of the board's independence, the membership of the board includes the secretary of Treasury, as well as provision for a senior public servant who is nominated by the secretary as an alternate member when the secretary cannot attend board meetings (ss. 14 and 22). At least five of the six board members appointed, in addition to the secretary and the RBA's governor and deputy governor, must not be RBA service staff or public servants (s. 14). This means that only a small minority of board attendees could ever have a current public service affiliation. Under long-standing practice, it also results in business leaders from various industry sectors forming a significant part of the RBB's external membership.

Even if the only person appointed with a dual board membership and public service role is the secretary to Treasury, the question is whether that alone jeopardises the much-heralded 'independence' of the board from governmental direction and control in setting monetary and banking policy. The secretary will have obligations to the treasurer as a senior public servant and the treasurer's departmental head, as well as to Treasury (and the government of the day) under the FMA Act, in addition to whatever obligations they might have as a member of the RBA's board. In particular, could the secretary ever be in a position where the secretary's other obligations realistically compromise or conflict with the secretary's obligations as a board member?

This question can be approached from a number of different angles. The structural framework established by the Reserve Bank Act still has to operate in a political and behavioural context, where both hard and soft aspects of governance are relevant (chapter 1). So, from that perspective, a board member's expertise, behaviour, and judgment are not reducible to matters of formal independence from government alone. At the same time, the post-Uhrig reinvigoration of the role of secretaries in agency and portfolio oversight for ministers arguably cuts across such representative roles for departmental secretaries and other senior public servants (see chapter 9).

Distinctions must also be kept in mind here between individual board members' legal responsibilities, their collective responsibility as a decision-making organ, and the impact (if any) of divided loyalties for a minority of individual members. Still, the burden of wearing too many hats is at its worst when the employment, professional, ministerial, parliamentary, and public service obligations of public servants pull them in different directions (Finn 1993: 51–2; and Finn 1995: 22–3, 26). This potential fragmentation of otherwise interlocking accountabilities makes it even more important, for the sake of institutional integrity, to ensure that systemic safeguards of independence are in place and followed.

The question here is whether the perceived or actual influence of government over public service members of the RBB undermines, or even compromises, its independence as a collective decision-making organ, on legal or other governance grounds. At the very least, factors such as overseas models of central bank independence, the relationship between Commonwealth ministers and departmental secretaries, and the legislative requirement for official liaison between the RBA's governor and Treasury secretary all condition perceptions of the secretary's place on the RBB and also distinguish the secretary from other board members.

In an opinion piece on governance in public institutions, former leader of the federal opposition, John Hewson, focuses at first upon the governance issue of separation of board roles, as applied to the RBA (Hewson 2007: 90):

> The RBA's board and governance processes, for example, are almost farcical. The governor, as chief executive, is also chairman of the board, a practice increasingly frowned on and discouraged in governance circles.

The separation of the chairmanship and CEO roles on the board is a long-standing issue of corporate governance regulation of the private sector in Australia, the United Kingdom and elsewhere, with different approaches prevailing across jurisdictions at different times. To the extent that current Australian corporate governance thinking in the private sector favours separation of the two roles, the RBA's governance arrangements may seem exceptional (e.g. Uren 2011; Kalokerinos 2007). The question is whether the public sector context, past practice and the regulatory results justify that divergence.

Turning his attention to the question of the RBA's independence, Hewson says (2007: 90):

> Much is made of the independence of the RBA. True, it's pretty independent of government these days, but it is still not independent within government. There is no reason for the secretary of the Treasury to be a designated member of the RBA board. This is a relic of the past when Treasury was the dominant source of advice to the government — indeed, the bank used to report to the Treasurer only through Treasury.

Other financial press commentary also singles out the anomalous position of the Treasury secretary on the RBB, in terms of both prevailing governance trends and international benchmarks, as follows (Uren 2011):

> The presence of the Treasury secretary on the board is a further oddity. The Campbell committee in the late-70s reviewed this and concluded it should be continued in the interests of coordinating both the fiscal and the monetary policymaking.

> In practice, whenever there is a question of whether interest rates should rise or remain steady, the Treasury secretary can nearly always be counted on to advocate steady rates.

> The New Zealand model, in which the Treasury secretary plays no part, appears to be closest to best practice for central bank independence. It would be assumed that the Treasury secretary and the governor would be in frequent discussion on economic policy, which ought to be enough for coordination purposes.

Importantly, these comments collectively expose different meanings and contexts for arguments about independence as a governance design issue. As in the private sector, a board member can be subject to a range of influences and relationships, not all of which necessarily compromise their independence of mind for board decision-making purposes. Independence from formal government direction and control is different from independence from all executive government involvement and influence. All of these aspects of independence are different again from independence from accountability arrangements that are applicable to institutions within the executive arm of government.

The question of board representation of senior public servants straddles these different standpoints from which considerations of independence might be assessed. The presence and appropriateness of such representation varies from one organisation to another. No Commonwealth employee or full-time public office holder is eligible to sit as a board member on the Future Fund's Board of Guardians, for example (s. 38(4)). Whatever the differences between such major institutions, there is a question of consistency and justification here from a whole-of-government perspective.

The question of the RBB's independence also attracts attention from legal experts on governance. Noting both the status of the secretary of Treasury as a board member and the secretary's alleviation of responsibility as a board member when acting in accordance with any conflicting obligations as a senior public servant, Shaun Gath evaluates the position as follows (2006: 6–7):

> How, then, is one to regard the role of the government director on the Reserve Bank Board now that he/she is freed from any fiduciary obligation to consider the interests of the Bank when performing her role and is, rather, it seems duty bound as a public servant to represent the views of the Treasurer?

> Might it not be said that the changes made to the CAC Act have had the practical (even if unintended) effect of circumventing the formal process for resolution of disputes between the Board and the Government established by the *Reserve Bank Act 1959* by ensuring that the Treasurer will have as a powerful and direct voice for his views at least one director who has no other function other than to directly report the Treasurer's opinions, untrammelled by any considerations going to the interests of the Bank itself?

> So, one may feel prompted to ask: is the Board of the Reserve Bank really 'independent' or not? ... Perhaps, when one takes into account the fact that there are other directors who will always outnumber the government director, the answer, on balance, is still 'yes' ... But this much seems to me to be unarguable: it is certainly not as independent as it was.

This passage contains a number of important steps in the development of Gath's argument — hence its reproduction here in full. The generic problem — which has the potential to create conflicts of interests and duties, particularly for governmental board directors — was identified more than 25 years ago by the Senate Standing Committee on Finance and Government Operations (SSCFGO 1982: 76, as cited in Gath 2006: 2):

> (A) departmental officer, as a member of the executive government, is placed in an impossible position in reconciling that role with his role as a member of a statutory authority. It is by no means inconceivable that the interests of an authority could conflict with those of a minister ... (M)embers of authority boards have a corporate responsibility to put the interests of the authority before any other interests. Consequently, department officers who are also members of authorities could be faced with very painful conflicts of interest.

Underpinning Gath's concern about the scope of the board's independence is his view of the CAC Act's conditioning of board members' duties when acting in accordance with their obligations as public officials. Under the CAC Act, directors and other officers of government authorities have duties that closely mirror their equivalents in the Corporations Act, with suitable modifications to account for their transition to a public sector context (chapter 6). Here, performance of an officer's statutory duties must also interact with and accommodate ministerial and portfolio oversight, adherence to applicable government policy, and compliance with financial management, reporting and other public sector regulatory requirements.

Since the turn of the century, the chief mechanism for alleviating such concerns is the exemption of an officer of a Commonwealth authority from breaching at least some of the designated duties where the officer is doing something required elsewhere under the CAC Act or else, where the officer is also a public servant, the officer acts 'in the course of the performance of his or her duties as a public servant'. However, this legal sidestep around such conflicts is criticised by Gath for leaving government directors and other officers 'effectively removed from the scheme of accountability established under the CAC Act ... with a stroke of the parliament's pen' (Gath 2006: 5).

Taking all of these issues into account, the question remains whether or not the reporting of ministerial views and relevant policy for the information of a board, by someone with multiple obligations as a board member, ministerial adviser and senior public servant, inevitably compromises the board's collective decision-making, either in how other board members treat such views or in the perceptions of others. In light of such strong concerns about board member independence and loyalty, how does the Uhrig review deal with the RBA and its board? Consistent with the principle that governing board members should be appointed for their expertise and not simply the constituencies they represent, the Uhrig review takes a general stance against representational appointments on boards (Uhrig 2003: 98–9):

> The review does not support representational appointments to governing boards as representational appointments can fail to produce independent and objective views. There is the potential for these appointments to be primarily concerned with the interests of those they represent, rather than the success of the entity they are responsible for governing. While it is possible to manage conflicts of interest, the preferred position is to not create circumstances where they arise.

Focusing in particular upon the appointment of public servants (especially departmental secretaries) to governing boards in the public sector, the Uhrig review maintains a healthy scepticism about such appointments, and views their appropriateness as being the exception rather than the norm (Uhrig 2003: 99):

> Similarly, care should be exercised when appointing public servants to boards. In circumstances where a departmental staff member is appointed on the basis of representing the government's interests or having a 'quasi' supervision approach, conflicts of interest may arise and poor governance is likely. Through participation in decision-making, either directly or implied, the departmental representative may become an advocate for the organisation rather than contributing critical comment. This also has the potential to create an incentive for the other members of the board to meet to discuss and agree on important issues separately from formal meetings, without involving the departmental representative, thereby removing the formal board meeting as the main decision-making forum of governance. *Membership of the board by the related departmental secretary is unwise unless there are specific circumstances which require it.* (emphasis added)

In short, representational appointments present governance risks of a lack of true independence, an inhibition of candour in boardroom discussion, a potential mixing of hat-wearing roles, and a 'constituency representation' focus (instead of a 'best interests of the organisation' focus). The common governance problem of wearing multiple hats is particularly acute in the case of departmental secretaries, who have a fundamental obligation as public servants to follow and communicate government policy as well as comply with lawful government directions. They also have a statutory obligation under the FMA Act to ensure 'proper use' of their department's resources, along with a governmental advisory role on matters concerning public sector bodies within their ministerial portfolio. Avoiding or managing potentially conflicted institutional loyalties is a key aspect of systemic integrity and the norms to which it gives effect.

Hewson's final comments on the RBA concern its non-executive directors and their governance function in context (Hewson 2007: 90):

> Similarly, the RBA's 'non-executive' directors — a spread of business people, a token academic — are political appointments who don't really function as non-executive directors should. They are, of course, expected to comment on economic circumstances from their own positions, but essentially they are fed the information the bank's management wants to give them to achieve the decisions management wants.

In an important sense, of course, most non-executive directors are dependent to one degree or another on the information that is provided and contextualised by management. This is a fact of life that leads to governance safeguards to ensure effective organisational oversight. Such safeguards include prudential supervision of management and corporate controls (especially over two-way information and communication flows), active questioning of information and advice from management (including drill-down enquiries beyond senior management where necessary), and resorting to more independent sources of advice from external experts (especially on major corporate decisions affecting a company's future). Still, the present law on differences between executive and non-executive directors is in a far from optimal state (Austin 2010, cited in Eyers 2010: 10-11).

Notwithstanding all of the concerns canvassed above, the Uhrig review recommended maintaining the RBA's existing governance and board arrangements. Citing the significance of a board's ability to appoint and remove the CEO, as well as the strength and effectiveness of the relationship between the CEO and the portfolio minister, the Uhrig review made an exception in the case of the RBA (Uhrig 2003: 41):

> One exception to this principle identified in the course of the review is the RBA. While the board does not have the power to appoint and terminate the CEO, based on evidence provided to the review, the board was assessed as providing effective governance in determination of RBA policies. The structure of the board and the nature of its responsibilities meet the expectations of the international financial community with respect to effective governance arrangements. Divergence from such arrangements may affect international confidence in the independence of the RBA. The governance arrangements should remain unchanged.

Testing these conclusions is difficult, given the conduct of the Uhrig review as an internal governmental review with select outside consultations and the absence of additional detail in the review itself on the basis for this assessment. At the very least, the exceptionalism with which the RBA is treated in the Uhrig review represents a pragmatic approach to the RBA's perceived success, independence and international reputation. Such considerations affecting the RBA are not necessarily in sync with the Uhrig review's strong emphasis upon enhancing the answerability of public sector bodies to the government of the day.

Still, the RBA was specifically identified in the review's terms of reference, and the Uhrig review's failure to address some aspects of the RBA's governing legislation and other aspects has been criticised (e.g. Wettenhall 2004–5). Senior RBA officials accept publicly that the importance of the banking industry to a national economy requires more than 'the normal principles of corporate governance', including acceptance that 'certain higher standards of prudence are required of banks than of the average corporate entity, and there is more intrusive supervision of their activities' (Stephens 2005). Similarly, the RBA's central role in economic and financial stability gives its independence and other governance arrangements a unique context, and also elevates them to a new level of significance (Stephens 2005), as tested in the GFC and its aftermath. Nevertheless, the countervailing considerations in this chapter point to substantive issues concerning appointments, membership, independence, oversight and other features that are likely to figure in ongoing scrutiny and any future official reviews of the RBA and its governance.

The Future Fund

The governance structure and arrangements for the Future Fund, and its amenability to governmental direction and influence, are important features in any debate about the ultimate policy uses of its investments. Governance arrangements for the Future Fund and its Board of Guardians are established under the *Future Fund Act 2006 (Cth)* (Parts 2 and 4). In the election year of 2007, political disputes occurred federally between the major political parties about the best use of the Future Fund. The government established it initially to meet at least expected public sector superannuation payments in coming decades, as indicated in the statutory objects of the Future Fund (s. 15). It later placed its residual Telstra shareholding in the Future Fund, with the opposition (and succeeding government) proposing to use the Future Fund for national broadband telecommunications infrastructure.

The legislation establishing the Future Fund draws much from the templates that were recommended by the Uhrig review. In establishing the Future Fund, Future Fund Board of Guardians, and Future Fund Management Agency, the Future Fund Act combines aspects of the Uhrig review's board and executive management templates in the one combined scheme. Moreover, as the Future Fund Act itself contemplates, both the CAC Act and the FMA Act apply to different component parts of that overall scheme. For example, members of the Future Fund Board of Guardians have statutory duties that closely correspond to those of board members of governmental corporations and authorities under the CAC Act, but the chair of the board cannot breach particular duties simply by doing what is required of them under the FMA Act, and the chair also cannot be directed by the board in relation to the chair's functions and powers under the FMA Act and PS Act concerning the agency (ss. 56–63 and 79).

Similarly, the Future Fund board and the Future Fund Management Agency that support it are together treated as a single agency for various FMA Act purposes, with the board's chair also responsible to the relevant minister for the agency's management (ss. 76–77 and 80). Indeed, the Future Fund's combination of regulatory features under the CAC and FMA acts is cited in a CFAR case study, as 'an example of an entity structure that involves a board and an FMA Act agency' (DFD 2012b: 33).

The basic legislative framework for the Future Fund under the Future Fund Act is as follows: decisions about investments for the Future Fund are the responsibility of the Future Fund Board of Guardians, and investments are made in its name (ss. 16–17); the board is constituted under the Future Fund Act (s. 34); the board is a body corporate that can execute contracts, hold property, and sue or be sued, but it holds any property or money 'for and on behalf of the Commonwealth' (ss. 36 and 37); the board comprises its chair and six other members, who must each have designated financial or corporate governance expertise (s. 38); board members are appointed part-time, and their appointment can be terminated by the relevant ministers for breach of duty and other deficiencies (ss. 40 and 44); the board also has ministerial reporting obligations (ss. 54 and 55); it is not a Commonwealth government authority, and so the CAC Act does not apply to the board, except where the Future Fund Act itself makes the CAC Act applicable to the board, most notably for the consequences of breaching any statutory duties owed by board members (s. 66).

Mirroring the directors' duties enshrined in the CAC Act and the Corporations Act, the main duties of board members cover duties of care and diligence (with a correlative business judgment defence), good faith, use of position, use of information, and conflicts of interest, with some of those duties applying to agency staff (ss. 56–62 and ss. 68–72). As with directors' duties in the CAC Act, these duties of board members are conditioned by their other statutory obligations concerning the Future Fund, so that they will not be in breach of duty simply because of compliance with those obligations (s. 63). As in both the CAC Act and the Corporations Act, other defences or safeguards for board members include reasonable reliance on information or advice that is provided by relevant agency staff, professional advisers or experts, or other board members or committees (s. 65).

The responsible ministers for the Future Fund set the Investment Mandate for the Future Fund (s. 18), in consultation with the board (s. 19); the board is bound by that Investment Mandate (s. 20). The board is advised and assisted by the Future Fund Management Agency, comprising the chair of the Future Fund Board of Guardians and the staff of the Future Fund Management Agency, which has no legal identity separate from the Commonwealth of Australia (s. 74). Relevant accounting, auditing, and reporting requirements under the FMA

Act apply to the board and the agency as though they comprise a single agency with the chair as its chief executive (s. 80). Similarly, the chair and the agency staff are treated as a statutory agency for the purposes of the PS Act (s. 77).

'In the performance of its investment functions, the Board must seek to maximise the return earned on the Fund over the long term, consistent with international best practice for institutional investment', which is the board's primary investment objective (s. 18(10)). This remains subject, however, to directions by the relevant ministers. In the case of any conflict between the board's primary investment objective and the ministerially directed investment mandate, the mandate prevails (ss 18(6) and 18(11)).

So, any future controversies about how governments use and influence the Future Fund are likely to centre at least upon the mechanisms for governmental direction and control that are built into the legislative framework for its investment mandate. The starting point is ministerial involvement in setting the investment mandate by giving directions: 'The responsible Ministers may give the Board written directions about the performance of its investment functions, and must give at least one such direction' (s. 18(11)).

The 'responsible Ministers' here are the treasurer and the finance minister (s. 5). Any directions given by them collectively form the investment mandate (s. 18(3)). The boundaries and content of those ministerial directions are framed under the Act, in terms of the considerations that must guide the ministers in giving directions (s. 18(2)):

(a) maximising the return earned on the Fund over the long term, consistent with international best practice for institutional investment; and

(b) such other matters as the responsible Ministers consider relevant.

The first consideration in that list accords with prudential investment advice and practice, and concentrates upon optimising the Fund's financial performance and returns, although it raises in-built issues about what optimises sustainable returns from a whole-of-investment-portfolio perspective (Horrigan 2010). Nothing in that consideration directly raises political or governance concerns. The same cannot necessarily be said, however, for the second consideration, which is not limited on its terms to additional matters that simply facilitate or support the first consideration. In theory anyway, it is pregnant with the possibility of political manipulation of the fund to the potential and even unintended detriment of its financial objectives. At the same time, it is difficult to foresee any conventional political purpose that would be at cross-purposes with optimising the value of the Future Fund, whatever political choices are made in the ultimate uses of the fund.

Hypothetically, there could be a direction to invest a particular proportion of investments in designated areas (e.g. to prefer Australian investments), or to give priority in investment decision-making to designated standards (e.g. to promote corporate responsibility and sustainability in the overall economy, consistent with other governmental policies to that effect (Horrigan 2010)). As this example shows, political and other socio-ethical motivations can shape investment approaches, although no government in reality will want an outcome of fewer financial returns for the Future Fund in the long run, whatever the government might do to the Future Fund's Investment Mandate in the short term. In other words, while the political capacity for shaping the fund's investment mandate exists, other systemic and institutional factors combine to inhibit directions that stray too far from the central objective of 'maximising the return earned on the Fund over the long term, consistent with international best practice for institutional investment'.

In practice, of course, the Future Fund Act facilitates close consultation between the government and the board in setting the investment mandate. All parties have a common commercial interest in optimising the fund's investment returns. The legislative governance framework for the Future Fund does other things to support this, such as making transparent and exposing to parliamentary scrutiny any board submission (and concern) about a draft ministerial direction affecting the investment mandate, and making public the board's investment policies in accordance with its investment mandate (ss. 18(2) and 24). Accordingly, ministerial directions above and beyond what is 'consistent with international best practice for institutional investment' are perhaps best reserved for matters that are truly ancillary, supplemental, and facilitative, rather than broader policy matters that risk being financially counterproductive in effect. At the very least, such mechanisms provide opportunities for scrutiny and dialogue concerning proposed governmental intervention of this kind.

The reputation of the Future Fund can be affected by other governance matters, in addition to management of its investment mandate. As with appointments to the RBA, the process and outcome of appointments to the Future Fund Board of Guardians can affect its reputation in the investment community and its future relations with governments of all political colours. The appointment of David Gonski as its chair in early 2012 is an example of a meritorious candidate emerging from a flawed appointment process (Edwards 2012: 71). This appointment generated considerable media debate, which surrounded Gonski's earlier involvement as an adviser to government on selecting a new chair, the degree of consultation with Future Fund board members about potential successors, the involvement of former politicians as board and chair appointees, and the publicly unknown aspects of the appointment process.[3] The controversy in the recent past surrounding various board appointments by government, including appointments to the Future Fund and RBA boards, reinforces the need for comprehensive, merit-based selection processes of sufficient transparency, independence and accountability (see chapter 9).

Conclusion

Such considerations return us to the central theme in this chapter, concerning the interplay between governance norms, frameworks and mechanisms in the design, implementation and review of governance arrangements. These features also relate to the systemic multi-order mechanisms that act as safeguards of institutional integrity and other public interests that are enshrined in the underlying political and legal architecture for the business of government.

As the discussion in this chapter shows, there are questions surrounding the creation and implementation of appropriate governance structures and other arrangements for public sector bodies that remain of ongoing significance. Despite the transition from the Uhrig review agenda to the respective agendas that are expressed in *Ahead of the Game* and the CFAR, each of those official milestones maintains at least some focus upon governance design and implementation. More broadly, governance design in the twenty-first century must also embrace a new order of shared governance challenges and responsibilities that require governance innovations in cross-governmental, trans-sectoral and even international coordination and leadership. This is a theme that is picked up in the final chapter, which addresses future governance challenges.

---

3   E.g. 'I Told Labor "Fund Board Wants Costello" But They Chose Me: Gonski', *Australian*, 15 March 2012, pp 1 and 4; 'Future Fund Wanted Costello', *Australian Financial Review*, 15 March 2012, pp 1 and 8; 'Judgment Day for Future Fund', *Australian*, 15 March 2012, p. 28; 'Costello: It's Been "a Shemozzle"', *Australian Financial Review*, 16 March 2012, pp 1–4; and 'Fund Job Cannot Be One for the Boys', *Australian Financial Review*, 16 March 2012, p 51.

9. Appointments and Boards

This chapter focuses on the senior appointment processes for the public sector bodies that were discussed in the last chapter. It deals with appointments at the Commonwealth level for authorities that operate under the *Commonwealth Authorities and Companies Act 1997 (Cth)* (CAC Act). As indicated in earlier chapters, these bodies have the power to make and implement decisions on matters related to the public purpose of the entity, unlike those that fall under the *Financial Management and Accountability Act 1997 (Cth)* (FMA Act) such as departments of state. There are guidelines for the selection of Australian Public Service (APS) agency heads and other relevant statutory office-holders, which come under the *Public Service Act 1999 (Cth)* (PS Act) (APSC 2009a). These guidelines are comprehensive in defining the role of key players, such as the secretary of a department, and how the merit-based process is to proceed. There are, however, no comparable guidelines for office-holders within Australian public bodies outside the PS Act; the Australian Public Service Commission (APSC) guidelines stop short of being applicable to the chairs and directors of such boards.

Most state governments have various procedures for making public sector appointments: New South Wales (New South Wales Government 2004), Queensland (Queensland Government 2006), Victoria (Victorian Government 2011) and Western Australia (Government of Western Australia 2010) each have a set of guidelines with the guidelines in South Australian currently under review (South Australian Government 2000). None of the states have procedures that are as comprehensive as international better practices.

In the last few years, two incidents have occurred that have the potential to undermine public confidence in Australia's appointment processes. One was the resignation of Adelaide businessman Robert Gerard from his position on the board of the Reserve Bank of Australia (RBA) in December 2005, after the opposition raised allegations of tax evasion. Another has been controversy over recent appointments to the board of the Australian Broadcasting Commission (ABC). The former was not a major crisis of confidence and, therefore, did not lead to pressure on the government to make the current processes more rigorous, transparent and independent. The second example, however, was sufficiently serious to spur the Labor Party into commitments for reform, as the case study in this chapter on the ABC indicates. The topic of board appointment processes is important because it can only be a matter of time before a political appointment to a high-profile board in Australia backfires enough to severely dent faith in public integrity and confidence in its key institutions.[1]

---

1 In March 2012, political controversy arose around the lack of systematic and transparent processes by which Mr David Gonski was appointed to chair the Future Fund.

This chapter first describes appointment processes to Australian public sector boards and briefly puts them in a comparative perspective; it then presents some findings from research conducted for this book (chapter 3) on the views of public sector officials about appointment processes and the consequent tensions that arise; and finally identifies some unresolved issues of principle and suggests some policy approaches that might best suit Australia into the future. Where relevant, the chapter refers to the ABC as a case study.

The Australian context and a comparative perspective

The Australian scene

Until recently in Australia, little interest was shown at the Commonwealth level in appointment processes to its boards. The Labor government under Kevin Rudd (2007–10) made some statements about what it intended to do, and the current government is pursuing that intent (see below). To date, however, there has been relatively little transparency about the appointment processes that have been, or are being, followed in relation to public sector boards at the Commonwealth level. What is known is that appointment processes are usually neither comprehensive nor systematic, and there is therefore much scope for reform.

The processes of selection and appointment are usually focused around the relevant minister, the prime minister, the governor-general and the Federal Executive Council, with assistance provided by cabinet, the Department of the Prime Minister and Cabinet (PM&C) and other relevant departments. Ministers are expected to make appointments on the basis of merit, and to take into account skills, qualifications and experience (PM&C 2009a). Boards may or may not be involved in identifying the skills and experiences that are required when vacancies arise. The *Cabinet Handbook* states that: 'Where a significant appointment process is proposed, the responsible minister must write to the Prime Minister seeking his or, at his discretion, Cabinet's approval of the appointment' (PM&C 2009a: 19–21). It also notes that ministers must ensure that the person being proposed is appropriately qualified and has relevant experience; due regard is paid to the government's policy of encouraging an increase in the number of appointments of women; and attention is paid to the need to have an appropriate geographical balance in appointments (2009a: 19–21).

In some cases, the enabling legislation relating to Commonwealth authorities does impose some important restrictions on ministers' powers of appointment. For example, a number of statutes require board members to have expertise in a specified area. There are also several acts that specify a process that must be followed before members are appointed, for example, the *Primary Industries and Energy Research and Development Act 1989 (Cth)* (PIERD Act). Yet, under legislation for these corporations (or authorities), ministers have broad statutory powers that seem to be subject to little or no formal oversight or transparency.

John Howard's Coalition government (1996–2007) carried out governance reform of its boards in the second half of the 2000s, especially through the leadership activities of the then Department of Finance and Administration (Finance) following the endorsement by the government of key recommendations in the *Review of the Corporate Governance of Statutory Authorities and Office Holders* (Uhrig review) (Uhrig 2003) (discussed in some detail in chapter 8). The Uhrig review, while noting how significant appropriate board appointments can be, and offering some guidance on how ministers could be supported in the appointment process to ensure the necessary experience and skills relevant for a particular appointment (Uhrig 2003: 86–7; 97–8), did not include a recommendation on this issue of appointment. Nor were its terms of reference directed primarily to this topic, which demonstrates that the Uhrig review was not intended to cover everything to do with governance.

As chapter 2 has indicated, some useful guidelines, which were devised by the Australian National Audit Office (ANAO), exist in the form of better practice guidance for incremental improvements. For example, its guidance paper on potential conflicts of interest for CAC bodies (2003a) suggests procedures for managing tensions in the board framework including: 'Develop with the Minister an agreed procedure to enable board members to have input to the appointment of new members, chair and organisation head' (2003a: 5). Similarly, its guidance paper on CAC boards provides a checklist on good board practices, including appointment protocols (ANAO 2003b: 4).

The most significant relevant reform of board appointment processes, discussed later in this chapter, is the legislation which has recently been drafted for appointments to the boards of the ABC and Special Broadcasting Service (SBS): the National Broadcasting Legislation Amendment Bill 2010 (Cth). If the elements in that legislation were to become broader and apply to all boards, then a comprehensive merit-based appointment process could be mandated. Whatever happens to this legislation (it is currently before the Senate), it contains useful steps in developing a comprehensive appointment process and is, therefore, worthy of close attention whether that be within or beyond the current electoral cycle.

A comparative perspective

In the United Kingdom and Canada there have been particular triggers for making improvements to appointment processes. Changes to reduce perceived cronyism in the United Kingdom were driven by a desire to lessen public cynicism in the mid 1990's, following a series of scandals (OCPA 2005a). The United Kingdom now has a relatively sophisticated appointment system, which is based around oversight and monitoring undertaken by various commissioners for public appointments. More recently, in Canada, which has a system of parliamentary scrutiny of appointments, change occurred in response to a crisis arising from a major sponsorship scandal and an adverse auditor-general's report in which the governance of several public bodies came under scrutiny (Treasury Board of Canada 2005). More limited reform has also occurred in New Zealand, where board appointments are made by ministers, but in accordance with guidelines and advice and assistance from a number of other bodies (NZ, SSC 2009). The United Kingdom has by far the most advanced and comprehensive appointment system of the countries mentioned, which has modelling relevance both within and beyond Australia.

It is because the United Kingdom system of public sector appointments is so much more comprehensive than that found at either the Commonwealth or state levels in Australia, or indeed in other comparable countries, that this chapter pays particular attention to the better practices to be found in that country and compares them to current Commonwealth government practices (see Edwards 2006b, for more detail on schemes in other countries.) Therefore, the lessons drawn from the UK experience could be seen to be relevant not only within Australia but to comparable overseas countries such as Canada and New Zealand.

Behaviour of main players and empirical findings

It is not surprising that current public sector appointment processes, which lack general guidelines, in many cases show a lack of transparency and accountability and, hence, integrity. This became clear in research conducted for this book through interviews with senior officials of the Australian government and chairs and CEOs of CAC boards in the 2000s (chapter 3). What was surprising was that appointment processes were so commonly mentioned, even in responses to questions that did not focus specifically upon appointment processes. This occurred, for example, even to questions that asked respondents to identify constraints to the implementation of effective corporate governance in their organisation and to nominate two or three major emerging governance issues that were facing their organisation.

Without any systematic approach to appointment processes across Commonwealth agencies, there exists much diversity and inconsistency in practice. Diversity in practice does reflect the difference in types of CAC bodies, but it also reflects the behavioural dynamics that operate between the board members and the minister or government. At one extreme is the use of the most systematic processes which permeate the generally accepted stages for good appointment processes: audit, advertisement, merit-based selection with eventual cabinet approval. The practice of appointing 'mates' with little due process is at the other end of the spectrum — it is a process highly focused around ministers (Edwards 2006a). So, while some good appointment practices occur, these practices are by no means common and overall could not be described as comprehensive or systematic.

In addition, lack of consistency in appointment processes leads to many tensions such as:

- among board members, particularly between ministerial appointments, on the one hand, and those seen to have a conflict of role, as government or industry 'representatives';
- between board members with informal links to the minister and other members of the board;
- between the chair and CEO, whether one or both are appointed by the minister;
- between the CEO, board and the portfolio department in attempting to gain the ear of the minister; and
- between the board and the minister where selection processes around the CEO leave some ambiguity.

These tensions and other consequences of the current appointment arrangements are elaborated below in the discussion of the role of ministers in appointments, the appointment of chairs and directors, the appointment of the CEO, and the role of appointed stakeholders and government representatives.

A few qualifications need to be kept in mind in what follows. There was much change in government policy during the period that the main interviews were conducted, arising principally from the Uhrig review (2003). One consequence, for example, was the increased relative power of portfolio secretaries compared with chairs of boards, and this was reflected in some interviews. Nevertheless, what follows is revealing about the attitudes of major players on whom we depend for effective governance of public sector bodies.

The role of the minister

In line with democratic principles, it is generally considered that it is the right of ministers to exercise ultimate responsibility for appointments — in terms of final decisions. This is certainly the case in Australia. Serious problems can arise, however, in perception or reality, when there is no formal process around the role of ministers in the appointment process. In these cases, it can be difficult for board members to perform their duties and to exercise the independent judgment that is expected of them (Edwards, Nicoll and Seth-Purdie 2003: 40).

Many practices occur at the Commonwealth level. At one end of the spectrum the enabling legislation is quite specific about the minister's role (as in the PIERD Act, referred to earlier). In others the process is more opaque and our research unveiled several and often unsolicited comments because of that. One CEO reflected the view of many in saying: 'What inhibits good governance in the public sector is the perception that directors (who are appointed by the minister) are doing what the minister wants rather than what is good governance'. Another reflected on a minister who had personally selected more than just a few 'mates' to chair boards who, according to this interviewee, did not necessarily have the most relevant skills. At least one of these chairs admitted to being a 'minister's chum'.

Board members, however, can display independent behaviour, irrespective of their relationship with the minister: once selected, members often operate both professionally and independently. As one chair of a board remarked: 'The minister is responsible for all appointments ... but despite this, the minister has no influence' (chair). And another: 'We are totally independent. We are absolutely independent despite the fact that board members are all mates with the PM'.

This independent behaviour of board members is also reflected in the case of the ABC. While the Labor government's position is that: '"Unlike the previous government, we are not going to stack the board with our mates", the relevant minister in 2007, Senator Stephen Conroy went on to admit that previous Labor governments "may have been guilty" of this'. (Sainsbury 2007). Despite that 'guilt', Ken Inglis reported, in his study of the ABC, that a member of the (old) ABC Commission once said to him (2002: 11):

> 'We leave our guns parked at the door'. Recent and present directors make the point more positively, saying that they feel beholden not to the government which invited them to come on board, however preferable they may find its overall policies to those of the opposition, but to the ABC. They develop a common sense of themselves as stewards, custodians, disinterested guardians of a national treasure.

Appointments can reflect 'merit-cronyism' (Prasser 2005), as illustrated by one CEO: 'I'm a pragmatist — what you need on a board is someone who your Minister trusts and not only skills expertise and talent. So I'm not supportive of an appointment process at such an arm's length as a purist approach. It has great practical advantage to have the trust of the minister'. Thus, it is not always easy to say appointees were 'mates' or were appointed on merit but what is important is the actual perception of the reason for appointment, which is likely to be more negative than otherwise when processes are not transparent.

Appointing chairs and directors

Diversity of approaches in appointing board chairs and directors can be expected when there is a lack of formal process, in the majority of cases, applied to the making of appointments. In the case of chairs of boards of CAC bodies, they are mostly appointed by the minister, rather than following the private sector practice of the chair being appointed by the board itself. A few chairs referred to a phone call from the minister inviting them to the position. What we were not able to find out was what happened prior to that call: to what extent the search for a chair involved people outside the minister's office. This is as yet largely unexplored territory and an obvious issue of lack of transparency. It is an important topic for, as Richard Leblanc and James Gillies have observed: 'it is the selection of a chair that matters most to the board process, not the separation (of the chair and CEO)' (2005: 12). One CAC CEO considered that: 'the more I think about it, the more I realise that the minister's appointment of the chair is the biggest issue'.

For director appointments, some of the practices include:

- responding to detailed specification in the legislation (e.g. research and development bodies which come under the PIERD Act);
- advice from the chair/board to the minister with or without a nominating committee; and
- advice from portfolio departmental heads to the minister, which may not include taking advice from the board or its chair.

Research for this book showed only a few examples of a systematic process by which the board identified skill gaps and informed the minister of what was needed in making appointments to the board. In other cases, even though there was a formal process, it was not considered effective because of the dominant role of the minister.

Many tensions can be expected to arise from more informal processes of selecting board directors, particularly as boards and departments compete to have the ear of the minister: 'We give formal advice directly to the minister, which is against the arrangements that (the secretary) put in place. He wanted all advice for board appointments to come directly from the department.' (CEO)

Appointing the CEO

The Uhrig review was categorical about the importance of the CEO of a CAC-type body being appointed by the board and not by the minister, although it stopped short of making that a specific recommendation. It could be argued, however, as one CEO did, that: 'It does not make sense to appoint someone the minister doesn't have faith in. Uhrig takes a technical, purist approach. I think this is not quite right or disingenuous'.

Tension can exist where there are provisions in the legislation for the board to select the CEO, but where there is the added requirement to have the appointment approved by the minister and cabinet. In one of these cases, we were informed by a CEO of the importance of a compromise candidate being selected, where necessary: The CEO is appointed by the board but the minister needs to find the person nominated acceptable, otherwise a compromise candidate is found. There is ambiguity over the minister's role in the appointment process. This needs to be addressed.'

Currently, practices around CEO appointments differ across CAC bodies, with some bodies having the capacity to select their own CEOs, some making recommendations that go to cabinet and some having no capacity to choose at all.

Stakeholders and government representatives

There are several issues around the fact that CAC boards frequently include stakeholders in one form or another (e.g. experts or government representatives). Lack of clarity about the role of a board director can occur for members of boards who have some representative role, such as for a (state) government, industry or organisation. As chapter 8 has indicated, the Uhrig review discouraged (but fell short of making a specific recommendation on) any representational appointments to boards because they 'can fail to produce independent and objective views' (2003: 98). It is worth noting, however, that this pure principle is difficult to practice in the public sector where expertise, as well as representative views (e.g. from state governments), is required — as is sometimes specifically stated in the enabling legislation.

There are some distinct advantages in stakeholders being represented on boards: one chair remarked that 'You do need some people who understand the business'. And then, there is the issue of balance: although some directors come with an industry background, they have to: 'tread a very fine line between letting us understand the issues but not acting for their own interests.' (CEO) If there is an awareness of the importance of managing conflicts of interest and there exist good processes in place to do that, then it could be argued that the Uhrig position is too 'pure'.

A different set of arguments applies in the case of departmental representatives on boards. Uhrig was opposed to departmental representatives being on boards but kept the door open: 'Membership of the board by the departmental secretary is unwise unless there are specific circumstances which require it' (2003: 99). On the one hand, there is the issue of potential conflicts, especially when budget proposals are being considered and funding is sought from the department. On the other hand, there can be significant advantages: these representatives can bring awareness of government thinking and priorities to board discussion, such as the membership of the head of Treasury on the RBA Board (chapter 8). Much depends on the quality and capacity of particular public servants with dual roles.

There are many possible conflicts of interest here and one departmental secretary saw three aspects to the role: acting in the interest of the body; as portfolio secretary acting for the portfolio as a whole ('because I carry the can'); and keeping a watch on things for the ministers ('shit management'). Another portfolio head was quite clear about the priority role: 'I'm portfolio secretary and I know that informally the minister and prime minister would expect me to keep an eye on them even though they have a CEO'. Since the recommendations of the Uhrig review have come into force, and the relative power of the portfolio secretary vis à vis the board chair has been enhanced, the case for a departmental representative on the board could arguably be said to be reduced.

Principles and better practice

This chapter now turns from current practice on appointment processes to better practice principles, and the implications for Australia if they were adopted and implemented.

Relevant principles from the United Kingdom[2]

In the mid 1990s, there was a particular trigger for the UK government to enhance public confidence in the integrity of the political process around public sector appointments. There was significant 'public and parliamentary disquiet over the issue of patronage, which fed into and exacerbated a broader decline in public trust in politicians and political institutions' leading the Conservative Party to be 'dogged by accusations of sleaze and corruption' (Flinders 2009: 555). The 'widespread public unease at standards in public life' (HOCPASC 2003: 10), including concerns about abuse of power, cronyism and political bias in public

---

2   See Edwards (2006b) for details on appointment practices in other comparable countries.

appointments led the then prime minister John Major, in 1994, to establish a committee to inquire into the standards of conduct of holders of public office (called the Committee on Standards in Public Life or The Nolan Committee).

Amongst a number of matters, the Nolan Committee was concerned to ensure that appointments to boards of non-departmental public bodies (so-called quangos) were made on the basis of merit, without undue political bias, and in accordance with a transparent and accountable process. To this end, the committee made a number of recommendations relating to appointments to public office, the 'Nolan rules' (each of which is discussed below), which were subsequently largely adopted by the government. Changes were made to reduce perceived cronyism and to lessen public cynicism; attention was paid to a more transparent process with a higher degree of independence and with close attention to merit-based appointment processes (OCPA 2005a).

Since the United Kingdom now has a comprehensive and relatively sophisticated appointment system that is based around the oversight and monitoring of various commissioners for public appointments, it is worth examining the relevance of the UK experience for Australia.[3] There is an additional reason for focusing on UK practices in this chapter. The Labor government committed to basing its appointments to the ABC Board on the UK Nolan principles, also known as the seven principles of public life. '"We are seeking advice as to the best way to implement the Nolan principles in terms of new appointments to the ABC" Minister Conroy said' (Sainsbury 2007). And the legislation before parliament as of March 2012 embodies these principles. For these reasons it is useful to trace events in the United Kingdom which led to the creation of its set of comprehensive principles and a code of practice around public sector appointments.

The position of commissioner for public appointments was established soon after the publication of the Nolan Committee's report. The Office of the Commissioner has since practiced under a *Code of Practice* (OCPA 2005b; 2009) (hereafter, the code) governing ministerial appointments to public boards that is based on principles that were enunciated by the committee. These principles, or 'Nolan rules' are as follows (OCPA 2009:19-20):

- *Ministerial responsibility* — the ultimate responsibility for appointments is with ministers.

- *Merit* — all public appointments should be governed by the overriding principle of selection based on merit, by the well-informed choice of

---

3   Prior to 2004, there existed a single UK commissioner. Since then, this system has been replaced by one commissioner for England and Wales and separate commissioners for Scotland (2004) and Northern Ireland (2005). These countries have separate institutions and processes that share similar principles as those outlined above, although the Scottish system is stricter in many regards (See OCPAS 2006).

individuals who through their abilities, experience and qualities match the need of the public body in question.

- *Independent scrutiny* — no appointment will take place without first being scrutinised by an independent panel or by a group including membership independent of the department filling the post.
- *Equal opportunities* — departments should sustain programmes to deliver equal *opportunity* principles.
- *Probity* — board members of public bodies must be committed to the principles and values of public service and perform their duties with integrity.
- *Openness and transparency* — the principles of open government must be applied to the appointments process, its workings must be transparent and information must be provided about the appointments made.
- *Proportionality* — the appointment procedures need to be subject to the principle of proportionality, that is they should be appropriate for the nature of the post and the size and weight of its responsibilities.

As a result of the application of these principles for more than a decade in England, Scotland and Wales, they have had in place a relatively systematic and transparent process of selection and appointment. The system requires appointments to be advertised and a shortlist to be compiled by a panel that includes or is overseen by an independent or impartial assessor. While the final decision on appointment still lies with the relevant minister, the processes that have been established reduce the scope for cronyism by increasing the probability that such decisions will be publicly exposed.[4]

In 2011, both the commissioner for appointments in England and Wales and the commissioner for appointments in Scotland announced revised and streamlined codes. Although the stated principles were reduced, the essence of the 'Nolan rules' was maintained in the codes;[5] hence the discussion to follow is based on those rules. The main difference now is that there is more devolution of responsibility to relevant government departments to ensure compliance with the code and a, related, stepped-up audit process that is overseen by the

---

4 The minister can select someone who is not on the shortlist provided by the panel, but this must be reported to the commissioner. In Scotland, the minister's decision on which candidate(s) is (are) appointed, and the reasons for this decision, is recorded and retained as part of the audit trail for the appointment round (OCPAS 2006: 24.5).

5 The principles have been reduced to three: merit; fairness and openness. The other 'Nolan rules' are incorporated in the following way: (a) the ultimate responsibility for public appointments resting with ministers is stated up front, prior to these three principles (OCPA 2012); (b) independent scrutiny is covered through an appointment panel which must have an external perspective and be chaired by an assessor appointed by the commissioner (OCPA 2012); (c) equal opportunity and diversity is explicitly woven through the code (2011); (d) probity is covered with the panel needing to satisfy itself that candidates are committed to the Nolan principles (2011); and (e) proportionality is covered with greater attention to a 'more proportionate independent assurance' process (OCPA 2011).

commissioner (OCPA 2012; OCPAS 2011). There will also be, for England and Wales, a centre of excellence for public appointments that will have the aim of widening the pool of candidates applying for vacancies.

Stages in a good appointment process

Identifying the main stages in appointment processes is the first step in reforming the appointments system. Different jurisdictions have identified a variety of ways of selecting and appointing to public sector boards. There is, however, widespread acknowledgement of several main stages if better practices are to be followed; these are described in appendix 3. Those stages involve: agreeing a vacancy profile and timeline for appointment; locating suitable candidates; assessing and vetting potential candidates, selecting and appointing; and, less commonly, auditing the appointment process.

A well-structured and managed process would cover all these stages in a way that not only makes merit a primary consideration, but is also transparent and accountable and has a suitable degree of independence. How that independence is actually exercised has been the subject of debate (e.g. Aucoin and Goodyear-Grant 2002). A related issue is whether parliamentary accountability for non-departmental boards, which has been adopted in the United Kingdom (see below) but is uncommon elsewhere (Flinders 2010), should be part of the process. Roger Wettenhall is of the view that any serious discussion of the role of statutory authorities can never advance far without considering the parliamentary relationship, since parliament creates them and specifies how they are to operate (2012). The issue is the extent to which parliament plays a role. Irrespective of who oversees the process, it is to be expected that it would be accompanied by establishing effective board charters that specify the roles and responsibilities of directors, with associated monitoring of board and director performance.

ABC case study

For decades, governments on all sides of politics have been accused of stacking the ABC board with their 'mates' or, as one interviewee called them, 'chums'. The current government announced its intention to change selection processes to: 'ensure that all appointments to the ABC and SBS Boards are conducted in a manner that fosters independence, transparency, accountability and public confidence' (Conroy 2008) and 'to end political interference in the ABC by introducing a transparent and democratic board appointment process that appoints non-executive directors on merit' (Albanese 2010). The government subsequently introduced into the parliament legislation to this effect but also, from October 2008, put into practice the merit-based assessment processes which are contained in that legislation.

The National Broadcasting Legislation Amendment Bill 2010 (hereafter the Bill) encompasses all of the stages in a good appointment process, as outlined above. Table 9.1 outlines the main proposals contained in the legislation which relate to the appointment stage. The Bill formalises a merit-based and independent appointment process that is based on the UK system of public sector board appointments. In fact, the basis for this policy goes back to the Labor policy *A Better ABC Board: Labor's Policy on the ABC Board Appointment Process*, which was announced in 2003 (Crean and Tanner 2003; ALP 2004). It proposed that there be an independent ABC appointment selection committee. The Bill that is currently before the Senate encompasses the principles, identified in this chapter, for merit-based appointments and so represents a model of better practice, which may be of use in the future and to other jurisdictions. The Bill:

- places responsibility for assessing candidates in the hands of an 'Independent Nomination Panel established at arm's length from the Government';
- specifies that vacancies are to be widely advertised;
- uses a set of core criteria (with additional criteria added if the minister so decides); and
- mandates a report from the panel to the minister, including a short-list of at least three recommended candidates.

The amending legislation specifies the functions of the panel and asserts that it would act independently from the government and would not be 'subject to direction by or on behalf of the Government of the Commonwealth' (s. 24C). The relevant department(s) is required to publish the processes by which such appointments were made in its annual report.

Importantly, if the minister wishes to appoint a person who has not been recommended by the panel, after notifying the prime minister of this, and once the appointment is made, the minister must table a statement of reasons to parliament for that decision. In the case of the chair of the board, the prime minister, on receiving the short list from the panel, will be required to consult the leader of the opposition before making a recommendation to the governor-general, and similarly, if choosing an individual who is not on the panel's recommended short list, provide reasons for the selection in a statement to parliament (s. 24X).

Table 9.1: Legislation by appointment stage

1. Preparation — the process and vacancy profile
Ministerial determination of selection criteria
Independent nomination panel established
2. Locating suitable candidates
Widely advertised positions
3. Assessing and vetting candidates
By 'independent' panel to set criteria
Background check by panel
4. Selection and Appointment
Shortlist of candidates — at least three names to minister
Ministers check on suitability of candidate — in relation to selection criteria
Minister gives reasons to parliament — if alternative candidate chosen
5. Audit
Department publishes annual statement on processes

Source: Based on DBCDE (2010).

The processes that are set out in the Bill represent a paradigm shift from the position adopted by governments up until now — on paper at least. As a result of the Bill's implementation, cronyism should be significantly reduced and the power of ministers should be significantly constrained. A major advance will occur if the articulated aims of the legislation to foster independence, transparency, accountability and public confidence are achieved. Even the most skillfully drafted legislation, however, carries risks that the government's intentions are not carried through. In that case, the UK implementation experience can alert us to potential pitfalls.

Unresolved issues of principle

This chapter ends by considering several critical issues of principle that need to be addressed if a comprehensive reform to processes of appointment to Commonwealth boards is to be achieved in Australia. What follows is broadly in line with the 'Nolan rules' and takes the reformed ABC board appointment process as its illustration.

The extent of ministerial involvement?

The breadth of the powers that are given to Commonwealth ministers in existing appointment processes, as outlined above, contrasts with the position in the United Kingdom, where the code has placed restrictions on ministerial involvement in the system and, most recently, has spelt out more clearly their role (OCPA 2012).

Despite the existence of the code, there has been a continual, and often heated, debate in the United Kingdom about the degree to which ministers should be involved — a tension between those that argue for a system completely independent of ministers as the only way to ensure appointment on the basis of merit and public confidence in the system, and those that argue that ministers must be involved in the process in line with the principle of representative democracy.[6] Until recently in England and Wales, ministers could be kept informed about the progress of an appointment round if they wished, but could not be actively involved between the planning stage and the submission of a short list of suitable candidates (OCPA 2005b; Gaymer 2007: 11). The previous commissioner for public appointments for England and Wales is on record as saying that some ministers had unrecorded involvement in the middle of an appointment process, which could be interpreted as political interference (Gaymer 2007: 12). Under the new code, ministers can convey to the panel views 'about the expertise, experience and skills of the candidates' at each stage of the process (OCPA 2012: 5) alongside a clearer statement of their role.

Recently, the process has become cumbersome, with parliamentary select committees being able to hold pre-appointment hearings to scrutinise candidates for key public board positions before they are appointed (such as the chair of the BBC Trust) (HOCPASC 2008; Flinders 2009).

Although the proposed ABC/SBS legislation spells out in some detail the functions of the nomination panel through the planning, advertising, assessing and recommending stages of the appointment process, it pays scant attention to the specific role of ministers between the setting of the selection criteria and receiving the short list of recommended candidates from the nomination panel. Without this attention in the Bill, or a separate code of practice, real difficulties can be expected and public confidence undermined for any government that is planning to adopt this approach.

If changes are going to be made across Commonwealth boards, a key issue to be resolved is what role ministers should play and, related to this, whether a more independent body or parliamentary committee should be involved in vetting appointments — if not also in the selection process. The related issue of independence in the process is discussed below.

---

6   Peter Aucoin and Elizabeth Goodyear-Grant (2002) argue for the independent decision-maker to appoint the most qualified applicant and not merely a qualified candidate (which is in fact the position in Novia Scotia). Their conclusion is that if the principle of relative merit is to be effective, then ministers should not have a say in appointments: 'the standard of relative merit demands a process that is separate and independent of ministers' (Aucoin and Goodyear-Grant 2002: 314).

What is the meaning of 'merit'?

Appointing on the basis of merit (the overriding principle in the United Kingdom, e.g. OCPA 2005b: 21) would seem to be an incontrovertible necessity but, over time, the principle has been interpreted in the United Kingdom in various ways. In line with the original recommendations of the Nolan Committee, the selection criteria take account of a balance of skills and background. Further, under the code, the concept of merit must be read in conjunction with the principles of equal opportunity and diversity, which are required to be 'inherent within the appointments process' (OCPA 2009: 23).

In practice, this means that ministers and departments are required to adopt a broad definition of merit that not only takes into account competencies and capabilities, but also takes into account non-traditional activities and career paths, while encouraging a greater number of women, people with disabilities and members of minorities to participate in selection processes.

In Australia, the APSC has set out the meaning of 'merit' for its appointment processes (2009a: 5). This definition is narrower than that which is contained in the code: although the guidelines do include a segment on representation of women, they do not specifically provide for the element of diversity. In the case of the ABC legislation, however, following closely the wording of the UK code, diversity and equal opportunity are specifically taken into account: 'A broad definition of merit will be applied to the ABC and SBS Board appointments whereby formal qualifications and traditional work experience will form only one element. Non-traditional activities and career paths are recognised and valued as suitable qualifications which contribute to an individual's overall suitability for appointment' (DBCDE 2010). In addition: 'The principles of equal opportunity and diversity will be followed throughout the selection process. In particular, consideration will be given to ensuring that the membership of boards encompasses diversity in gender and geographical representation' (2010).

Here, as elsewhere, what is contained in the legislation can differ from practice: there is some evidence that British bureaucrats have adopted a rather narrow definition of 'relevant experience' to favour appointees who have already had board experience (Flinders, personal correspondence 2010). And, a relevant consideration that is not emphasised in either the UK or Australian cases is the importance for board performance of having around the board table the most relevant set of expertise and competencies. This means defining merit broadly enough to encompass not only inherent skills or qualities of the applicant but also how well the applicant's expertise fits with the expertise of other board members and also fits with the job that is required to be done.

How is independent scrutiny to be assured?

A central part of appointment processes to public sector bodies in the United Kingdom has been independent scrutiny by an independent assessor. According to the previous commissioner for public appointments for England and Wales, independent scrutiny 'underwrites the integrity of the whole appointments process' (OCPA 2005b: 31). The assessors are selected either by the OCPA, or by departments, in a competitive process. Their job is to ensure that the appointment process meets the requirements of the code and is in line with its principles (UK Cabinet Office 2006: 15; OCPA 2012). The revised code removes the requirement for an independent assessor and transfers some of their role to the relevant department. The assessment panel, however, must include at least one member with an 'external perspective' (2012: 6).

How independent will the selection and workings of the Australian nomination panel for the ABC be in practice? The panel will be appointed by the secretary of PM&C and will include a chair and two or three other members (s. 24E–24P). The nomination panel in the original ALP policy consisted of the secretary of the relevant department and head of relevant division, the APSC merit commissioner and an eminent and independent person. But the Bill does not specify the criteria for selection of panel members, or how the process of selection is to take place: will the appointees be eminent people who will be expected to 'not rock the boat' or people appointed because of their institutional affiliations? This needs clarification. Independence would also be threatened if the relevant minister is briefed orally before the short list is formally lodged with him or her, and this part of the process is not made transparent. There is also an issue over the independence of the head of PM&C, when compared to the APS commissioner, who is a statutory appointment (Nethercote 2010). One possibility would be designating the commissioner as an 'independent officer of parliament'. It is worth noting that the current commissioner of public appointments for England and Wales is also the civil service commissioner (OCPA 2011).

Probity: How to handle conflicts of interest?

Conflicts of interest (including 'duty') arise where 'the impartiality of an officer in discharging their duties could be called into question because of the potential, perceived or actual influence of personal considerations' (ANAO 2003a: 1) (See also Finn 1993; OECD 2004b; 2005a, b). There can also be conflicts of role, especially in the public sector, with government members being appointed to public sector boards. Conflicts of role arise where 'a person is called upon to play incompatible professional roles, and may face pressure to bring selective memory to bear on privileged information and/or act with dual personality' (Howard and Seth-Purdie 2005: 61).

In Australia, under the CAC Act, a director of a Commonwealth authority who has a material personal interest in a matter that relates to the affairs of the authority is generally required to disclose the interest to the other directors, excuse themselves from meetings where the matter is considered and refrain from voting on the matter (CAC Act, s. 27F; 27K). The *Cabinet Handbook* (PM&C 2009a) and *A Guide on Key Elements of Ministerial Responsibility* (Howard 1998a) also contain some broad guidance on the procedures that should be followed to avoid conflicts of interest that can arise in appointment processes. The legal requirements contained in the CAC Act, and these statements of principle, leave considerable room for conflicts, or the perception of conflicts, to arise. This can undermine confidence in the integrity and independence of public sector boards.[7]

The Australian Fisheries Management Authority (AFMA) is one Commonwealth authority with an established process to deal with potential or perceived conflicts of interest, which goes beyond the requirements that are outlined in the CAC Act (AFMA 2006) (See also ANAO 2003a). The Bill is, in fact, brief in dealing with probity issues but the nomination panel has the responsibility for determining the level of background checks to be undertaken prior to appointment (DBCDE 2010).

Will public confidence be enhanced with openness and transparency?

The principle here is about accountability and ensuring that members of the public have confidence in the system as a result of having information on relevant aspects of appointment processes. The desire for a transparent process must, however, be weighed against privacy concerns. The response to this dilemma in England and Wales has been to establish mandatory publicising, confidentiality and audit requirements. Documentation in relation to appointment processes must be kept and retained for a minimum of two years.

The UK evidence is that, despite detailed legislation and oversight by the OCPA, more than a decade later serious breaches of the code still occurred, including a number of appointments that were made with the virtual absence of an audit trail (Hayward, Mortimer and Brunwin 2004; MORI 2005). Moreover, an independent study conducted for the Office of the Commissioner of Public Sector Appointments (OCPA) on the perception of ministerial appointments processes found, in 2005 (10 years after setting up the OCPA), poor public understanding of board appointment processes with only one in five UK citizens

---

7   The OECD has produced some guidelines and a toolkit (2005b) to assist governments who wish to minimise actual or perceived conflicts. These have already been the basis of tools used by the NSW Independent Commission against Corruption and the Queensland Crime and Misconduct Commission (OECD 2004b: 8).

having confidence in the public appointments system. A more recent study regards raising knowledge 'a significant challenge' on the basis of the current lack of knowledge about public appointment processes (Cameron and Skinner 2010: 6).

The current commissioner for public appointments intends to uses his powers of audit to rigorously enforce the merit principle and compliance with the new code through spot audits (OCPA 2012: 6). He will report publicly on a department's compliance with the code and will publicise good and poor performance.

In Australia, as this chapter has shown, there is no real transparency about how people are selected for board positions, unlike other countries where transparency has been regarded as essential to a process which gains and maintains public confidence. This is not just about who is selected, but also all the stages in the appointment process. The public should be provided with sufficient information to understand what processes are followed to fill positions on public boards — from identifying vacancies through to choosing suitable candidates.

In the case of the ABC, one of the stated aims of the current policy is to restore public trust in the ABC. The crucial question here is: to what extent can we expect the proposed reforms to enhance faith in the system? Obviously, any reforms will require a civic education component, transparency and independent monitoring processes to shift attitudes of distrust about politicians. If the British experience is anything to go by, however, even this may not be sufficient to ensure public confidence in the board appointment system.

On the audit issue, the department(s) will be required to provide a statement in relation to each process for each director or chair appointment processes in its annual report, but it would seem sensible to have an overall audit from beyond the department, for example from the APSC or the ANAO, if not parliament itself. This will be all the more important if the government decides to extend what will be significantly improved appointment processes beyond the ABC and SBS Boards to all boards in the public sector.

The above suggests that a key issue for Australia to address is how far and in what way it wants to go with more rigorous and transparent processes, beyond what is intended for the ABC/SBS board processes. The UK experience would suggest that a good and transparent communication process will be required if the government is to gain public confidence in its board appointment processes.

Can there be an efficient as well as an effective process?

An important consideration in the establishment of appointment processes is cost and timeliness: the need for greater accountability, independence and rigour must be balanced against the need to use scarce resources cost-effectively. One of the seven 'Nolan rules' that are taken into account in the code in England and Wales is proportionality — the notion that the processes 'should be appropriate for the nature of the post and the size and weight of its responsibilities' (OCPA 2009: 27).

A more structured, transparent and independent process for Commonwealth public sector board appointments in Australia would be more costly than the current informal system. An issue here is whether the additional costs that are associated with a more rigorous system could be expected to be offset by the advantages associated with greater accountability and public confidence in the process, as well as the improvements in organisational performance that stem from having a more competent and cohesive board (see Edwards and Clough 2005; Leblanc and Gillies 2005). Arguably, though, the UK system has gone too far in attempting to ensure transparency and accountability: Matthew Flinders claims that processes have become 'too cumbersome and inflexible' and are likely to put off some potential candidates (2010). This is particularly so, Flinders claims, since the introduction of pre-appointment processes that involve the parliament. A balance is obviously needed here between competing principles.

At the Commonwealth level in Australia, a workable balance between efficiency and accountability concerns could well be attained in a number of ways: for example, by requiring boards to routinely undertake a skills audit before each new appointment and by giving the APS commissioner the additional function of being commissioner of public appointments, as is now the case in England and Wales (Nethercote 2010). Given that the APSC already oversees merit-based appointment processes that occur under its current jurisdiction, this would not be an excessive burden but would give the perception (which would, hopefully, be the reality) of a more independent voice in the process of selecting and appointing members of public sector boards. A third way of gaining the balance would be to involve parliament (e.g. a senate committee), but only in the case of major appointments, such as the chair of the ABC or RBA.

Conclusion

This chapter has presented the current picture of board appointment processes, as they relate to Commonwealth boards. Over the past several years, improvements have been made or are intended, most notably with the processes around appointment of directors of the ABC and SBS boards. The findings of the empirical survey on the pervasiveness of political appointments and lack of current good processes across all boards, however, leave much room for improvement. The chapter has raised a number of in-principle questions, such as what should be the role of the minister in board appointment processes and how independent can the process in fact be with the minister having final say? Is there any role for parliament in this process? And can Australia expect, in the foreseeable future, to have the proposed reforms to the ABC appointment process expanded to cover all major public sector boards? Or is this only likely to happen, as the experience in the United Kingdom suggests, after there has been a crisis in public confidence?

There is an opportunity now to begin a measured process of reform that could help enhance and protect public confidence in the governance of public institutions. As a newcomer to reform in this area, and in line with the encouragement that was given in *Ahead of the Game* to learn lessons from other jurisdictions, much can be gained from examining the changes that have been made in recent years in the United Kingdom, as indeed the current government has done for its Broadcasting Legislation Bill. The principles that are articulated in the code provide a framework for improving outcomes and public confidence. While there is considerable scope for variation in the processes that are adopted, departing from these general principles could jeopardise the integrity of the appointment process and the institutions that those boards are intended to serve.

Good governance around appointment processes to public sector boards requires the exercise of the norms or values which are contained in the framework provided in chapter 1: values of trust, public accountability and transparency in the context of legitimate exercises of political authority by elected representatives. Public servants and board members must be able to distinguish between what is legitimate and what might be informal government pressures, which, in the longer term, only serve to undermine the integrity of public institutions.

10. Public Governance: Challenges and Issues in an Age of Uncertainty

This concluding chapter has four purposes: to identify system-wide challenges arising from recent governance trends; to review the continuing tensions that emerge from contemporary public sector governance; to assess the implications of these for good governance and performance; and to canvass possible ways forward, given the contradictory agendas and uncertainties in the current environment. These include the ability to deliver on official objectives, such as an adaptable public governance system for the twenty-first century. The analysis draws on key themes and issues from the preceding chapters, and relates them to ongoing and emerging governance priorities and challenges.

Governance trends and challenges

New forms of governance

A decade ago, the Organisation for Economic Co-operation and Development (OECD) foreshadowed fundamental changes in the way in which public governance would be viewed in the future. The main messages that it identified were threefold. First, traditional forms of government had become ineffective. Secondly, new forms of governance that were expected to become important in the future would involve a wider range of actors. Thirdly, primary features of governance systems were expected to change, in particular, the permanency and power of organisational structures (OECD 2001b: 3).

These OECD messages, like those in this book, point to the observable shift over recent decades from hierarchical governance relationships, in which the boundaries around the organisation, sector or country are clear, to more horizontal or collaborative forms of governance with boundaries that blur across organisations and sectors, nationally and globally. Power is seen as shifting (although neither mainly nor fully) from decision-makers in government towards the many actors outside of government who are now involved in public policy processes. How governments engage in governance is adapting accordingly. This trend presents fundamental public governance challenges, which are discussed below.

Challenges of policy complexity and global interdependency

On the policy side, problems are increasingly complex, politically sensitive and inherently multidisciplinary in character. Regulation increasingly comes in a variety of state-backed and other forms. Service (Wanna, Butcher and Freyens 2010) is also more complex today, compared, even, to 10 years ago, with the involvement of more players from government and non-government organisations having often diffuse responsibilities.

A number of whole-of-government priorities, which currently confront the Commonwealth government, present the challenge of interdependency, such as: a sustainable environment (especially water and energy reform: Gillard 2010), rural and regional affairs, productivity improvements and service delivery to Indigenous Australians. That these types of issue are not new (compare former prime minister John Howard's policy statement in 2002), underscores how they have become a permanent part of the policy landscape. The major domestic policy challenges, according to the secretary of Treasury (Parkinson 2012), cover complexity in fields such as health, aged care, infrastructure and service delivery, as well as issues such as productivity performance and the sustainability of cities, and a disgruntled citizenry.

Similar examples of complex governance challenges can be found at the international level. External challenges have usually been fiscal in nature and economic factors (e.g. international competitiveness) have remained a driver, although nothing compares to the global financial crisis (GFC) of 2008. At the very least, the GFC presented ongoing governance challenges in the form of shared responsibility for global governance problems, vulnerability of interdependent systems, coordination and harmonisation of global regulatory responses, and enhanced expectations of governmental regulators of markets.

It is worthy of note that the chair of the Australia 2020 Summit and public governance expert, Glyn Davis, at the turn of the century observed that 'The challenges for governance … are not directly those of globalisation or an information economy. Rather they are the difficulties of adjustment, of finding a coherent course as change works through the economy and society' (Davis and Keating 2000: 242). In a continuing age of uncertainty, these issues remain central to effective governance.

The challenge of permeable boundaries

It is generally accepted that the future direction for public governance will require greater use of new forms of interactive processes and structures to manage complex issues alongside more traditional ones. It will no longer be simply enough to draw boundaries around sectors more clearly — innovative ways of bridging boundaries will be needed for effective governance. Into the future, it will be necessary to find better ways of matching problems with appropriate governance arrangements, if complex policy and delivery issues are to be effectively handled across the main players in governance decision-making processes. But, more than this will be required, given the blurring of boundaries around government and non-government sectors, as well as matters of national and global concern. Non-government players are increasingly found within bureaucracies as part of decision-making processes, government players are increasingly found working alongside non-government players in communities, and coordination and cooperation between different governments increasingly comes to the fore.

Governability and governance

Australia has institutional stability and continuity, together with a well-performing system of government. Yet significant questions exist about effectiveness in decision- making and its implementation. The major issues of the day are not experiencing resolution, principally for two reasons. First, political leadership appears to be ailing, if public perceptions are taken into account. In the space of three years, former prime minister Kevin Rudd's position soared to enviable heights and then plunged as his exalted agenda was found to lack grounding. His successor, Prime Minister Julia Gillard, has struggled to consolidate her position as the country's leader. The political realities of minority government also affect delivery of the legislative and policy agenda. Secondly, while complexity undoubtedly plays a significant part, other questions about capacity, connectivity and the roles of government are relevant. The series of official governance reviews that were undertaken in the first decade of this century and beyond are a testament to that. The implications for government are discussed below.

Governance regulatory frameworks

Whole-of-government frameworks and regulation are characteristically conceived in terms of what a particular level of government can control and legislate. As this book demonstrates, governance interactions within one level of government, across different levels of government, and amongst governmental and non-governmental parties are increasingly important in the twenty-first century. This development presents challenges for the ongoing evolution and adaptation of governance regulatory frameworks. Recurring issues of appropriate governance structures, public accountability mechanisms, performance and risk management, and multi-stakeholder engagement permeate the governance discussions in the *Review of the Corporate Governance of Statutory Authorities and Office Holders* (Uhrig review) (2003), *Ahead of the Game: Blueprint for the Reform of Australian Government Administration* (AGRAGA 2010) and the Commonwealth Financial Accountability Review (CFAR) (DFD 2012b).

These challenges are particularly evident in shared responsibilities and outcomes, cross-governmental governance initiatives, and governmental use of regulatory tools in addition to laws in governing the community. For example, governments now have a range of regulatory drivers that are available to them and which relate to governance concerns in one way or another, along a spectrum that includes conventional law-making and regulatory enforcement, official standard-setting, policy and regulatory incentives, multi-stakeholder initiatives, and whole-of-government frameworks (Horrigan 2010). This reinforces the connections and interactions between different forms of contemporary governance and regulation.

Continuing and emerging tensions

The several dimensions of governance that are addressed in this book raise a number of basic tensions. These are of varying degrees of saliency and immediacy, and may be continuing or emerging. Three sets of tensions are reviewed below.

Tensions in horizontal and vertical governance

At its heart, public sector governance is about managing some fundamental tensions, which have been identified as a theme of this book and which will need to be confronted by Anglophone governments into the future. The most pressing would appear to be that between the traditional vertical or hierarchical accountabilities of the Westminster system through ministers and parliament, and the horizontal responsibilities of departments and agencies out toward other government organisations and beyond toward non-government organisations and citizens. This is not a matter of which, but of a balance between the two. There are important accountability and other implications in managing this tension, which are discussed later in this chapter.

Many dimensions of this ongoing but growing tension can be identified. First, there are those that arise as part of the relationship between a public department or agency and other departments or agencies of government, which were discussed in chapter 5. The *Public Service Act 1999 (Cth)* (PS Act) and *Financial Management and Accountability Act 1997 (Cth)* (FMA Act) give the departmental secretary responsibilities for the administration of his or her department under the minister, but also responsibilities for management of the department. Increasingly, however, the government is expecting collaborative behaviour of a department of state with other Commonwealth organisations in delivering on the government's agenda and in forging cross-portfolio networks. The tension in the roles of the secretary could be intensified with the added responsibility that is placed on the public service today as a result of the inclusion in *Ahead of the Game* of a responsibility for Australian Public Service (APS)-wide 'stewardship', in partnership with other secretaries.

Secondly, there are the difficulties that arise in multi-level governance, and specifically the relationship between Commonwealth and state agencies under the Council of Australian Governments (COAG) agenda as discussed in chapter 4. Here, there is a tension between the Commonwealth and the states in collaborating on outcomes, such as for health, education and policy relating to Indigenous Australians, with the Commonwealth intervening on methods of state delivery to ensure value for money from Commonwealth funds. Not to be forgotten are the relationships that are place- and locality-based, or devolved systems of governance, which are needed to achieve whole-of-government objectives for both state and Commonwealth governments.

The final set of vertical and horizontal tensions was identified in chapter 7 as governments increasingly attempting to engage with non-government organisations and citizens, not only in delivery of services but also in the policy development process. For officials, a particular challenge today is between serving democratically elected representatives of the people and working directly with citizens in participatory democratic processes (chapter 1). The demands by government to deliver on budget and on time conflict with the time it takes to both build up policy capacity and for officials to engage outside of government to gain broader ownership of policy objectives. So, pursuit of the most efficient practices can conflict with the resources that are required to gain trust and work collaboratively over lengthy periods of time for possibly more effective outcomes, which is particularly so in the areas of relevance to Indigenous Australians.

Tensions in central coordination

There are four significant areas of potential tension in central coordination. The first is the relationship between the political executive and the machinery that exists to support its agenda and priorities. There have been dramatic reminders of how much central effectiveness is dependent on political leadership as well as the capacity of the system to respond. If leaders' aspirations exceed this ability to respond, a likely result is shortfalls in capacity and possible dysfunctions. If the development of capability is miscalculated — which can easily occur when there are skill shortages — a mismatch also results. Successful system governance requires mastering several intricate levels of relationship within central government and nationally, and the reconciling of contending political and environmental pressures.

The second source of tension derives from the question of how to organise the machinery of government and the design conundrum that arises from the system imperative for central steering, coherence and coordination, and the need for specialised agencies to undertake managing and delivery. Enhancing central policy capacity and coherence, may, as in the United Kingdom, lead to centralisation (Smith 2011). An ongoing challenge is the extent to which degrees of centralisation and decentralisation are appropriate.

A third tension arises from the question of where to locate capacity: internal to the APS or through external support and third parties. The internal capacity building of the public service runs up against pressures to respond to the supply conditions for expertise and the environmental demands for choice and customer focus. External sourcing provides expertise and flexibility but at the cost of developing internal capacity.

A final tension stems from the federal impulses to provide policy and executive direction to jurisdictions within the federal system and/or to improve the performance of delivery systems. The evolving COAG agenda has set new levels of aspirations, but has floundered in some respects on jurisdictional politics (COAG Reform Council 2011).

Tensions in agency and board governance

Several institutional tensions have been identified in chapter 3, which arise from the Commonwealth government's adoption of corporate governance concepts and practices into its public administration practices. Tensions arise, for example, where independence is accorded to statutory authorities under the *Commonwealth Authorities and Companies Act 1997 (Cth)* (CAC Act), but within a public sector context where the relevant minister may have broader governmental objectives to achieve. There is also a related tension between the independence of the CAC body and the fact that ministers are responsible for appointment of the members of that body. Internally, CAC bodies must work through ongoing tensions in the different roles of the board and management. These tensions are exacerbated by the addition of more people (e.g. political advisers) and mechanisms (e.g. advisory groups) to the information and communication flows between ministers and public sector bodies — hence, the need for protocols or guides such as the APS Commission's (APSC) *Supporting Ministers, Upholding the Values — A Good Practice Guide* (2006), which deals with how public servants relate to ministerial advisers.

This book has also addressed the tension arising between the duties and obligations of public servants to the government of the day and the duties and obligations of board directors to the organisation on whose board they sit. This is recognised in *Ahead of the Game*, which recommended the development of better guidance for all directors of Commonwealth companies, whether they are APS employees or not, including 'the legal obligations of government employees appointed to company boards, particularly on conflicts between public servants' duties under the *Public Service Act 1999*, and directors' duties under the *Corporations Act 2001*' (AGRAGA 2010: 69). Many of these tensions will continue into the future because they are endemic to particular relationships in the public sector, and must therefore be recognised and managed appropriately.

Implications for government

The above catalogue of issues and tensions are of varying significance. Tensions between institutions and actors engaged in governance are par for the course, and can be regarded, particularly where governments and politicians are involved, as a part of democratic processes. They nevertheless point to potential hot spots or areas where vulnerabilities may exist and weaknesses in the governance fabric may be exposed, if not handled properly. It is also clear from several cases that a concentration of factors accounts for governance failure.

There are four types of implications raised for government. They are: reform of governance regulatory architecture; disconnects and mismatches in both processes of governance and in the capacity to handle complexity and to adjust to the changing environment; modernisation and the potential efficacy of the official reform agenda; and areas where best practice has received insufficient attention.

Reform of architecture

The 2012 CFAR (DFD 2012b) has signalled that the twin-track model of governance structures exemplified in the CAC and FMA acts, and their respective 'board' and 'executive management' templates, no longer match (if they ever did) the array and complexities of public sector bodies and the governance challenges that they now face. At the same time, there is emerging disquiet in the Australian business sector about the respective roles and liabilities of boards and management, as fuelled by a series of landmark cases (e.g. the Australian Securities and Investments Commission (ASIC) litigation involving the James Hardie, Centro and Fortescue Metals companies). This has flow-on implications for the interpretation and application of the legal duties of public sector boards and management, given how closely the CAC Act tracks developments under the *Corporations Act 2001*. In turn, this correlation between these acts has other significance in a public sector context, such as the reform option of having the official corporate regulator (i.e. ASIC) investigate and prosecute breaches of directors' and officers' duties in both public and private sector contexts (DFD 2012b: 100).

Disconnects and mismatches

A transition is occurring in structures, processes, culture, policy, delivery tools and organisational relationships in the public sector to cope with the above trends and tensions, particularly to deal with the complexity of weaving together the aspects of horizontal and vertical governance. These transitional changes of the last decade or so have been, however, slow to adapt to the increased interdependencies of government and non-government players.

Implementation has long been the neglected part of the policy development process and most affected by these interdependencies. The implementation of government policy was an issue at the beginning of the reform era, in the 1980s, as a result of political concern with program failures and public service independence, which produced a sustained process of redistributing power between politicians and public servants (Halligan 2001). Despite the use of different instruments, political control and performance continued to be an issue for governments, with the concern in the 2000s being that political priorities were not sufficiently reflected in policy directions, and were not followed through in program implementation and delivery.

Failures in implementation have become more acute with the increasing prevalence of complex whole-of-government policy priorities, crossing organisational and jurisdictional boundaries. The auditor-general's view is that the public sector needs to focus, not so much on governance frameworks, as on implementation (McPhee 2009a: 5).

Delivery systems are failing to match the problems that they are meant to solve. As Donald Kettl (2009: 25) puts it, 'many of the most important problems we face simply do not match the institutions we have created to govern them'. He goes on to argue that there are 'interlocking public–private–non-profit systems that lack adequate governance or a clear government role', and that in the United States there are many systems for dealing with important issues 'in which no one is in control' (2009: 26).

A real danger in the future is that, because of the increasing mismatch between the political demands for policy capacity and the lack of capability to meet those demands, a dysfunctional public sector will emerge.

Managing system complexity and unintended consequences

It will often be the case that, while the purpose of system-change may be clear — for example, in the complex area of natural resource management — the decision-maker or decision-makers may not be able to mandate the actions required to achieve that purpose (Stewart 2010: 3). The behaviour of the system will emerge *as a result* of the many interactions within it (Ryan et al 2010: 17). Stephen Dovers (2010: 4) explains this, in the context of natural resource management:

> Institutions are singular, but a resource complex like water and the many human activities that interact with it (agriculture, industry, emergency management, recreation, etc) draw into the picture multiple institutions, organisations, policy processes, actors, and so on. Adjustment to one element may or may not have the desired effect if other elements provide countervailing incentives or disincentives. The idea of an institutional system reminds us of the multitude of organisations, rules, norms and players to be considered, their interdependencies, and that important systems characteristics such as feedbacks, time lags and path dependencies will be at play.

Those who work in the public sector are increasingly confronted with outcomes that are not what were intended in the policy or delivery design — for example, a tougher approach to crime may not lead to better public safety but only overcrowded prisons (Stewart and Ayres 2001: 79). Jenny Stewart and Russell Ayres explain this failure as partly 'due to a failure to anticipate the implications of change in one part of an interconnected system. In many cases, policy advisers are only too aware of these interconnections and are frustrated by structures and procedures which fail to bring actors together in productive ways, or by political imperatives which force ill-considered choices' (2001).

Stewart and Ayres (2001: 83) go on to recommend applying systems thinking to complex public policy problems, along the lines that are suggested in chapter 1 and elsewhere in this book: 'Rather than selecting instruments to fit a particular kind of policy problem (the conventional approach to policy design) systems analysis suggests that the nature of the problem cannot be understood separately from its solution'. An example of this is in the reduction of illicit drug use which, if conventional tools were used, would probably involve sanctions on users and sellers of drugs. However, a systems approach would 'examine relationships between sellers, users, suppliers, health professionals and the law and attempt to model responses to different types of interventions, before selecting one or more to apply' (2001: 84). They argue that, in the future, there will need to be a searching for 'distinctive ways of connecting goals and instruments, in that new approaches to causation, intervention and evaluation are implied' (2001: 91). These systemic, relational and other connections are part of the evolving governance landscape.

System reform as an approach to complexity and modernising governance

A reform agenda can be distinguished according to whether: the focus is limited to fine-tuning; extends to introducing new instruments and techniques; or represents a fundamental form of change that subsumes the others, and which can be observed in the historic shift to new public management. A further type, system design and maintenance, addresses systemic coherence and balance in which there is systematic refurbishing of the components. This type is in the tradition of a comprehensive review and provides a reform context in which fine-tuning and new techniques can be introduced. The Australian reform agenda fits this type as a large-scale crafting of the system. The influence of the previous head of the Department of Prime Minister and Cabinet, Terry Moran, as a systemic thinker and operator was important here. He argued that the reform agenda in *Ahead of the Game* for the public service was 'more than the sum of the parts' (Moran 2010a).

Ahead of the Game provides a generalised road map for an extended reform process to be managed by the public service. There is a rolling agenda for change with a large range of elements that encompasses many players, in particular, two leadership groups, the Secretaries Board and APS 200, a senior leadership forum for supporting the secretaries. Numerous processes have been under way to implement *Ahead of the Game* recommendations. One of the most significant was the augmentation of the APSC's powers to make it the lead agency for around half the recommendations. The A$39 million allocated under the 2010 budget was, however, subsequently cut by Prime Minister Gillard when projecting fiscal rectitude in the election campaign, leaving uncertainty about the pace and direction of reform.

Significant resources have not been allocated to the reform task. But, assuming that implementation proceeds in part, to what extent can fundamental change be expected to flow from the agenda in *Ahead of the Game?* Much of the language of new governance is there: citizen engagement, whole-of-government, shared outcomes across portfolios, cooperative federalism, and external relationships and partnerships. While the strength of the reform agenda is its focus on attending to a wide range of aspects of the existing public service system, less convincing is how it will produce changes to cultures, mind-sets and practices that derive from how that system is constituted. There remain, therefore, a number of issues with the reform agenda and process.

Fundamentals for future public governance

The changing governance environment, with its many interconnections, multi-faceted problems and cross-sector boundaries, can be expected to lead to governance practices that are out of tune with the standard set of good governance principles. As already indicated, the next decade may well see a good governance system being recognised, not so much for the focus on appropriate internal governance processes, but more for achieving good organisational and broader societal outcomes through effective interactions between system components (Ryan et al 2010: 21).

What follows is an examination of the condition of public governance and several dimensions that are likely to be needed for good governance into the future. In doing this, standard sets of principles of good public sector governance are drawn on (ANAO 2003c; APSC 2008). Key principles will be strong and consistent leadership of a type to manage complexity and its inherent tensions, and clear and applicable concepts of accountability. Additional relevant principles permeate *Ahead of the Game* (such as integration, innovation, collaboration, participation and shared responsibility).

Leadership

Modern leadership approaches are much more team-based and collaborative than they were a decade or so ago; emphasis is now required on gaining commitment at all levels. The traditional hierarchical approach to leadership relied more on compliance, where strong personalities tended to dominate and, hence, responsiveness to the broader public and its involvement in the policy process was not emphasised (Althaus and Wanna 2008: 123).

Having said that, rhetoric around collaborative governance and inclusive leadership can be at odds with the practice, as in John Howard's Coalition government's Northern Territory intervention in 2007. In practice, there may be a real tension for a government attempting to achieve horizontal and vertical alignment — in connecting policy intent with delivery and integrating organisational goals and performance. Nevertheless, increasingly we can expect successful leadership in the public sector to display a capacity to drive complex multi-organisational networks that encourage individual and institutional contributions to shared goals, if not also shared leadership.

Accountability

The traditional hierarchical view of accountability is now being challenged (McPhee 2008a: 3). If, in some complex and interdependent policy and delivery circumstances, as indicated above, no one can be said to be in charge, how can accountability be pinpointed? (Kettl 2009: 123). We have moved into a new era of multiple and interactive accountabilities.

The United Nations has identified several challenges to be faced in terms of coming to grips with accountability issues in the new governance environment (2007: 32–3):

- an increase in accountability conflicts (e.g. between 'output' or performance accountability and multiple stakeholder accountability);
- for public officials, a need to 'increasingly exercise judgment over which form of accountability to prioritise in a given circumstance';
- increasingly important professional and personal accountabilities for public officials;
- less dominance of political accountability; and
- increasing accountability roles for political representatives 'i.e. monitoring the "accountabilities system" for its overall results and integrity.'

These challenges can make life hard for senior government officials; as Catherine Althaus and John Wanna state (2008: 123, relying on Shergold 2004a; 2007b):

> Public officials appear now to pay more attention to interdepartmental cooperation and horizontal alignment. They are meant to work in dynamic partnership with private and non-governmental organisations, to show initiative and take calculated risks to achieve exemplary social outcomes … All this at the same time as they are supposed to be responsive to community demands and have been placed under strict accountability regimes that demand almost excessive process requirements.

This, with the dangers that accompany diminishing trust, puts the relationship between senior public servants and their ministers under greater pressure.

In part, it could be argued that some of the more recent implementation problems of the Australian government are due to the often long and complex chains (which Jeffrey Pressman and Aaron Wildavsky called 'the complexity of joint action' quoted in Kettl 2009: 216) that go through government, out to non-government organisations and back to government as various market, regulatory and other mechanisms are used in complex partnering or contracting arrangements (Kettl 2009: 216; Edwards 2011).

To this list of challenges can be added those complications that federalism brings, especially with an active COAG agenda of complex issues. Refinement of accountability to government at the federal level of government through the Uhrig review templates, recognition of shared governance responsibility through *Ahead of the Game*, and improvement of financial performance and accountability through the CFAR process still leaves all three to be integrated with another order of public responsibility and accountability.

These 'internal to government' mechanisms must additionally be aligned with 'external to government' mechanisms that are becoming prominent as democratic government evolves to embrace new forms of participatory, deliberative and monitory democracy (chapter 1), and as a technologically innovative digital society embraces new forms of networking, collaborating, and communicating, both nationally and globally. In addition, it can be argued that there is a need for accountability systems to move from 'a focus on organisations inside ... to an assessment of the system's results from the outside' (Kettl 2009: 233). Managing and integrating these 'inside out' and 'outside in' perspectives are part of the organisational governance challenges for public sector bodies too.

Towards shared outcomes and accountabilities

The need for effective interagency, intersectoral and interjurisdictional collaboration is well established, yet, a system of shared accountability for system-wide and societal results is lacking (Bourgon 2011; Halligan 2010d). Achieving public results is increasingly challenging because the process is multi-dimensional, multi-level and multi-sectoral; but demands have been increasing for such solutions.

There is an expanding range of experiments involving sharing of outcomes and accountabilities. At the interface between levels, the Australian Intergovernmental Agreement on Federal Financial Relations is designed to improve the wellbeing of Australians through collaborative working arrangements and enhanced public accountability, which covers outcomes achieved and outputs delivered. The arrangement provides for public accountability for outcomes at the federal level, with state-level flexibility regarding how these outcomes are to be delivered (APSC 2010a).

Stewart provides an example of lower-level public servants working in an area related to Indigenous Australians who had to operate 'under the radar' in order to gain good outcomes on the ground. This required not only sharing outcomes and responsibilities, but, most importantly, prior establishment of trusting relationships (2010: 7). One example is of a community request for air conditioning that did not appear to be a government priority. The provision of air conditioning, however, not only established trust but led to discussion about other mutual objectives, such as improved school attendance, which the air conditioning enhanced. By opening up to ideas in this way, public servants tapped into 'virtuous possibilities of system interconnection'. Important here was that resources could be made available to adapt to outcomes, rather than being rigidly confined to set 'pots' of money (Stewart 2010: 8).

Ahead of the Game recommends the introduction of shared outcomes across portfolios. It is not clear, however, for public servants and those who co-produce with them in policy or delivery, whether accountabilities, as well as outcomes, are to be shared. When outcomes are shared, what are the accountability mechanisms? Roles should be distinct even if responsibilities are shared, but does this mean that accountabilities are also shared and, if so, how is this to work in practice? In addition, when are risks also to be shared across departments, with other governments or with non-government partners? These are issues that need the attention of government if there is to be alignment between collaboration and accountability and quality shared governance is to become a reality (see Edwards 2011 for more detail on these issues).

Governance for the twenty-first century

The Australian Government today needs to give priority to designing and participating in a public governance system that is sufficiently flexible to deal with new challenges as they arise. This will test its relationships with other sectors operating at its boundaries.

There is also the important question of what type of public governance system will emerge from uncertainty about the roles of the Commonwealth, new policy issues and the turbulent international environment. How much will its role veer towards society-centric governance, and what changes does this entail for how government manages its relations with others? Given the APS's mixed performance on service delivery and citizen engagement, how viable is 'service transformation' and co-design (Dutil et al 2010; Lenihan and Briggs 2010)? These questions will be answered by what is accomplished in the rest of this decade.

Leveraging governance: The new role for government

Just as government has recently relied heavily on outsourcing many of the activities it traditionally undertook, into the future it is likely that non-government organisations will operate from within the public arena as partners in policy development and service delivery, which will necessitate attention to new processes, structures and relationships. Governments will therefore be increasingly faced with boundary issues, which in turn raise questions about the respective roles for government and non-government players. As Kettl (2009: 239) has remarked:

> The importance of boundary spanning ... suggests a new approach for government — an approach that democratizes the process by spreading participation, privatizes government by relying more on nongovernment partners, governmentalizes the private sector by drawing its organizations more into strong public roles, and ultimately challenges the framework of ... democratic institutions.

Public officials will need to emphasise more the serving and empowering of citizens to better meet their needs. In terms of accountability, this means public servants will need to interact with and listen to citizens in a way that empowers them as members of a democratic community (Denhardt and Denhardt 2007: 23, 134). The existing tension between serving the bureaucracy hierarchically and meeting the demand of democracy will intensify and, hence, require careful management.

The role of government into the future, therefore, will be much less 'active' and more one of stewardship — enabling, and leveraging — than in the past. According to one scenario, it is envisaged that government leaders will effectively align public, private, non-profit, national and global players across messy boundaries; responsibility will be broadly shared and full control less apparent; and leadership, management and coordination mechanisms will be less able to be institutionalised (Kettl 2009: 178, 186; Schick 2011).

Apart from predicting a democratising governance future for the reasons stated, and the tensions that this may create, good governance into the future can also be expected to have built into its processes the ability for decision-making units to learn from past practices. This will necessarily involve ongoing monitoring of implementation structures and processes to see if they remain appropriate to the task as it unfolds. The potential tension here, between project management-type systems and a learning process, 'can only be resolved by building into our organisations effective monitoring and communication and the will and capacity to make change in response' (Shergold 2007b: 14). This may well emerge as a result of the capability departmental reviews that the APS is intending to implement as part of the *Ahead of the Game* agenda and the proposed delivery boards (Moran 2010b).

New capabilities

The skills of public servants in the future may well need to embrace a total shift to making 'networking' and a set of 'enablement skills' a prime focus, wherever third parties and/or citizens need to be engaged. This was recognised some years ago by Lester Salamon (2002: 16):

> Unlike both traditional public administration and the new public management, the 'new governance' shifts the emphasis from management skills and the control of large bureaucratic organisations to enablement skills, the skills required to engage partners arrayed horizontally in networks, to bring multiple stakeholders together for a common end in a situation of interdependence.

Multiple capabilities are needed in the new era of public governance and for a high performing public service, which *Ahead of the Game* aims to achieve. Public servants will now need to be more responsive to medium and longer-term issues; better equipped to handle complexity; more effective users of current information and communications technology, and more active networkers and collaborators within and beyond the public service.

In addition, there will be an increasing role for people who can broker knowledge across the boundaries at which public servants work — with industry, non-government organisations and academics, as well as citizens. As yet, the role of knowledge brokers is not clearly defined in the literature and in practice, whether for individuals or organisations (Knight and Lightowler 2010: 547), but that can be expected to occur as the need for them becomes more apparent.

Conclusion

This book has sought to outline the main features of Australian public governance at the national level, and to give careful attention to several important dimensions. The basics of governance are in good shape, but attention needs to be paid to the challenges that have been identified in this book and recent international studies (Pollitt and Bouckaert 2011; Bourgon 2011; Pal 2011).

The public sector faces distinctive issues in an era of governance that involves a wide range of players, but also because it is up against the demands of the international sphere at a time of great uncertainty (Cohen and Roberts 2012). In terms of the dimensions of governance that are covered in this book, the Australian public sector is better equipped to handle the issues of today than many others internationally and, to date, has been more comfortable with 'government' rather than 'governance'. How effectively the public sector will absorb the governance orientation *and* maintain the strengths of a central government is the ultimate meta-challenge.

Appendix 1: Methodology for Interview Study 2004–07

In the period 2004–07, the authors undertook a total of 43 formal interviews with departmental secretaries, chief executives of agencies reporting under the *Financial Management and Accountability Act 1997 (Cth)* (FMA Act), and representatives of authorities and companies reporting under the *Commonwealth Authorities and Companies Act 1997 (Cth)* (CAC Act).

A total of 25 interviews, including 13 with departmental secretaries and 12 chief executives, were undertaken with interviewees from departments and agencies reporting under the FMA Act. The 18 interviews with bodies reporting under the CAC Act covered authorities, companies and government business enterprises and included interviews with six board chairs, six chief executives and six directors/managing directors.

Following the authors' findings in earlier interviews that were undertaken in 2002–03, this new series of interviews sought to obtain clearer qualitative data with respect to the adoption of concepts and principles of corporate governance (and governance generally) within the federal public sector. In particular, the interviewers sought the views of relevant participants as to the roles and operation of executive and management boards within government departments and central agencies, and as to the authority and operation of authorities and companies reporting under the CAC Act.

The Interview Schedule comprised three sets of questions. The first set comprised open questions for both FMA and CAC interviewees and they addressed three general areas of interest that are associated with public sector governance: interviewees' understanding of the meaning of corporate governance (and governance generally across the Australian public sector), their understanding of the governance 'system' as a whole (i.e. the legislative framework for accountability, performance and stakeholder participation), and their views as to who should bear responsibility for the oversight of public sector governance.

The second set of questions was directed specifically to the representatives of FMA bodies. These questions required interviewees to consider the role and operation of executive and advisory boards that were utilised within departments and the role of the chief executive and boards in central agencies reporting under the FMA Act. Interview questions sought to explore the character of these boards given the adoption of the decision-making board and more prescriptive 'corporate' governance requirements of the CAC Act.

Questions also sought to establish the arrangements of departments and agencies to achieve whole-of-government coherence through the use of representatives on each other's committees.

The final set of questions was directed specifically to those representing CAC bodies and sought to test the perception of interviewees regarding the independence of government given their role as participants in a corporate entity within the public sector. In particular, how did they see their independence manifested in practice, how were the 'corporate' requirements of the CAC Act being adopted in practice and how compatible were the requirements of the CAC Act with the requirements of the FMA Act in reflecting the authority of the chief executive and the chief executive's responsibility to the minister? Specific issues that were raised by these questions included the role of government policy in the work of boards, the processes for appointment of the chair and directors by ministers, and whether these processes affected the dynamics of the board in making collective decisions.

Appendix 2: Flipchart of FMA Act Agencies and CAC Act bodies, 15/2/12

Australian Government
Department of Finance and Deregulation

Chart of 111 Agencies under the *Financial Management and Accountability Act 1997* (FMA Act)#

20 Departments of State [Ω] under the *Public Service Act 1999*

1. Department of Agriculture, Fisheries and Forestry
2. Attorney-General's Department
3. Department of Broadband, Communications and the Digital Economy
4. Department of Climate Change and Energy Efficiency *
5. Department of Defence *
6. Department of Education, Employment and Workplace Relations
7. Department of Families, Housing, Community Services and Indigenous Affairs
8. Department of Finance and Deregulation
9. Department of Foreign Affairs and Trade
10. Department of Health and Ageing
11. Department of Human Services
12. Department of Immigration and Citizenship
13. Department of Industry, Innovation, Science, Research and Tertiary Education
14. Department of Infrastructure and Transport
15. Department of the Prime Minister and Cabinet
16. Department of Regional Australia, Local Government, Arts and Sport
17. Department of Resources, Energy and Tourism
18. Department of Sustainability, Environment, Water, Population and Communities
19. Department of the Treasury
20. Department of Veterans' Affairs †
(part of the Defence portfolio)

Note: there are 20 Departments of State and 22 Cabinet Ministers

5 prescribed agencies are non-statutory and staffed through a Department of State

Defence: 1/1
Defence Materiel Organisation [M]
Industry, Innovation, Science, Research and Tertiary Education: 1/1
IP Australia ^
Resources, Energy and Tourism: 1/2
Geoscience: 2/14
Treasury: 2/14
Australian Office of Financial Management (AOFM) [M]
Royal Australian Mint

2 prescribed agencies are statutory, but staffed through a Department or agency

Education, Employment and Workplace Relations: 1/7
Seafarers Safety, Rehabilitation and Compensation Authority (Seacare Authority)
Treasury: 1/14
Commonwealth Grants Commission

67 prescribed agencies also encompass a "Statutory Agency" under the *Public Service Act 1999* (PS Act)

Agriculture, Fisheries and Forestry: 3/3
Australian Fisheries Management Authority †
Australian Pesticides and Veterinary Medicines Authority (APVMA) † [Ω]
Wheat Exports Australia †
Attorney-General's: 15/19 #
Administrative Appeals Tribunal
Australian Commission for Law Enforcement Integrity (ACLEI)
Australian Crime Commission [Ω]
Australian Customs and Border Protection Service [M]
Australian Human Rights Commission †
Australian *Institute* of Criminology [Ω]
Australian Law Reform Commission
Australian Transaction Reports and Analysis Centre (AUSTRAC)
Family Court of Australia [M]
Federal Court of Australia
Federal Magistrates Court of Australia
National Native Title Tribunal
Office of the Australian Information Commissioner
Office of Parliamentary Counsel
Office of the Director of Public Prosecutions *
Broadband, Communications and the Digital Economy: 1/1
Australian Communications and Media Authority (ACMA) † [M]
Climate Change and Energy Efficiency: 1/1
Office of the Renewable Energy Regulator
Education, Employment and Workplace Relations: 4/ 5
Fair Work Australia (FWA)
Office of the Australian Building and Construction Commissioner
Office of the Fair Work Ombudsman
Safe Work Australia [Ω]
Families, Housing, Community Services and Indigenous Affairs: 2/ 2
Australian Institute of Family Studies (AIFS) *
Equal Opportunity for Women in the Workplace Agency
Finance and Deregulation: 3/ 3
Australian Electoral Commission * [M]
ComSuper
Future Fund Management Agency † [M]
Foreign Affairs and Trade: 2/ 4
Australian Centre for International Agricultural Research (ACIAR)
Australian Trade Commission (Austrade) [M]
Health and Ageing: 10/ 11
Australian National Preventive Health Agency (ANPHA) [Ω]
Australian Radiation Protection and Nuclear Safety Agency (ARPANSA)
Cancer Australia
Independent Hospital Pricing Authority [Ω]
National Blood Authority [M] [Ω]
National Health and Medical Research Council (NHMRC)

National Health Performance Authority [Ω]
Organ and Tissue Authority (Australian Organ and Tissue Donation and Transplantation Authority)
Private Health Insurance Ombudsman
Professional Services Review Scheme
Immigration and Citizenship: 1/1
Migration Review Tribunal and Refugee Review Tribunal (MRT-RRT)
Industry, Innovation, Science, Research and Tertiary Education: 1/2
Australian Research Council [M]
Infrastructure and Transport: 1/1
Australian Transport Safety Bureau (ATSB)
Prime Minister and Cabinet: 5/7
Australian National Audit Office
Australian Public Service Commission (APS Commission)
Office of National Assessments *
Office of the Commonwealth Ombudsman
Office of the Inspector-General of Intelligence and Security
Regional Australia, Local Government, Arts and Sport: 4/ 6
Australian Sports Anti-Doping Authority (ASADA)
Australian Skills Quality Authority (National Vocational Education and Training Regulator)
National Capital Authority [M]
Tertiary Education Quality and Standards Agency
Resources, Energy and Tourism: 1/2
National Offshore Petroleum Safety and Environmental Management Authority (NOPSEMA) † [Ω]
Sustainability, Environment, Water, Population and Communities: 3/ 4
Great Barrier Reef Marine Park Authority † [Ω]
Murray–Darling Basin Authority † [Ω]
National Water Commission [Ω]
Treasury: 10/ 14
Australian Bureau of Statistics * [M]
Australian Competition and Consumer Commission † [Ω]
Australian Securities and Investments Commission (ASIC) † * [M]
Australian Taxation Office [M]
Corporations and Markets Advisory Committee (CAMAC) † *
Inspector-General of Taxation
National Competition Council
Office of the Auditing and Assurance Standards Board (AUASB)*
Office of the Australian Accounting Standards Board (AASB)*
Productivity Commission

8 prescribed agencies also encompass an "Executive Agency" under the *Public Service Act 1999*

Attorney-General's: 2/19
CrimTrac Agency [Ω]
Insolvency and Trustee Service Australia (ITSA) † ^ Σ
Foreign Affairs and Trade: 1/4
Australian Agency for International Development (AusAID) [M]
Health and Ageing: 1/ 11
Interim Independent Hospital Pricing Authority [Ω]

Prime Minister and Cabinet: 1/ 7
National Mental Health Commission
Regional Australia, Local Government, Arts and Sport: 2/ 5
National Archives of Australia [M] Σ
Old Parliament House
Sustainability, Environment, Water, Population and Communities: 1/ 4
Bureau of Meteorology [M] Σ

4 Departments of the Parliament, under the *Parliamentary Service Act 1999*

Department of the Senate
Department of the House of Representatives
Department of Parliamentary Services [M]
Parliamentary Budget Office

5 prescribed agencies engage personnel under their own Act, and not the PS Act

Attorney-General's: 2/19 #
Australian Federal Police [M] [Ω]
Australian Security Intelligence Organisation [M]
Foreign Affairs and Trade: 1/4
Australian Secret Intelligence Service
Prime Minister and Cabinet: 1/7
Office of the Official Secretary to the Governor-General
Treasury: 1/14
Australian Prudential Regulation Authority (APRA) †

Key to Symbols

FMA Act agencies comprise all Departments of State, Departments of the Parliament and "prescribed agencies" named in the FMA Regulations. These agencies are all able to receive appropriations in their own right.
Also, note that all FMA Act agencies are in the "General Government Sector".
[M] 41 agencies are material entities. Material entities comprise 99% of revenues, expenses, assets and liabilities. Note too, that all of the 20 Departments of State are "material in nature".
† 15 agencies also encompass bodies corporate formed under statute.
[Ω] 17 agencies are interjurisdictional in nature, eg, involving the States or Territories in their governance structure or establishment.
* 10 agencies can engage personnel under their enabling legislation as well as under the *Public Service Act 1999*. These include Defence, under the *Defence Act 1903*, *Naval Defence Act 1910* and the *Air Force Act 1923*.
Σ 3 Executive Agencies have statutory functions.
^ ITSA handles money other than public money.
^ IP Australia encompasses some office holders, ie: for registering patents, trademarks and designs.
15/ 19 – Indicates number of prescribed agencies of that type (e.g. statutory agencies) out of the total prescribed agencies in the portfolio.
The Attorney-General's portfolio includes the High Court of Australia, which is part of the Commonwealth, and is in the "General Government Sector". However, it is not an agency under the FMA Act, due to its status under its enabling legislation, which also sets its employment framework.

62 statutory authorities are Commonwealth authorities for CAC Act purposes

Agriculture, Fisheries and Forestry: 7
- Cotton Research and Development Corporation
- Fisheries Research and Development Corporation
- Grains Research and Development Corporation [M] Ⓟ
- Grape and Wine Research and Development Corporation
- Rural Industries Research and Development Corporation
- Sugar Research and Development Corporation
- Wine Australia Corporation (Wine Australia)

Attorney-General's
- Australian Government Solicitor [M] Ⓡ

Broadband, Communications and the Digital Economy: 3
- Australian Broadcasting Corporation [M]
- Australian Postal Corporation [M]
- Special Broadcasting Service Corporation [M]

Defence: 7
- Army and Air Force Canteen Service (Frontline Defence Services)
- Australian Military Forces Relief Trust Fund (Army Relief Trust Fund)
- Defence Housing Australia [M]
- Royal Australian Air Force Veterans' Residences Trust Fund
- Royal Australian Air Force Welfare Trust Fund
- Royal Australian Navy Central Canteens Board
- Royal Australian Navy Relief Trust Fund

Education, Employment and Workplace Relations: 3
- Australian Curriculum, Assessment and Reporting Authority [||]
- Coal Mining Industry (Long Service Leave Funding) Corporation [M]
- Comcare [M] Ⓟ *

Families, Housing, Community Services and Indigenous Affairs: 8
- Anindilyakwa Land Council
- Central Land Council
- Indigenous Business Australia [M]
- Indigenous Land Corporation
- Northern Land Council
- Tiwi Land Council
- Torres Strait Regional Authority
- Wreck Bay Aboriginal Community Council

Finance and Deregulation: 2
- Albury-Wodonga Development Corporation (Albury-Wodonga Corporation) [M] [||]
- Commonwealth Superannuation Corporation

Foreign Affairs and Trade
- Export Finance and Insurance Corporation [M] Ⓟ ^

Health and Ageing: 5
- Australian Institute of Health and Welfare Ⓟ *
- Food Standards Australia New Zealand [||]
- Health Workforce Australia [||]
- Private Health Insurance Administration Council
- Australian Commission on Safety and Quality in Health Care [||]

Human Services
- Australian Hearing Services (Australian Hearing) [M]

Industry, Innovation, Science, Research and Tertiary Education: 5
- Australian Institute of Aboriginal and Torres Strait Islander Studies
- Australian Institute of Marine Science Ⓟ [||]
- Australian National University
- Australian Nuclear Science and Technology Organisation [M] Ⓟ
- Commonwealth Scientific and Industrial Research Organisation [M] Ⓟ

Infrastructure and Transport: 4
- Airservices Australia [M]
- Australian Maritime Safety Authority [M]
- Civil Aviation Safety Authority [M]
- National Transport Commission [||] *

Regional Australia, Local Government, Arts and Sport: 9
- Australia Council
- Australian Film, Television and Radio School Ⓟ
- Australian National Maritime Museum Ⓟ
- Australian Sports Commission (Australian Institute of Sport) [M]
- National Film and Sound Archive of Australia
- National Gallery of Australia [M] Ⓟ
- National Library of Australia [M]
- National Museum of Australia [M] Ⓟ
- Screen Australia *

Resources, Energy and Tourism
- Tourism Australia [M]

Sustainability, Environment, Water, Population and Communities: 2 #
- Director of National Parks Ⓟ Ⓡ
- Sydney Harbour Federation Trust Ⓟ [||]

Treasury: 2
- Australian Reinsurance Pool Corporation [M]
- Reserve Bank of Australia [M] Ⓟ

Veterans' Affairs
- Australian War Memorial [M] Ⓟ

#1 statutory corporation is subject only to certain CAC Act provisions

Sustainability, Environment, Water, Population and Communities
- NEPC Service Corporation * [||]
- Sections 9, 18, 20 and Schedule 1

22 Commonwealth companies under the CAC Act
(ie. the Commonwealth controls the company)

14 limited by guarantee — Corporations Act 2001

Climate Change and Energy Efficiency
- Low Carbon Australia Limited

Defence: 3
- AAF Company
- Australian Strategic Policy Institute Limited
- RAAF Welfare Recreational Company

Education, Employment and Workplace Relations
- Australian Institute for Teaching and School Leadership Limited [||]

Families, Housing, Community Services and Indigenous Affairs
- Aboriginal Hostels Limited Σ

Health and Ageing: 2
- Aged Care Standards and Accreditation Agency Ltd Ⓟ
- General Practice Education and Training Limited

Industry, Innovation, Science, Research and Tertiary Education
- Australian Learning and Teaching Council Limited

Prime Minister and Cabinet
- National Australia Day Council Limited

Regional Australia, Local Government, Arts and Sport: 4
- Australia Business Arts Foundation Ltd
- Australian Sports Foundation Limited Σ
- Bundanon Trust

Resources, Energy and Tourism
- Australian Solar Institute Limited

8 limited by shares — Corporations Act 2001

Broadband, Communications and the Digital Economy
- NBN Co Limited [M] Σ

Families, Housing, Community Services and Indigenous Affairs
- Outback Stores Pty Ltd

Finance and Deregulation: 3
- Australian River Co. Limited
- ASC Pty Ltd [M]
- Medibank Private Limited [M]

Industry, Innovation, Science, Research and Tertiary Education
- IIF Investments Pty Limited

Infrastructure and Transport
- Australian Rail Track Corporation Limited [M]

Treasury
- HIH Claims Support Limited

---

14 bodies encompass a Statutory Agency under the *Public Service Act 1999* (PS Act). These comprise a Commonwealth company and 13 Commonwealth authorities, with 4 marked * as they can engage personnel under their enabling Act along with the PS Act. # There is 1 statutory corporation, subject only to certain CAC Act provisions, that is a Statutory Agency under the PS Act and can employ its own staff (*).

7 Commonwealth authorities are established by regulations; comprising 5 of the 6 research and development corporations, plus both the Army and Air Force Canteen Service and the Royal Australian Navy Central Canteens Board.

2 Commonwealth companies are being wound up.

3 Commonwealth authorities and 4 Commonwealth companies are also government business enterprises (GBEs) under section 5 of the CAC Act.

2 Commonwealth authorities are exempt from being notified of general policies of the Australian Government, under sections 28 and 48A of the CAC Act.

1 Commonwealth authority is partially exempt from ss 28 and 48A of the CAC Act.

1 Commonwealth authority is a statutory marketing authority (SMA) (*Wine Australia Corporation (Wine Australia)*).

69 General Government Sector (GGS) bodies. The National Interest Account is also classified as GGS, but is administered by the Export Finance and Insurance Corporation (EFIC) ^ which is a Public Financial Corporation.

9 Public Non-financial Corporations (PNFC).

5 Public Financial Corporations (PFC). ^ EFIC also administers the National Interest Account, which is classified as GGS.

2 Unclassified bodies (plus there is 1 statutory corporation # which is unclassified and subject only to certain CAC Act provisions).

[M] 28 CAC Act bodies are material entities (comprising 99% of revenues, expenses, assets and liabilities). 24 are Commonwealth authorities and 4 are Commonwealth companies, limited by shares.

Ⓟ 16 Commonwealth authorities and 1 company are also subject to section 47A of the CAC Act, which allows for directions on procurement matters.

[||] 8 Commonwealth authorities, 1 Commonwealth company and 1 statutory corporation are inter-jurisdictional in nature, e.g. involving the States or Territories or New Zealand in the governance structure or establishment.

Σ 4 Commonwealth companies are mentioned in statute.

Ⓡ 3 Commonwealth authorities have a single person at their apex, rather than a multi-member board.

1 statutory corporation is only subject to the provisions of the CAC Act mentioned beneath its entry.

Appendix 3: The Stages in a Good Appointment Process

(1) *Preparation — the process and vacancy profile.* The first step is to agree on a process and timeline for the appointment. After the process has been agreed, the board should carry out an assessment of its current skills and expertise so as to identify gaps that need to be filled. The assessment would need to consider required expertise in line with the current and emerging priorities of the board. It would also need to consider personal qualities that are required for board members generally. Following this process, selection criteria for a specific vacancy or vacancies would be drawn up in line with the criteria that has been set for board membership as a whole.

(2) *Locating suitable candidates.* Suitable candidates who meet the position profile (or selection criteria) need to be located and encouraged to apply in accordance with the agreed appointment process. To promote transparency and diversity, this would typically involve the publication of a job advertisement. For certain appointments, there may also be a need to target particular individuals on the recommendation of ministers, departments, professional recruiters and other relevant organisations. An important part of this stage in the process is the provision of information to potential candidates. Under the *Code of Practice for Ministerial Appointments to Public Bodies* for England and Wales, for example, information packs must be sent to all applicants. These packs must contain an application form, a role description and position profile, an indication of the required time commitment, remuneration details, information on the organisation and a complaints leaflet on the commissioner for public appointment's complaints procedure (OCPA 2005b: 30).

(3) *Assessing and vetting potential candidates.* After suitable candidates have been identified, a selection committee needs to assess candidates against the selection criteria. The candidates' qualifications and prior experience also need to be verified and an understanding gained of the extent of the candidates' commitment to fulfilling the responsibilities of the position (i.e. probity check). Part of this process involves the evaluation of potential conflicts of interest.

(4) *Selection and appointment.* This stage in the process usually involves the selection of a candidate from a shortlist in accordance with relevant statutory and customary requirements. At the federal government level, this often involves a decision being made by a minister after consultation with the prime minister, Cabinet and other relevant individuals. Whatever processes are followed, they need to comply with any pre-determined, merit-based procedures and all applicable legal requirements.

(5) *Audit*. A less common element of assessment processes is auditing, whereby an internal or external group reviews the documentation that has been kept throughout the assessment so as to determine how appointments have been made. As discussed, the *Code of Practice* for England and Wales now dictates that regular audits be conducted on appointments that are made by organisations that fall within the remit of the Commissioner for Public Appointments. No such process currently applies in Australia, although it offers a number of potential advantages, including greater rigor and transparency, which can help to promote public confidence in public sector boards and appointment processes.

References

AAP 2011, 'Shorten Revives ATO Advisory Board Plan', *Sydney Morning Herald*, 5 October.

ABC 2006, '"Public Service" to Blame for Immigration Failures', 8 September, *ABC News Online*, <http://www.abc.net.au/news/2006-09-08/public-service-to-blame-for-immigration-failures/1258456>.

Abelson, J. and Gauvin, F-P. 2006, *Assessing the Impacts of Public Participation: Concepts, Evidence and Policy Implications: Research Report 06*, Canadian Policy Research Networks, Ottawa.

Abetz, E. 2003a, 'Minister's View: Corporate Governance Requires Vigilance and Constant Review', *Federal Risk Manager*, 14.

—2003b, 'The Role of Corporate Governance in Improving Transparency and Accountability in the Public Sector', speech given at the IQPC Implementing, Managing and Evaluating Corporate Governance in the Public Sector Conference, Sydney.

Adlam, N. and Gartrell, A. 2007, 'Martial Law — Howard Mobilizes Cops, Military as he Declares "National Emergency"', *NT News*, 22 June.

AFMA (Australian Fisheries Management Authority) 2006, *Fisheries Administration Paper Series No. 4 — Corporate Governance*, Commonwealth of Australia, Canberra.

AGRAGA (Advisory Group on the Reform of Australian Government Administration) 2009, *Reform of Australian Government Administration: Building the World's Best Public Service*, Commonwealth of Australia, Canberra.

—2010, *Ahead of the Game: Blueprint for the Reform of Australian Government Administration*, Commonwealth of Australia, Canberra.

Ahn, B-M., Halligan, J. and Wilks, S. 2002, *Reforming Public and Corporate Governance: Management and the Market in Australia, Britain and Korea*, Edward Elgar, London.

Albanese, A. (Minister for Infrastructure and Transport) 2010, 'National Broadcasting Legislation Amendment Bill, Second Reading', speech to the House of Representatives, 30 September.

Alford, J. 2002, 'The Necessity and Difficulty of Trust in Partnerships between Government and Non-government Organisations', paper presented to the International Political Science Association, Structure and Organisation of Government Research, Melbourne, June.

Allen, G. 2006, 'The Evolving Government–Community Paradigm: Challenges for the Public Sector', paper presented to the Governments and Communities in Partnership Conference, Melbourne, September.

Althaus, C. and Wanna, J. 2008, 'The Institutionalisation of Leadership in the Australian Public Service' in P. t' Hart and J. Uhr (eds), *Public Leadership: Perspectives and Practices*, ANU E Press, Canberra.

ANAO (Australian National Audit Office) 1999, *Principles and Better Practices: Corporate Governance in Commonwealth Authorities and Companies — Discussion Paper*, Commonwealth of Australia, Canberra.

— 2003a, *Better Practice Guide: Conflicts of Personal Interest and Conflicts of Role*, guidance paper no. 6, Commonwealth of Australia, Canberra.

— 2003b, *Better Practice Guide: CAC Boards*, guidance paper no. 3, Commonwealth of Australia, Canberra.

— 2003c, *Public Sector Governance: Better Practice Guide*, Commonwealth of Australia, Canberra.

— 2004, *Audit Report No. 6 2004–05: Performance Management in the Australian Public Service*, Commonwealth of Australia, Canberra.

— 2005, *Public Sector Audit Committees: Having the Right People is the Key, Better Practice Guide*, Commonwealth of Australia, Canberra.

— 2007, *Whole of Government Indigenous Service Delivery Arrangements*, audit report no. 10, 2007–08, Commonwealth of Australia, Canberra.

— 2010, *Audit Report No. 9 2010–11: Green Loans Program: Department of the Environment, Water, Heritage and the Arts; Department of Climate Change and Energy Efficiency*, Commonwealth of Australia, Canberra.

— 2011, *Development and Implementation of Key Performance Indicators to Support the Outcomes and Programs Framework, Audit Report No. 5 2011–12*, Commonwealth of Australia, Canberra.

— and CPA Australia 2008, *Monitoring and Reporting Financial and Non-financial Performance of Australian Government Organisations, ARC Project on Corporate Governance, Issue Paper No. 5*, Commonwealth of Australia, Canberra.

— and Department of the Prime Minister and Cabinet 2006, *Implementation of Programme and Policy Initiatives: Making Implementation Matter, Better Practice Guide*, Commonwealth of Australia, Canberra.

APSC (Australian Public Service Commission) 2004, *State of the Service Report 2003–04*, Commonwealth of Australia, Canberra.

— 2005, *State of the Service Report 2004–05*, Commonwealth of Australia, Canberra.

— 2006, *Supporting Ministers, Upholding the Values — A Good Practice Guide*, Commonwealth of Australia, Canberra.

— 2007a, *Agency Health: Monitoring Agency Health and Improving Performance*, Commonwealth of Australia, Canberra.

— 2007b, *Tackling Wicked Problems: A Public Policy Perspective*, Commonwealth of Australia, Canberra.

— 2007c, *Building Better Governance*, Commonwealth of Australia, Canberra.

— 2007d, *State of the Service Report 2006–07*, Commonwealth of Australia, Canberra.

— 2008, *State of the Service Report 2007–08*, Commonwealth of Australia, Canberra.

— 2009a, *Merit and Transparency: Merit-based Selection of APS Agency Heads and Statutory Office Holders*, Commonwealth of Australia, Canberra.

— 2009b, *Contemporary Government Challenges: Delivering Performance and Accountability*, Commonwealth of Australia, Canberra.

— 2009c, *State of the Service Report 2008–09*, Commonwealth of Australia, Canberra.

— 2010a, *State of the Service Report 2009–10*, Commonwealth of Australia, Canberra.

— 2010b, *Case Study: Australia's New Cooperative Federal Financial Agreement: Focusing on Better Outcomes for Citizens*, Commonwealth of Australia, Canberra.

Arnstein, S. 1969, 'A Ladder of Citizen Participation', *Journal of the American Institute of Planners*, 35(4).

ASX Corporate Governance Council 2003, *Principles of Good Corporate Governance and Best Practice Recommendations*, Australian Stock Exchange Lt., Sydney.

Aucoin, P. 1990 'Administrative Reform in Public Management: Paradigms, Principles Paradoxes and Pendulums', *Governance*, 3(2).

— and Goodyear-Grant, E. 2002, 'Designing a Merit-based Process for Appointing Boards of ABCs: Lessons from the Nova Scotia Reform Experience', *Canadian Public Administration*, 45(3).

Auditor General of Canada 1999, 'Collaborative Arrangements — Issues for the Federal Government' (chapter 5, April) and 'Involving Others in Governing — Accountability at Risk' (chapter 23, November), in *Report of the Auditor-General 1999*, Minister of Public Works and Government Services Canada, Ottawa.

Austin, B. 2010 in J. Eyers, 'Getting the Blame Game Right', *Australian Financial Review*, 2 June.

Austin, The Hon. R. 2010, *The McPherson Lecture Series: Three Lectures on the Roles and Duties of Australian Company Directors*, University of Queensland Press, Brisbane.

— 2011, 'Directors' Duties after James Hardie and Centro', speech given at the Supreme Court of Victoria Commercial Law Conference, Melbourne.

Australian Government 2008, *One Year Progress Report*, Commonwealth of Australia, Canberra.

— 2010, *Government Response to the Report of the Government 2.0 Taskforce: Engage: Getting on with Government 2.0*, Commonwealth of Australia, Canberra.

Australian Labor Party (ALP) 2004, 'Our Arts, Culture and Heritage', in *National Platform and Constitution 2004*, Canberra.

ASX (Australian Securities Exchange) Corporate Governance Council 2010, *Corporate Governance Principles and Recommendations with 2010 Amendments*, Australian Securities Exchange, Sydney.

Barker, G. 2007, 'The Public Service', in C. Hamilton and S. Maddison (eds), *Silencing Dissent*, Allen & Unwin, Sydney.

Barker, L. 2004, *Building Effective Boards: Enhancing the Effectiveness of Independent Boards in Executive Non-departmental Public Bodies*, Her Majesty's Stationary Office, London.

Barrett, P. 1996, 'Managing Risk as Part of Good Management: An ANAO Perspective', speech given at the launch of MAB–MIAC Report No. 22, Canberra.

— 1997, 'Corporate Governance and Accountability for Performance', speech given at Joint Seminar by IPAA and ASCPA.

— 2000, 'What's New in Corporate Governance?', speech given to CPA Australia's Annual Congress, Adelaide.

— 2002a, 'Expectation, and Perception, of Better Practice: Corporate Governance in the Public Sector from an Audit Perspective', speech given to CPA Australia's Government Business Symposium, Melbourne.

— 2002b, 'Achieving Better Practice Corporate Governance in the Public Sector', speech given to the International Quality & Productivity Centre Seminar, Achieving Better Practice, Corporate Governance in the Public Sector, 26 June.

— 2003, *Better Practice Public Sector Governance*, National Institute for Governance, Canberra.

Bartos, S. 2008, 'When Integrity Breaks Down: The Australian Wheat Board example', in B. Head, A.J. Brown and C. Connors (eds), *Promoting Integrity: Evaluating and Improving Public Institutions*, Ashgate, Farnham.

Bayne, P. 1999, 'The Court, the Parliament and the Government — Reflections on the Scope of Judicial Review', *Federal Law Review*.

— 1991, 'The Court, the Parliament and the Government, Reflections on the Scope of Judicial Review' (1991) 20 (1) Federal Law Review 1, 17.

Bell, S. and Hindmoor, A. 2009, *Rethinking Governance: The Centrality of the State in Modern Society*, Cambridge University Press, Melbourne.

Bhagat, S. and Black, B. 2002, 'The Non-correlation between Board Independence and Long-term Firm Performance', *Journal of Corporation Law*, 27.

Bingham, L.B., Nabatchi, T. and O'Leary, R.O. 2005, 'The New Governance Practices and Processes for Stakeholder and Citizen Participation in the Work of Government', *Public Administration Review*, 65(5).

Bishop, P. and Davis, G. 2002, 'Mapping Public Participation in Policy Choices', *Australian Journal of Public Administration*, 61(1).

Blacher, Y. and Adams, D. 2007, 'Working Together for Stronger Victorian Communities' in S. Parker and N. Gallagher (eds), *The Collaborative State: How Working Together can Transform Public Services*, Demos, London.

Blackman, D., Buick, F., Halligan, J., O'Flynn, J. and Marsh, I. 2010, 'Australian Experiences with Whole of Government: Constraints and Paradoxes in Practice', paper presented to Panel Track 32, 'Working Across Boundaries: Barriers, Enablers, Tensions and Puzzles', IRSPM Conference, University of Bern, Switzerland, April 9.

Blind, P. 2006, 'Building Trust: Government in the Twenty First Century: Review of Literature and Emerging Issues', background paper for 7th Global Forum on Reinventing Government, Vienna, 26–29 June 2007.

Bond, S., De Vera, J., Makoriws, S., Ong-Reyes, M.C., Simpson, J.B. and Zoo, J. 2007, *Institutionalizing Civic Engagement for Building Trust: The Case of the Economic and Social Councils, On-Line Network in Public Administration and Finance*, United Nations, New York.

Botterill, L. and McNaughton, A. 2008, 'Laying the Foundations for the Wheat Scandal: UN Sanctions, Private Actors and the Cole Inquiry', *Australian Journal of Political Science*, 43(4).

Bottomley, S. 1994, 'Regulating Government-owned Corporations: A Review of the Issues', *Australian Journal of Public Administration*, 53(4).

— 1997, 'From Contractualism to Constitutionalism: A Framework for Corporate Governance', *Sydney Law Review*, 19.

— 2000, 'Government Business Enterprises and Public Accountability through Parliament', Research Paper 18 1999–2000, Commonwealth Parliamentary Library, Canberra.

Bouckaert, G. and Halligan, J. 2006, 'Performance: Its Measurement, Management, and Policy' in B.G. Peters and J. Pierre (eds), *Handbook of Public Policy*, Sage, London.

— 2008, *Managing Performance: International Comparisons*, Routledge, London.

Bouckaert, G., Peters, B.G. and Verhoest, K. 2010, *The Coordination of Public Sector Organizations: Shifting Patterns of Public Management*, Palgrave Macmillan, Basingstoke.

Bourgon, J. 2007a, 'Responsive, Responsible and Respected Government: Towards a New Public Administration Theory', *International Review of Administrative Sciences*, 73(1).

— 2007b, 'Citizen Expectations and Trust in the State', speech to Plenary Session 1, 7th Global Forum on Reinventing Government: Building Trust in Government, United Nations, Vienna, June 26.

— 2008, 'The Future of Public Service: A Search for a New Balance', *Australian Journal of Public Administration*, 67(4).

— 2011, *A New Synthesis of Public Administration: Serving in the 21st Century*, McGill-Queen's University Press, Montreal.

Bovens, M. and P. 't Hart 1996, *Understanding Policy Fiascoes*, Transaction Publishers, New Brunswick, NJ.

Bowen, C. (Minister for Financial Services and Superannuation) 2009, 'Service Delivery Reform: Designing a System that Works for You', address to the National Press Club, Canberra, 16 December.

Boxelaar, L., Paine, M. and Beilin, R. 2006, 'Community Engagement and Public Administration: Of Silos, Overlays and Technologies of Government', *Australian Journal of Public Administration*, 65(1).

Bradley, M. et al 1999, 'The Purposes and Accountability of the Corporation in Contemporary Society: Corporate Governance at a Crossroad', 62 *Law and Contemporary Problems*, 9.

Braithwaite, J., and Drahos, P. 2000, *Global Business Regulation*, Cambridge University Press.

Braithwaite, V. and Levi, M. (eds) 2003, *Trust and Governance*, Russell Sage Foundation, New York.

BRDO (Board Resourcing and Development Office) 2007, 'Appointment Guidelines — Governing Boards and Other Public Sector Organizations', British Columbia, Canada, July.

Brans, M. and Vancoppenolle, D. 2005, 'Policy-Making Reforms and Civil Service Systems: An Exploration of Agendas and Consequences' in M. Painter and J. Pierre (eds), *Challenges to State Policy Capacity: Global Trends and Comparative Perspectives*, Palgrave Macmillan, Basingstoke.

Briggs, L. 2009, 'All Those Who Stand and Wait: Putting Citizens at the Centre', *Public Policy*, 4(1).

— and Fisher, R. 2006, 'Fashions and Fads in Public Sector Reform', paper presented to the CAPAM Conference, Sydney, October.

Brooke, V.G. 1993, 'Portfolio Organisation in the Commonwealth Public Sector', Master of Administration thesis, University of Canberra.

Brown, A.J. and Bellamy, J.A. (eds) 2007, *Federalism and Regionalism in Australia: New Approaches, New Institutions?*, ANU E Press, Canberra.

Bryson, J.M. 2004, 'What to do when Stakeholders Matter: Stakeholder Identification and Analysis Techniques', *Public Management Review*, 6(1).

Bryson, J.M., Crosby, B.C. and Stone, M.M. 2006, 'The Design and Implementation of Cross-Sector Collaborations: Propositions from the Literature', *Public Administration Review*, 66(s1).

Burris, S., Drahos, P. and Shearing, C. 2005, 'Nodal Governance', *Australian Journal of Legal Philosophy*, 30.

Cameron, D. and Skinner, G. 2010, *Public Appointments — Awareness, Attitudes and Experiences*, Government Equalities Office, London.

Campbell, C. 1998, 'Conclusion' in C. Campbell and B.G. Peters (eds), *Organizing Governance, Governing Organizations*, University of Pittsburgh Press.

— and Halligan, J. 1993, *Political Leadership in an Age of Constraint: The Australian Experience*, University of Pittsburgh Press.

Cane, P. and McDonald, L. 2009, *Principles of Administrative Law: Legal Regulation of Governance*, Oxford University Press, Melbourne.

Caruana, J. 2010, 'Financial Stability: Ten Questions and about Seven Answers', in C. Kent and M. Robson (eds), *Reserve Bank of Australia 50th Anniversary Symposium, Proceedings of a Conference held in Sydney on 9 February 2010*, Sydney, Reserve Bank of Australia.

Cavaye, J. 2004, 'Governance and Community Engagement: The Australian Experience', in W.R. Lovan, M. Murray and R. Shaffer (eds), *Participatory Governance: Planning, Conflict Mediation and Public Decision-making in Civil Society*, Ashgate, Aldershot.

CCMAU (Crown Company Monitoring Advisory Unit) 2002, *Owner's Expectations Manual*, New Zealand.

CFACG (Committee on the Financial Aspects of Corporate Governance) (Chairman: A. Cadbury) 1992, *Report of the Financial Aspects of Corporate Governance*, Gee and Co Ltd, London.

Charkham, J.P. 1994, *Keeping Good Company: A Study of Corporate Governance in Five Countries*, Oxford University Press.

Chen, P. 2007, *Electronic Engagement: A Guide for Public Sector Managers*, ANU E Press, Canberra.

Chhotray, V. and Stoker, G. 2009, *Governance Theory and Practice: A Cross-Disciplinary Approach*, Palgrave Macmillan, Basingstoke.

Christensen, T. and Laegreid, P. (eds) 2006, *Autonomy and Regulation: Coping with Agencies in the Modern State*, Edward Elgar, Cheltenham.

Cioffi, J. and Cohen, S. 2000, 'The State, Law and Corporate Governance: The Advantage of Forwardness', in S. Cohen and G. Boyd (eds), *Corporate Governance and Globalization: Long Range Planning Issues*, Edward Elgar, Cheltenham.

CIPFA (Chartered Institute of Public Finance and Accountancy in the United Kingdom) 1995, *Corporate Governance: A Framework for Public Service Bodies*, London.

COAG (Council of Australian Governments) 2002, *COAG Communique*, 5 April.

COAG Reform Council 2011, *Seamless National Economy: Report on Performance*, Report to the Council of Australian Governments, Sydney, 23 December.

Cohen, D. and Roberts, A. 2012, 'A New Age of Uncertainty', *Governance*, 25(1).

Cole, S. 2002, 'Developing Trends in Corporate Governance and Director Duties', paper presented at the IQPC Conference on Performance Measures for Corporate Governance, Sydney, 25–26 February.

Cole, T.R.H. (Commissioner) 2006, *Report of the Inquiry into Certain Australian Companies in Relation to the UN Oil-for-Food Programme Vols. 1–4*, Commonwealth of Australia, Canberra.

Collier, B. and Pitkin, S. (eds) 1999, *Corporatisation and Privatisation in Australia*, CCH, Sydney.

Committee on Standards in Public Life 1995, *Standards in Public Life: First Report of the Committee on Standards in Public Life*, Her Majesty's Stationary Office, London.

— 2005, *Getting the Balance Right — Implementing Standards of Conduct in Public Life: Tenth Report of the Committee on Standards in Public Life*, Her Majesty's Stationary Office, London.

Commonwealth Ombudsman 2005, *Inquiry into the Circumstances of the Vivian Alvarez Matter*, Commonwealth Ombudsman, Canberra.

— 2007, *Lessons for Public Administration: Ombudsman Investigation of Referred Immigration Cases*, Commonwealth Ombudsman, Canberra.

Conroy, S. (Minister for Broadband, Communications and the Digital Economy) 2008, 'Measures to Ensure Strong and Independent National Broadcasters', media release, 16 October.

Considine, M. and Painter, M. (eds) 1997, *Managerialism: The Great Debate*, Melbourne University Press.

Cornish, S. 2010, *The Evolution of Central Banking in Australia*, Reserve Bank of Australia, Sydney.

CPA Australia 2005, *Excellence in Governance for Local Government*, CPA Australia, Melbourne.

Crean, S. and Tanner, L. 2003, *A Better ABC Board: Labor's Policy on the ABC Board Appointment Process*, Parliament of Australia, Canberra.

Curtain, R. 2001, 'The Australian Public Policy Network: Promoting New Approaches to Public Policy', *Canberra Bulletin of Public Administration*, 102.

— 2004, 'Engaging Citizens to Solve Major Public Policy Challenges' in H.K. Colebatch (ed.), *Beyond the Policy Cycle: The Policy Process in Australia*, Allen & Unwin, Sydney.

Dahlström, C., Peters, B.G. and Pierre, J. (eds) 2011, *Steering from the Centre: Strengthening Political Control in Western Democracies*, University of Toronto Press.

Davis, G. 2008, 'One Big Conversation: The Australian 2020 Summit', *Australian Journal of Public Administration*, 67(4).

— and Keating, M. 2000, *The Future of Governance*, Allen & Unwin, St Leonards.

Denhardt, J.V. and Denhardt, R.B. 2007, *The New Public Service: Serving, not Steering*, M.E. Sharpe, New York.

DBCDE (Department of Broadband, Communications and the Digital Economy) 2010, 'The Merit-Based Appointment Process', <http://www.dbcde.gov.au/television/abc_and_sbs_board_appointments/the_merit-based_appointment_process>.

Department of Climate Change and Energy Efficiency 2010, *Department of Climate Change and Energy Efficiency's Response to the Hawke Report on the Home Insulation Program and the Faulkner Inquiry into the Green Loans Program*, <http://www.climatechange.gov.au/~/media/publications/energy-efficiency/departmental-response-to-hawke-and-faulkner.pdf>.

Department of Defence 2010, *Incoming Government Brief*, <http://www.defence.gov.au/foi/docs/disclosures/101_1011_igb.pdf>.

DFA (Department of Finance and Administration) 1997, 'Governance Arrangements for Commonwealth Government Business Enterprises', <http://www.finance.gov.au/publications/governance-arrangements/index.html>.

— 2001, *Department of Finance and Administration Annual Report 2000–2001*, Commonwealth of Australia, Canberra.

— 2003, *Policy Guidelines*, Commonwealth of Australia, Canberra.

— 2004, *Annual Report 2003–04*, Commonwealth of Australia, Canberra.

— 2005a, *Financial Management Reference Material No. 2: Governance Arrangements for Australian Government Bodies*, Commonwealth of Australia, Canberra.

— 2005b, *Governance Arrangements for Australian Government Bodies*, Commonwealth of Australia, Canberra.

— 2005c, *Governance Implementation Update (Uhrig Review): The Implementation Process, Guidance Material and the Timeline for Assessments*, Commonwealth of Australia, Canberra.

— 2005d, *List of Australian Government Bodies and Governance Relationships* (as at 31 December 2004), Financial Management Reference Material No. 1, Commonwealth of Australia, Canberra.

— 2007, *Governance Implementation Update (Uhrig Review): Outcomes of the Uhrig Review Process*, Commonwealth of Australia, Canberra.

DFD (Department of Finance and Deregulation) 2009, *List of Australian Government Bodies and Governance Relationships*, 3rd edn (as at 1 October 2009), Financial Management Reference No. 1, Commonwealth of Australia, Canberra.

— 2011a, 'Foundations for Better Government', Issues Paper No. 1, Commonwealth Financial Accountability Review, Australian Government, Canberra.

— 2011b, *Commonwealth Government Business Enterprise: Governance and Oversight Guidelines*, Australian Government, Canberra.

— 2012a, Flipchart of FMA Act Agencies/CAC Bodies, <http://www.finance.gov.au/publications/flipchart/index.html>

— 2012b, *Is Less More: Towards Better Commonwealth Performance*, discussion paper, Commonwealth Financial Accountability Review, Australian Government, Canberra.

Department of Human Resources 2005, *Annual Report 2004–2005*, Commonwealth of Australia, Canberra.

Dobell, R. and Bernier, L. 1997, 'Citizen Centered Governance: Implications for Inter-governmental Canada' in R. Ford and D. Zussman (eds), *Alternative Service Delivery: Sharing Governance in Canada*, IPAC/KPMG, Toronto.

Dovers, S. 2010, 'Institutional Change and Water Policy', unpublished background paper prepared for the National Water Commission, April.

Dunn, D.D. 1997, *Politics and Administration at the Top: Lessons from Down Under*, University of Pittsburgh Press.

Dutil, P., Howard, C., Langford, J. and Roy, J. 2010, *The Service State: Rhetoric, Reality and Promise*, University of Ottawa Press.

Dworkin, R. 2011, *Justice for Hedgehogs*, The Belnap Press of Harvard University Press, Cambridge, Massachusetts.

Edwards, M. 2002, 'Public Sector Governance — Future Issues for Australia', *Australian Journal of Public Administration*, 61(2).

— 2003, 'Participatory Governance', *Canberra Bulletin of Public Administration*, 107.

— 2006a, 'Corporate Governance in the Public Sector, Lessons from the Research, Some Perceptions on Appointment Processes to Public Sector Bodies', paper presented at Corporate Governance in the Public Sector — from Theory to Practice Conference, Canberra, March.

— 2006b, *Appointments to Public Sector Boards in Australia: A Comparative Assessment*, issues paper no. 3, ARC Corporate Governance Project, University of Canberra.

— 2008, *Participatory Governance*, issues paper no. 6, ARC Corporate Governance Project, University of Canberra.

— 2011, *Shared Accountability in Service Delivery: Concepts, Principles and the Australian Experience*, paper presented at the UN Committee of Experts on Public Administration (CEPA) Meeting, Vienna, July.

— 2012, 'Time to fix Future Fund Process', *Australian Financial Review*, 15 March.

— and Clough, R. 2005, *Corporate Governance and Performance: An Exploration of the Connection in a Public Sector Context*, issues paper no. 1, ARC Corporate Governance Project, University of Canberra.

— and Langford, J. (eds) 2002, *New Players, Partners and Processes: A Public Sector Without Boundaries?*, National Institute for Governance, University of Canberra and University of Victoria, British Columbia.

— Nicoll, G. and Seth-Purdie, R. 2003, *Conflicts and Tensions in Commonwealth Public Sector Boards*, National Institute for Governance, University of Canberra.

Farrar, J. 2005, *Corporate Governance: Theories, Principles and Practice*, 2nd edn, Oxford University Press, Melbourne.

— 2008, *Corporate Governance: Theories, Principles and Practice*, 3rd edn, Oxford University Press, Melbourne.

— 2010, 'The Global Financial Crisis and the Governance of Financial Institutions', *Australian Journal of Corporate Law*, 24(3).

Faulkner, P. 2010, *Independent Inquiry — Green Loans Program: Review of Procurement Processes and Contractual Arrangements*, Commonwealth of Australia, Canberra.

Finn, P. 1993, *Integrity in Government. Second Report, Abuse of Official Trust: Conflict of Interest and Related Matters*, Australian National University, Canberra.

— 1994, 'Public Trust and Public Accountability', *Griffith Law Review*, 3(2).

— 1995, 'A Sovereign People, a Public Trust', in P. Finn (ed.), *Essays On Law and Government (Volume 1)*, Law Book Company Ltd, Sydney.

— 2010, 'Public Trusts, Public Fiduciaries', *Federal Law Review*, 38.

Finnis, J. 2006, 'On "Public Reason"', *Notre Dame Legal Studies Paper*, no. 06–37.

Flinders, M. 2009, 'The Politics of Patronage in the United Kingdom: Shrinking Reach and Diluted Permeation', *Governance*, 22(4).

— 2010, 'The Politics of Public Appointments', *Guardian*, 31 March.

Frederickson, D.G. and Frederickson, H.G. 2006, *Measuring the Performance of the Hollow State*, Georgetown University Press, Washington D.C.

Freebairn, P. 2011, 'RBA Puts Man on Ground in Beijing', *Australian Financial Review*, 1–2 October.

French, R. 2009, 'International Law and Australian Domestic Law', speech to the Supreme Court of New South Wales Annual Conference, Hunter Valley, 21 August.

Fung, A. 2006, 'Varieties of Participation in Complex Governance', *Public Administration Review*, 66(s1).

— 2009, 'Participate, but do so Pragmatically' in OECD 2009, *Focus on Citizens*, OECD, Paris.

Funnell, W. 2001, *Government By Fiat: The Retreat From Responsibility*, University of New South Wales Press, Sydney.

Gath, S. 2004, *Company Law and Governance Update: Focus on Public Sector*, Blake Dawson Waldron, Canberra.

— 2005, 'Good Governance and Whole of Government: The Challenge of Connecting Government', *Public Administration Today*, July–Sept, 18.

— 2006, 'The Peculiar Case of the Government Director', speech to the Corporate Governance in the Public Sector — from Theory to Practice Conference, Canberra, March.

Gaymer, J. 2007, *Appoint the Best of the Best in Public Life — the British Experience*, Portugal Institute of Corporate Governance, Lisbon.

Gillard, J. 2010, 'The Measure of Progress is in the Years', speech to the Rotary Club of Adelaide, Adelaide, 10 November.

— 2011, Garran Oration, speech given at the Institute of Public Administration Annual Conference, Hobart, 26 August.

Gourley, P. 2010, 'The Advocate? Henry's Public Talk Walks Perilously Close to Politics', Public Sector Informant, *The Canberra Times*, 1 June, 4–5.

Government of Western Australia 2010, *The Principles of Good Corporate Governance for West Australian Public Sector Boards and Committees*, Public Sector Commission.

Grantham, R. 2005, 'The Governance of Government Owned Corporations', *Companies and Securities Law Journal*, 23, 181–94.

Grattan, M. 2007, 'Silence of the Service', *Age*, 31 August.

Gray, W. 2006, *COAG Trial Evaluation: Wadeye, Northern Territory: An Independent Evaluation*, Council of Australian Governments, Australia.

— and Sanders, W.G. 2006, *Views from the Top of the 'Quiet Revolution': Secretarial Perspectives on the New Arrangements in Indigenous Affairs*, discussion paper no. 282/2006, Centre For Aboriginal Economic Policy Research, Australian National University, Canberra.

Gregory, R.J. 1998, 'Political Responsibility for Bureaucratic Incompetence: Tragedy at Cave Creek', *Public Administration*, 76(3).

Gutmann, A. and Thompson, D. 2004, *Why Deliberative Democracy?*, Princeton University Press.

Halligan, J. 1987, 'Reorganising Australian Government Departments 1987', *Canberra Bulletin of Public Administration*, 52.

— 1997, 'New Public Sector Models: Reform in Australia and New Zealand', in J-E. Lane (ed.), *Public Sector Reform: Rationale, Trends and Problems*, Sage, London.

— 2001, 'Politicians, Bureaucrats and Public Sector Reform in Australia and New Zealand', in B.G Peters and J. Pierre (eds), *Politicians, Bureaucrats and Administrative Reform*, Routledge, London.

— 2003a, 'Public Sector Reform and Evaluation in Australia and New Zealand', in H. Wollmann (ed.), *Evaluation in Public Sector Reforms*, Edward Elgar, Cheltenham.

— 2003b 'Australian Public Service: Redefining Boundaries', in J. Halligan (ed.) *Civil Service Systems in Anglo-American Countries*, Edward Elgar, Cheltenham.

— 2006, 'The Reassertion of the Centre in a First Generation NPM System', in T. Christensen and P. Lægreid (eds), *Autonomy and Regulation: Coping with Agencies in the Modern State*, Edward Elgar, Cheltenham.

— 2007a, 'Anglo-American Systems: Easy Diffusion', in J.C.N. Raadschelders, T.A.J. Toonen and F.M. Van der Meer (eds), *The Civil Service in the 21st Century, Comparative Perspectives*, Palgrave Macmillan, Basingstoke.

— 2007b, 'Reintegrating Government in Third Generation Reforms of Australia and New Zealand', *Public Policy and Administration*, 22(2).

— 2008a, 'The Search for Balance and Effectiveness in the Australian Public Service', in C. Aulich and R. Wettenhall (eds), *Howard's Fourth Government: Australian Commonwealth Administration 2004–2007*, University of New South Wales Press, Sydney.

— 2008b, *The Centrelink Experiment: An Innovation in Service Delivery*, Australian National University Press, Canberra.

— 2010a, 'Reforming Management and Management Systems: Impacts and Issues', in P. Ingraham and J. Pierre (eds), *Public Change And Reform: Moving Forward, Looking Back: A Festschrift To Honor B. Guy Peters*, McGill-Queens UP, Montreal & Kingston.

— 2010b, 'Australian Public Service: New Agendas and Reform', in C. Aulich and M. Evans (eds), *The Rudd Government: Australian Commonwealth Administration 2007–2010*, ANU E-Press, Canberra.

— 2010c, 'Shared Accountability for Shared Results', paper presented at the New Synthesis Project's Canada Roundtable, Ottawa, 4–5 May.

— 2010d, 'Post-NPM Responses to Disaggregation through Coordinating Horizontally and Integrating Governance', in Per Laegreid and Koen Verhoest (eds.), *Governance of Public Sector Organizations — Proliferation, Autonomy and Performance*, Basingstoke: Palgrave.

— 2011a, 'The Evolution of Public Service Bargains of Australia's Senior Public Servants', paper presented at the 6th European Consortium for Political Research Conference, Panel 284: The Evolution of Public Service Bargains of Top Civil Servants in State Administration in a Comparative Perspective, University of Iceland, Reykjavik, 25–27 August.

— 2011b, 'The Conundrum of Agencies within Australian Public Sector Reform, Permanent Study Group VI: Governance of Public Sector Organisation, 'Agencies in Crisis? States in Search of Better Coordination and Rationalisation of Agencification', speech given to the 33rd Annual Conference of the European Group of Public Administration, Bucharest, 7–10 September.

— 2011c, 'Central Steering in Australia', in C. Dahlström, B.G. Peters and J. Pierre (eds), *Steering from the Centre: Strengthening Political Control in Western Democracies*, University of Toronto Press.

— Buick, F. and O'Flynn J. 2011, 'Experiments with Joined-Up, Horizontal and Whole-of-Government in Anglophone Countries', in A. Massey (ed.), *International Handbook on Civil Service Systems*, Edward Elgar, Cheltenham.

— and Horrigan, B. 2005, *Reforming Corporate Governance in the Australian Federal Public Sector: From Uhrig to Implementation*, issues paper no. 2, ARC Corporate Governance Project, University of Canberra.

— Miller, R. and Power, J. 2007, *Parliament in the Twenty-first Century: Institutional Reform and Emerging Roles*, Melbourne University Publishing.

— and Power, J. 1992, *Political Management in the 1990s*, Oxford University Press, Melbourne.

— and Sadleir, C. 2011, 'Australian Public Service System', in A. Massey (ed.), *International Handbook on Civil Service Systems*, Edward Elgar, Cheltenham.

— and Tucker, T. 2008, 'Governance Failure in a Department of State: The Case of Immigration in Australia', paper presented at the European Group of Public Administration Conference, Erasmus University, Rotterdam, 3–6 September.

— and Wettenhall, R. 1990, 'Major Changes in the Structure of Government Institutions' in John Power (ed.), *Public Administration in Australia: A Watershed*, Hale & Iremonger, Sydney.

Hamburger, P. 2007, 'Coordination and Leadership at the Centre of the Australian Public Service', in R. Koch and J. Dixon (eds), *Public Governance and Leadership*, Deutscher Universitats-Verlag, Wiesbaden.

't Hart, P. 2010, 'Lifting its Game to Get Ahead: The Canberra Bureaucracy's Reform by Stealth', *Australian Review of Public Affairs*, July.

Hawke, A. 2010, *Review of the Administration of the Home Insulation Program*, Commonwealth of Australia, Canberra.

Hawke, L. 2012, 'Public Sector Performance in Australia — Success or Stagnation?', *International Journal of Productivity and Performance Management*, 61(3).

— and Wanna, J. 2010, 'Australia after Budgetary Reform: A Lapsed Pioneer and Decorative Architect?' in J. Wanna, L. Jensen and J. de Vries (eds), *The Reality of Budgetary Reform in OECD Countries: Trajectories and Consequences*, Edward Elgar, Cheltenham.

Hayward, B., Mortimer, E. and Brunwin, T. 2004, *Survey of Public Attitudes Towards Conduct in Public Life*, Committee on Standards in Public Life, UK Government, United Kingdom.

Head, B. 2006, 'Network-Based Governance — How Effective?', paper presented at Governments and Communities Conference, Centre for Public Policy, University of Melbourne, September.

— 2007, 'Community Engagement: Participation on Whose Terms?', *Australian Journal of Political Science*, 42(3).

— 2010, 'How Can the Public Sector Resolve Complex Issues? Strategies for Steering, Administering and Coping', *Asia-Pacific Journal of Business Administration*, 2(1).

Heracleous, L. 2001, 'What is the Impact of Corporate Governance on Organisational Performance?', *Corporate Governance: An International Review*, 9(3).

Her Majesty's Treasury 2005, *Corporate Governance in Central Government Departments: Code of Good Practice*, Her Majesty's Stationary Office, London.

Henry, K. 2007, 'Treasury's Effectiveness in the Current Environment', speech to Treasury staff, 14 March.

Hewson, J. 2007, 'Governance Needs Fixing', *Australian Financial Review*, 30 March.

Higgs, D. 2002, *Review of the Role and Effectiveness of Non-executive Directors*, Department of Trade and Industry, London.

HIH Royal Commission (The Hon. Justice Owen, Commissioner) 2003, *The Failure of HIH Insurance*, Volume 1, Commonwealth of Australia, Canberra.

HOCPASC (House of Commons Public Administration Select Committee) 2003, *Government by Appointment: Opening up the Patronage State: Fourth Report of Session 2002–03*, vol. 1: HC 165–1, The Stationery Office, London.

— 2008, *Parliament and Public Appointments: Pre-appointment Hearings by Select Committees: Third Report of Session 2007–08: HC 152*, The Stationery Office, London.

Holmes, B. 2011, *Citizens' Engagement in Policymaking and the Design of Public Services*, research paper no. 1, 2011–12, Australian Parliamentary Library, Canberra.

Holmes, M. 1989, 'Corporate Management: A View from the Centre', in G. Davis, P. Weller and C. Lewis (eds), *Corporate Management in Australian Government*, Macmillan, Melbourne.

Hood, A. 1998, 'Public Officials, Government and the Public Trust: Schizophrenia?', *Australian Journal of Public Administration*, 57(1).

Hood, C. 1991, 'A Public Management for All Seasons?', *Public Administration*, 69(1).

Horrigan, B. 2001, 'How do Executive Boards for Public Sector Agencies Differ from Corporate Boards?', *Canberra Bulletin of Public Administration*, 101.

— 2002, 'Fault Lines in the Intersection between Corporate Governance and Social Responsibility', *University of New South Wales Law Journal*, 25.

— 2003, 'Governance, Liability and Immunity of Government Business Enterprises and Their Boards', in M. Whincop (ed.), *From Bureaucracy to Business Enterprise*, Ashgate, Aldershot.

— 2010, *Corporate Social Responsibility in the 21st Century: Debates, Models and Practices Across Government, Law and Business*, Edward Elgar, Cheltenham.

Howard, C. and Seth-Purdie, R. 2005, 'Governance Issues for Public Sector Boards', *Australian Journal of Public Administration*, 64(3).

Howard, J. 1998a, *A Guide on Key Elements of Ministerial Responsibility*, Commonwealth of Australia, Canberra.

— 1998b, 'A Healthy Public Service is a Vital Part of Australia's Democratic System of Government,' *Australian Journal of Public Administration*, 57(1).

— 2002, 'Strategic Leadership for Australia: Policy Directions in a Complex World', speech to the Committee for Economic Development of Australia, 20 November.

IAPP (International Association for Public Participation) 2007, *IAP2 Spectrum of Public Participation*, <http://www.iap2.org/associations/4748/files/spectrum.pdf>.

Inglis, K. 2002, 'Aunty at Seventy: A Health Report on the ABC', speech to the ANU National Institute of Social Sciences at the National Museum of Australia, Canberra, 13 November.

Involve 2005, *People and Participation: How to Put Citizens at the Heart of Decision-making*, London.

Kalokerinos, J. 2007, *Developments in the Role of the Chair in the Private and Public Sectors*, issues paper no. 4, ARC Corporate Governance Project, University of Canberra.

Keane, J. 2009, *The Life and Death of Democracy*, W.W. Norton & Company, New York.

Keasey, K., Thompson, S. and Wright, M. 1997, *Corporate Governance — Economic, Management and Financial Issues*, Oxford University Press.

Keast, R., Mandell, M., Brown, K. and Woolcock, G. 2004, 'Network Structures: Working Differently and Changing Expectations', *Public Administration Review*, 64(3).

Keating, M. and Holmes, M. 1990, 'Australia's Budgetary and Financial Management Reforms', *Governance*, 3(2).

— Wanna, J. and Weller, P. 2000, *Institutions on the Edge? Capacity for Governance*, Allen & Unwin, St Leonards, NSW.

Kent, C. and Robson, M. 2010, 'Introduction', in C. Kent and M. Robson (eds), *Reserve Bank of Australia 50th Anniversary Symposium, Proceedings of a Conference held in Sydney on 9 February 2010*, Reserve Bank of Australia, Sydney.

Kernaghan, K. and Siegel, D. 1987, *Public Administration in Canada*, Methuen, Toronto.

Kerr, P. 2011, 'RBA Board Structure Invokes Debate', *Weekend Australian Financial Review*, 10–11 September.

Kettl, D.F. 2009, *The Next Government of the United States: Why our Institutions Fail Us and How to Fix Them*, W.W. Norton and Company, New York.

Keys, J. 1997, *Getting on Board: A Guide to Recruitment and Induction of Members of Western Australian Government Boards and Committees*, Public Sector Management Office, Ministry of the Premier and Cabinet, Western Australian Government, Perth.

Kickert, W. 1993, 'Complexity, Governance and Dynamics, Explorations of Public Network Management', in J. Kooiman (ed.), *Modern Governance*, Sage, London.

Kirchner, S. 2008, 'A "New Era" for the Reserve Bank?', *Policy*, 24(1).

— 2011, 'Time to Revise RBA Board', *Australian Financial Review*, 7 September.

Knight, C. and Lightowler, C. 2010, 'Reflections of "Knowledge Exchange Professionals" in the Social Sciences: Emerging Opportunities and Challenges for University-based Knowledge Brokers', *Evidence & Policy: A Journal of Research, Debate and Practice*, 6(4).

Kooiman, J. 1999, 'Social Political Governance: Overview, Reflections and Design', *Public Management Review*, 1.

Kooiman, J. 2003, *Governing as Governance*, Sage Publications, London.

Larcker, D., Richardson, S., Tuna, I. 2004, *How Important is Corporate Governance?*, The Wharton School, Philadelphia.

Leblanc, R. and Gillies, J. 2005, *Inside the Boardroom: How Boards Really Work and the Coming Revolution in Corporate Governance*, John Wiley and Sons, Canada.

Lenihan, D. 2009, *Rethinking the Public Policy Process: A Public Engagement Framework*, Public Policy Forum, Ottawa.

Lenihan, D. and Briggs, L. 2010, 'Co-Design: Toward A New Service Vision for Australia?' *Public Administration Today*, January–March.

Lewis, S. 2007, 'Labor Vows to Depoliticise the ABC Board', *Australian*, 5 June.

Lindquist, E. 2001, 'Reconceiving the Centre: Leadership, Strategic Review and Coherence in Public Sector Reform', in Organisation for Economic Co-operation and Development, *Government of the Future*, OECD, Paris.

— 2004, 'Strategy, Capacity and Horizontal Governance: Perspectives from Australia and Canada', *Optimum*, 34(4).

— 2010, 'From Rhetoric to Blueprint: The Moran Review as a Concerted, Comprehensive and Emergent Strategy for Public Service Reform', *Australian Journal of Public Administration*, 69(2).

Lovan, W.R., Murray, M. and Shaffer, R. 2004, *Participatory Governance; Planning, Conflict Mediation and Public Decision-making in Civil Society*, Ashgate, Aldershot.

MAC (Management Advisory Committee) 2001, *Performance Management in the Australian Public Service: A Strategic Framework*, Commonwealth of Australia, Canberra.

— 2004, *Connecting Government: Whole of Government Responses to Australia's Priority Challenges*, Commonwealth of Australia, Canberra.

— 2005, *Working Together: Principles and Practices to Guide the Australian Public Service*, Australian Government, Canberra.

— 2010, *Empowering Change: Fostering Innovation in the Australian Public Service*, Commonwealth of Australia, Canberra.

McCabe, A., Keast, R. and Brown, K. 2006, 'Community Engagement: Towards Community in Governance', paper presented to the Governments and Communities in Partnership Conference, Melbourne, September.

MacDermott, K. 2008, *Whatever Happened to Frank and Fearless? The Impact of New Public Management on the Australian Public Service*, ANU E Press, Canberra.

McKay, K. 2003, 'Two Generations of Performance Evaluation Management Systems in Australia', *Canberra Bulletin of Public Administration*, 110.

— 2004, *Two Generations of Performance Evaluation and Management System in Australia*, ECD Working Paper Series, No. 11, The World Bank Washington, D.C.

McKenzie, N. and Baker, R. 2011, 'RBA Officials Hid Details of Secret Commissions', *Age*, 5 October.

McPhee, I. 2005, 'Outcomes and Outputs: Are We Managing Better as a Result?' speech to the CPA National Public Sector Convention, 20 May.

— 2008a, 'Public Sector Governance — Showing the Way', address to the Australian Institute of Company Directors and The Institute of Internal Auditors — Australia Public Sector Governance Forum, Canberra, 4 September.

— 2008b, 'Accountability for the 21st Century — the Powers and Responsibilities of Commonwealth Auditors-General', paper presented at the 20th Commonwealth Auditors-General Conference, Bermuda, 7 July.

— 2009a, 'Different Perspectives of Public Sector Governance: Asia and Australia', address to the AICD Public Sector Governance Conference, Canberra, 14 October.

— 2009b, 'The Business of Government: Why Public Sector Management Must Evolve', 2009 Brookes Oration, Deakin Business School, Melbourne, 27 August.

MAG (Ministerial Advisory Group) 2002, *Report of the Advisory Group of the Review of the Centre*, State Services Commission, Wellington.

Maiden, M. 2011, 'Reserve Bank Still Not Off the Hook on Securency', *Sydney Morning Herald*, 2 July.

Maley, M. 2000, 'Too Many or Too Few? The Increase in Federal Ministerial Advisers 1972–1999', *Australian Journal of Public Administration*, 59(4).

— 2010, 'Australia', in C. Eichbaum and R. Shaw (eds), *Partisan Appointees and Public Servants: An International Analysis of the Role of the Political Adviser*, Edward Elgar, Cheltenham.

Mandell, M. 2006, 'Do Networks Matter: The Ideals and Realities', paper presented to the Governments and Communities in Partnership Conference, Melbourne, September.

Mant, A. 2007, 'The Triumph of Big Business-think', *The International Journal of Leadership in the Public Services*, 3(1).

Mantziaris, C. 1998, 'Interpreting Ministerial Directions to Statutory Corporations: What Does a Theory of Responsible Government Deliver?', *Federal Law Review*, 26.

Metcalfe, A. 2007, 'Post-Palmer Reform of DIAC and Regulation of the Migration Advice Industry', address to the Inaugural CPD Immigration Law Conference, Melbourne, 9 February.

— 2011, 'Whole-of-government Issues in Policy Making', Presentation to Centre for Defence and Strategic Studies, Canberra, 9 November.

Metcalfe, L. 1994, 'International Policy Co-ordination and Public Management Reform', *International Review of Administrative Sciences*, 60(2).

Miller, R. and Sanders, K. 2006, 'Implementing the Uhrig Templates — A Time to Pause and Get it Right', *Keeping Good Companies*, 26–28 August.

Millstein, I. and MacAvoy, P. 1998, 'The Active Board of Directors and Performance of the Large Publicly Traded Corporation', *Columbia Law Review*, 98.

Minister for Finance and Administration (Senator Nick Minchin) 2004, 'Australian Government Response to Uhrig Report', media release, 12 August.

— 2006, 'Uhrig Review: Progress with Implementation', media release, 5 January.

Minter Ellison 2010, *Directors of Commonwealth Authorities and Companies — Legal Duties & Liabilities (A Guide)*, Australia.

Moran, T. 2008, 'Splicing the Perspectives of the Commonwealth and States into a Workable Federation', speech at the ANZSOG Annual Conference on Federalism, Melbourne, 11–12 September.

— 2009, 'Challenges of Public Sector Reform', speech to Institute of Public Administration Australia, Canberra, 15 July, <http://www.dpmc.gov.au/media/speech_2009_07_15.cfm>.

— 2010a, 'How to Stay Ahead of the Game', presentation to APS staff by the Secretary of Department of the Prime Minister and Cabinet, Canberra, 21 May, <http://www.dpmc.gov.au/reformgovernment/resources/2010-06-19_secretary.cfm>.

— 2010b, 'Citizens, Culture and Leadership', speech to Institute of Public Administration Australia, Canberra, 8 December.

— 2011, The John Paterson Oration 2011, Australia and New Zealand School of Government Annual Conference, 28 July.

Morgan Disney & Associates Pty. Ltd with Tracey Whetnall Consulting and Wis-Wei Consulting Pty Ltd 2006, *Synopsis Review of the COAG Trial Evaluations, Report to the Office of Indigenous Policy Coordination (OIPC)*, <http://www.fahcsia.gov.au/sa/indigenous/pubs/evaluation/coag_trial_site_reports/overiew/Documents/COAG_Trials_Overview.pdf>.

MORI (Market and Opinion Research International) 2005, *Perceptions of the Ministerial Public Appointments Process — Combined Qualitative and Quantitative Report*, Office of the Commissioner for Public Appointments, London.

Moro, G. 2003, 'Governance: A Citizens' Perspective', in OECD, *Open Government: Fostering Dialogue with Civil Society*, OECD, Paris.

Mulgan, G. 2007, *Good and Bad Power: The Ideals and Betrayals of Government*, Penguin Books, London.

Mulgan, R. 1998, 'Politicisation of Senior Appointments in the Australian Public Service', *Australian Journal of Public Administration*, 57(3).

— 2003, *Holding Power to Account: Accountability in Modern Democracies*, Palgrave Macmillan, Basingstoke.

Myners, P. 1995, *Developing a Winning Partnership: How Companies and Institutional Investors are Working Together*, Department of Trade and Industry, London.

Nethercote, J.R. 2010, '"Independent" Board that's Still Within Power's Thrall', *Public Sector Informant*, *Canberra Times*, 2 March.

New South Wales Government 2004, *Guidelines for NSW Board and Committee Members: Appointments and Remuneration*, Sydney.

—— 2008, *Merit Selection Guide for NSW Public Sector Panels: Picking the Best Person for the Job*, NSW Department of Premier and Cabinet, Sydney.

NSW PBRC (New South Wales Public Bodies Review Committee) (Chair: M. Morris) 2006, *Report on Corporate Governance: Follow-Up Review of Performance Audit Report on Corporate Governance*, Parliament of New South Wales, Sydney.

Newman, J. 2002, 'The New Public Management, Modernization and Institutional Change: Disruptions, Disjunctures and Dilemmas', in K. McLaughlin, S.P. Osborne and E. Ferlie (eds), *New Public Management: Current Trends and Future Prospects*, Routledge, London, 76–91.

Nicoll, G. 2001, 'Ownership Structures for the Governance of Companies in the Public and Private Sectors' in National Institute for Governance, *Current Issues in Public Sector Governance*, University of Canberra.

—— 2002, 'New Ownership Structures and the Governance of Australian Corporations', in B-M. Ahn, J. Halligan and S. Wilks, *Reforming Public and Corporate Governance: Management and the Market in Australia, Britain and Korea*, Edward Elgar, London.

NIG (National Institute for Governance) 2004, *Review of Stakeholder Engagement for Planning in the ACT, Report on Consultancy for the ACT Government*, University of Canberra.

Norman, R. and Gregory, R. 2003, 'Paradoxes and Pendulum Swings: Performance Management in New Zealand's Public Sector', *Australian Journal of Public Administration*, 62(4), 35–49.

NZ, SSC (State Services Commission) 2009, *Board Appointment and Induction Guidelines*, revised November, Wellington,

OCPA (Office of the Commissioner for Public Appointments) 2005a, *Internal Research Project Examining the Role and Development of the Office of the Commissioner for Public Appointments*, London.

—— 2005b, *Code of Practice for Ministerial Appointments to Public Bodies*, London.

—— 2009, *Code of Practice for Ministerial Appointments to Public Bodies*, London.

— 2011, *Review of Public Appointments Regulation: Outcome of Consultation*, Commissioner of Public Appointments, London, November.

—2012, *Code of Practice for Ministerial Appointments to Public Bodies*, London.

OCPAS (Office of the Commissioner for Public Appointments in Scotland) 2006, *Code of Practice for Ministerial Appointments to Public Bodies in Scotland*, Edinburgh.

— 2011, *Revised Code of Practice for Ministerial Appointments to Public Bodies in Scotland*, Edinburgh.

OECD (Organisation for Economic Co-operation and Development) 1999, *Principles of Corporate Governance*, Paris.

— 2000, *Government of the Future*, Paris.

— 2001a, *Citizens as Partners: Information, Consultation and Public Participation in Policy Making*, Paris.

— 2001b, *Governance in the 21st Century: Future Studies*, Paris.

— 2002, *Distributed Public Governance: Agencies, Authorities and other Government Bodies*, Paris.

— 2003a, *Open Government: Fostering Dialogue with Civil Society*, Paris.

— 2003b, *The e-Government Imperative*, Paris.

— 2004a, *Principles of Corporate Governance*, Paris.

— 2004b, 'Managing Conflict of Interest in the Public Service', background document to the Forum on Implementing Conflict of Interest Policies in the Public Service, Rio de Janeiro, Brazil, 5–6 May, <http://www.oecd.org/dataoecd/3/46/31571370.pdf>.

— 2005a, *Evaluating Public Participation in Policy Making*, Paris.

— 2005b, *Guidelines for Managing Conflict of Interest in Public Service*, Paris.

— 2005c, *Managing Conflict of Interest in the Public Sector: A Toolkit*, Paris.

— 2006, 'Can Governments be Trusted', *OECD Civil Society Newsletter*, 6.

— 2009a, *Focus on Citizens: Public Engagement and Better Policy and Services*, Paris.

— 2009b, *How Good is Trust? Measuring Trust and its Role for the Progress of Societies*, OECD statistics working paper, Paris.

O'Flynn, J., Buick, F., Blackman, D. and Halligan, J. 2011, 'You Win Some, You Lose Some: Experiments with Joined-up Government', *International Journal of Public Administration*, 34(4).

—— and Wanna, J. (eds) 2008, *Collaborative Governance: A New Era of Public Policy in Australia?*, ANU E Press, Canberra.

OPM (Office for Public Management Ltd) and CIPFA (The Chartered Institute of Public Finance and Accountancy) 2004, *The Good Governance Standard for Public Services*, London.

Orts, E. 2002, 'Corporate Governance, Stakeholder Accountability, and Sustainable Peace', *Vanderbilt Journal of Transnational Law*, 35(2).

Osborne, S.P. 2006, 'The New Public Governance?' *Public Management Review*.

Osborne, S. 2010, *The New Public Governance? Emerging Perspectives on the Theory and Practice of Public Governance*, Routledge, New York.

Osmani S.R. 2007, 'Participatory Governance for Efficiency and Equity: An Overview of Issues and Evidence', paper presented to 7th Global Forum on Reinventing Government, 'Building Trust in Government', Vienna, June.

Painter, M. 1987, *Steering the Modern State*, Sydney University Press.

—— and Carey, B. 1979, *Politics between Departments: The Fragmentation of Executive Control in Australian Government*, University of Queensland Press, St Lucia.

—— and Pierre, J. 2005, 'Unpacking Policy Capacity: Issues and Themes', in M. Painter and J. Pierre (eds), *Challenges to State Policy Capacity: Global Trends and Comparative Perspectives*, Palgrave MacMillan, Basingstoke.

Pal, L.A. 2011, *Frontiers of Governance: The OECD and Global Public Management Reform*, Palgrave Macmillan, Basingstoke.

Palmer, M.J. 2005, *Inquiry into the Circumstances of the Immigration Detention of Cornelia Rau: Report*, Commonwealth of Australia, Canberra.

Parker, S., Paun, A., McClory, J. and Blatchford, K. 2010, *Shaping Up: A Whitehall for the Future*, Institute for Government, London.

Parker, C., Scott, C., Lacey, N. and Braithwaite, J. (eds) 2004, *Regulating Law*, Oxford University Press.

Parkinson, M. 2012, *Investing in the Future: Nurturing Greater Diversity in Treasury's Leadership*, APSC Leader to Leader series, 28 February.

Parliament of Australia 2010, *National Broadcasting Legislation Amendment Bill 2010, Explanatory Memorandum*, Canberra.

Parliament of Australia, Senate Select Committee on the Administration of Indigenous Affairs 2005, *After ATSIC: Life in the Mainstream?*, Commonwealth of Australia, Canberra.

Parnell, S. and Dodd, M. 2010, 'Defence comes Clean on Failures', *Weekend Australian*, 30 October.

Parsons, W. 2004, 'Not just Steering but Weaving: Relevant Knowledge and the Craft of Building Policy Capacity and Coherence', *Australian Journal of Public Administration*, 63(1).

Pechtold, A. 2005, 'Statement by the Chairman', speech to the Public Governance Committee at Ministerial Level, OECD, Rotterdam, 28 November.

Peters, B.G. 2005, 'Policy Instruments and Policy Capacity' in M. Painter and J. Pierre (eds), *Challenges to State Policy Capacity: Global Trends and Comparative Perspectives*, Palgrave Macmillan, Basingstoke.

—— 2006, 'Concepts and Theories of Horizontal Policy Management', in B.G Peters and J. Pierre (eds), *Handbook of Public Policy*, Sage, London.

—— and Pierre, J. 1998, 'Governance without Government? Rethinking Public Administration', *Journal of Public Administration Research and Theory*, 8(2).

—— and Pierre, J. 2000, *Governance, Politics and the Modern State*, Macmillan, London.

Pierre, J and Peters, B. G. 2000, *Governance, Politics and the State*, Palgrave Macmillan, Basingstoke.

Plibersek, T. (Minister for Human Services) 2011, 'Service Delivery Reform — Redesigning What We Do and How We Do It', speech to National Press Club, Canberra, 21 June.

PM&C (Department of the Prime Minister and Cabinet) 2003, *Annual Report 2002–03*, Commonwealth of Australia, Canberra.

—— 2004, *Annual Report 2003–04*, Commonwealth of Australia, Canberra.

—— 2008a, *Annual Report 2007–08*, Commonwealth of Australia, Canberra.

—— 2008b, *Australia 2020 Summit: Final Report*, Commonwealth of Australia, Canberra.

—— 2009a, *Cabinet Handbook: Sixth Edition*, Commonwealth of Australia, Canberra.

—— 2009b, *Federal Executive Council Handbook*, Commonwealth of Australia, Canberra.

—— 2011, *Requirements for Annual Reports for Departments, Executive Agencies and FMA Act Bodies*, <http://www.dpmc.gov.au/guidelines/docs/annual_report_requirements_2010-11_markedup.pdf>.

Podger, A. 2007, 'What Really Happens: Department Secretary Appointments, Contracts and Performance Pay in the Australian Public Service', *Australian Journal of Public Administration*, 66(2).

—— 2009, *The Role of Departmental Secretaries: Personal Reflections on the Breadth of Responsibilities Today*, ANU E Press, Canberra.

Pollitt, C. 1993, *Managerialism and the Public Services*, 2nd edn, Basil Blackwell, London.

—— 2005, 'Ministries and Agencies: Steering, Meddling, Neglect and Dependency', in M. Painter and J. Pierre (eds), *Challenges to State Policy Capacity: Global Trends and Comparative Perspectives*, Palgrave Macmillan, Basingstoke.

—— and Bouckaert, G. 2004, *Public Management Reform: A Comparative Analysis*, 2nd edn, Oxford University Press.

—— and Bouckaert, G. 2011, *Public Management Reform. A Comparative Analysis: New Public Management, Governance and the Neo-Weberian State*, 3rd edn, Oxford University Press.

Prasser, S. 2005, 'Choose Mates of Merit', *Courier Mail*, 5 December.

PS (People and Strategy) and IPAA (Institute of Public Administration, ACT Division) 2001, *Performance Management: A Guide to Good Practice*, IPAA, Canberra.

PSAB *Public Service Amendment Bill 2012*

Queensland Government 2006, *Welcome Aboard: A Guide for Members of Queensland Government Boards, Committees and Statutory Authorities*, Department of Premier and Cabinet, Brisbane.

—— 2010, *Engaging Queenslanders — A Guide to Community Engagement Methods and Techniques*, Queensland Government, Brisbane.

Reddel T. and Woolcock, G. 2004, 'From Consultation to Participatory Governance? A Critical Review of Citizen Engagement Strategies in Queensland', *Australian Journal of Public Administration*, 63(3).

Review of the Measures of Agency Efficiency, Department of Finance and Deregulation 2011, *Report*, Commonwealth of Australia, Canberra.

Rhodes, R. 1997, *Understanding Governance*, Open University Press, M. Keynes.

Rhodes, R.A.W. and Wanna, J. 2009, 'Bringing the Politics Back In: Public Value in Westminster Parliamentary Government', *Public Administration*, 87(2).

Rhodes, R.A.W., Wanna, J. and Weller, P. 2008, 'Reinventing Westminster: How Public Executives Reframe their World', *The Policy Press*, 36(4).

— 2009, *Comparing Westminster*, Oxford University Press.

Richards, D. and Smith, M. 2006, 'The Tensions of Political Control and Administrative Autonomy: From NPM to a Reconstituted Westminster Model', in T. Christensen and P. Laegreid (eds), *Autonomy and Regulation: Coping with Agencies in the Modern State*, Edward Elgar, Cheltenham.

Rudd, K. 2008, Address to Heads of Agencies and Members of Senior Executive Service, April 30.

— 2009a 'John Paterson Oration', speech given to the Australia New Zealand School of Government Annual Conference, Canberra, 3 September.

— 2009b, 'Equipping the Australian Public Service for Australia's Future Challenges: Sir Robert Garran Oration', speech given to the Institute of Public Administration Australia, Brisbane, 20 November.

Ryan, S., Broderick, K., Sneddon, Y. and Andrews, K. 2010, *Australia's NRM Governance System: Foundations and Principles for Meeting Future Challenges*, Australian Regional NRM Chairs, Canberra.

Sainsbury, M. 2007, 'Media', *Australian*, 6 December.

Salamon, L.M. (ed.) 2002, *The Tools of Government: A Guide to the New Governance*, Oxford University Press.

Sankar, M. 2005, 'Bridging the Gap between Policy, Research and Practice: Experiences from a Community Economic Development Action Research Project in New Zealand', *Social Policy Journal of New Zealand*, 26.

Schick, A. (2011) 'Leveraged Governance: Avoiding Fracture and Getting Results', in OECD, *Government at a Glance 2011*, Paris.

Sedgwick, S. 2010a, 'Commissioner's Overview', in APSC, *State of the Service Report*, Commonwealth of Australia, Canberra.

—— 2010b, 'The New Whole of Government Framework', keynote address, Conference on Connecting Across Boundaries —— Making the Whole of Government Agenda Work, Canberra, 19 November.

—— 2011a, Canberra Evaluation Forum: Evaluation and Australian Public Service Reform, 17 February.

—— 2011b, 'Public Service Commissioner's Overview', in Australian Public Service Commission, *Annual Report 2010–11*, Commonwealth of Australia, Canberra.

—— 2011c, State of the Service Report 2010–11, launch, 5 December.

Seldon, A. 2009, *Trust: How We Lost It and How to Get It Back*, Biteback Publishing, London.

Sen, A. 2009, *The Idea of Justice*, The Belnap Press of Harvard University Press, Cambridge, Massachusetts.

Senate Environment, Communications, Information Technology and the Arts References Committee 2001, *Above Board? Methods of Appointment to the ABC Board*, Commonwealth of Australia, Canberra.

SFPARC (Senate Finance and Public Administration References Committee) 2003, *Staff Employed under the Members of Parliament (Staff) Act 1984*, Parliament of Australia, Canberra.

SSCFGO (Senate Standing Committee on Finance and Government Operations) 1982, *Statutory Authorities of the Commonwealth: Fifth Report*, Australian Government Publishing Service, Canberra.

Shergold, P. 2004a, '"Lackies, Careerists, Political Stooges?" Personal Reflections on the Current State of Public Service Leadership', *Australian Journal of Public Administration*, 63(4).

—— 2004b, 'Plan and Deliver: Avoiding Bureaucratic Hold-ups', speech given to the Australian Graduate School of Management/Harvard Club of Australia, Canberra, 17 November.

—— 2005a, 'Government and Communities in Partnership: Sharing Responsibility', speech given to the Government and Communities in Partnership Conference, Melbourne, May.

—— 2005b, 'Foundations of Governance in the Australian Public Service', speech given at the launch of Foundations of Governance in the Australian Public Service, Canberra, 1 June.

— 2006, 'Governance in the Australian Public Service: Challenges for the Future', paper presented to the Corporate Governance in the Public Sector — from Theory to Practice Conference, Canberra, March.

— 2007a, 'Driving Change to Bring About Better Implementation and Delivery' in J. Wanna (ed.), *Improving Implementation: Organizational Change and Project Management*, ANU E Press, Canberra.

— 2007b, 'What Really Happens in the Australian Public Service: An Alternative View', *Australian Journal of Public Administration*, 66(3).

Six, P. 2005, 'Joined-Up Government in the West beyond Britain: A Provisional Assessment', in V. Bogdanor (ed.), *Joined-Up Government*, Oxford University Press.

Slaughter, A-M. 2004, *A New World Order*, Princeton University Press.

Smith, D. 2007, 'From COAG to Coercion: A Story of Governance Failure, Success and Opportunity in Australian Indigenous Affairs', paper delivered at ANZSOG Conference on Collaboration, ANU, Canberra, June.

Smith, M. 2011, 'The Paradoxes of Britain's Strong Centre: Delegating Decisions and Reclaiming Control', in C. Dahlström, B.G. Peters and J. Pierre (eds), *Steering from the Centre: Strengthening Political Control in Western Democracies*, University of Toronto Press.

Smith, R.C. 2010, *The Roles and Responsibilities of Departmental Secretaries: A Paper Prepared for the Remuneration Tribunal, Remuneration Tribunal 2010*, appendix 2, Commonwealth of Australia, Canberra.

Sossin, L. 2002, 'Democratic Administration' in C. Dunn (ed.), *Handbook of Public Administration in Canada*, Oxford University Press, Toronto.

South Australian Government 2000, *Government Boards and Committees: Guidelines for Agencies and Board Directors*, Department of the Premier and Cabinet, Adelaide.

Stapledon, G.P. 1996, *Institutional Shareholders and Corporate Governance*, Clarendon Press, Oxford.

Stephens, G. 2005, 'Governance Arrangements for Effective Public Financial Policies: A Central Banker's Perspective', presentation to the APEC Business Advisory Council, Asian Bankers' Association and Pacific Economic Cooperation Council Symposium on Promoting Good Corporate Governance and Transparency in APEC Financial Institutions, Melbourne.

Stewart, J. and Ayres, R. 2001, 'Systems Theory and Policy Practice: An Exploration', *Policy Sciences*, 34(1).

— 2010, 'Transcending Bureaucracy: The Possibilities of Systems Theory', paper presented to Panel Track 32, 'Working Across Boundaries: Barriers, Enablers, Tensions and Puzzles', IRSPM Conference, University of Bern, Switzerland, 8 April.

Stokes, M. 1986, 'Company Law and Legal Theory' in W.L. Twining (ed.), *Legal Theory and Common Law*, Basil Blackwell, Oxford.

Taggart, M. 1991, 'Corporatisation, Privatisation and Public Law', *Public Law Review*, 2.

Tanner, L. (Minister for Finance and Deregulation) 2008, *Operation Sunlight: Enhancing Budget Transparency*, Australian Government, Canberra.

TFMI (Task Force on Management Improvement) 1993, *The Australian Public Service Reformed: An Evaluation of a Decade of Management Reform*, Australian Government Publishing Service, Canberra.

Thompson, E. 2001, 'The Constitution and the Australian System of Limited Government, Responsible Government and Representative Democracy: Revisiting the Washminster Mutation', *University of New South Wales Law Journal*, 24(3).

Thynne, I. and Wettenhall, R. 2002, 'Public Enterprise and Privatization in a New Century: Evolving Patterns of Governance and Public Management', *Public Finance and Management*, 2(1).

Tiernan, A. 2007, *Power without Responsibility? Ministerial Staffers in Australian Governments from Whitlam to Howard*, UNSW Press, Sydney.

— and Weller, P. 2010, *Learning to be a Minister: Heroic Expectations, Practical Realities,* Melbourne University Publishing.

Townsend, T. 2009, *Capacity, Collaboration and Culture: The Future of the Policy Research Function in the Government of Canada*, Policy Research Initiative, Ottawa.

Treasury Board of Canada 2005, *Meeting the Expectations of Canadians: Review of the Governance Framework for Canada's Crown Corporations*, Canadian Government, Ottawa.

Tucker, T.R. 2010, *Corporate Governance in the Australian Public Service*, LAP LAMBERT Academic Publishing, Saarbrücken.

Uhr, J. 2005, *Terms of Trust: Arguments over Ethics in Australian Government*, UNSW Press, Sydney.

Uhrig, J. 2003, *Review of the Corporate Governance of Statutory Authorities and Office Holders*, Commonwealth of Australia, Canberra.

— 2005, 'Seminar Comments', *The Uhrig Report: Its Implications for the Australian Government, National Institute for Governance Seminar Transcript of Proceedings*, National Institute for Governance, Canberra.

UK (United Kingdom) Cabinet Office 2006, *Making and Managing Public Appointments: A Guide for Departments*, 4th edn, UK Government, London.

— 2009, *Power in People's Hands: Learning from the World's Best Public Services*, UK Government, London.

UK (United Kingdom) Government 2005, *The Government's Response to the Tenth Report of the Committee on Standards in Public Life*, Her Majesty's Stationary Office, Norwich, England.

UN (United Nations) 2003, *World Public Sector Report: E-Government at the Crossroads*, New York.

— 2007, *Toward Participatory and Transparent Governance: Reinventing Government*, New York.

Uren, D. 2011, 'RBA Riddled with Conflicts of Interest', *Australian*, 4 April.

Uslaner, E.M. 2002, *The Moral Foundations of Trust*, Cambridge University Press.

Verhoest, K. and Bouckaert, G. 2005, 'Machinery of Government and Policy Capacity', in M. Painter and J. Pierre (eds), *Challenges to State Policy Capacity: Global Trends and Comparative Perspectives*, Palgrave Macmillan, Basingstoke.

Victorian Government 2007, *A Matter of Trust: Trust in Government, State Services Authority*, occasional paper no. 2, State Services Authority, Melbourne.

— 2009, *Guidelines for Victorian Government Boards, Statutory Authorities and Advisory Committees*, Department of Premier and Cabinet, Melbourne, December.

— 2011, *The Appointment and Remuneration of Part-time Non-executive Directors of State Government Boards, Statutory Bodies and Advisory Committees*, Department of Premier and Cabinet, Melbourne, July.

Walter, J. 2006, 'Ministers, Minders and Public Servants: Changing Parameters of Responsibility in Australia', *Australian Journal of Public Administration*, 65(3).

Walters L.C., Aydelotte, J. and Miller, J. 2000, 'Putting more Public in Policy Analysis', *Public Administration Review*, 60(4), 349–59.

Wang, X.H. and Van Wart, M. 2007, 'When Public Participation in Administration Leads to Trust: An Empirical Assessment of Managers' Perceptions', *Public Administration Review*, 6(2).

Wanna, J. 2006, 'From Afterthought to Afterburner: Australia's Cabinet Implementation Unit,' *Journal of Comparative Policy Analysis*, 8(4).

— 2007, 'Introduction — Improving Implementation: the Challenge Ahead', in J. Wanna (ed.), *Improving Implementation: Organizational Change and Project Management*, ANU E Press, Canberra.

— 2008, 'Independence and Responsiveness — Re-tying the Gordian Knot', *The Australian Journal of Public Administration*, 67(3).

— and Bartos, S. 2003, '"Good Practice: Does it Work in Theory?" Australia's Quest for Better Outcomes', in J. Wanna, L. Jensen and J. de Vries (eds), *Controlling Public Expenditure: The Changing Role of Central Budget Agencies — Better Guardians?*, Edward Elgar, Cheltenham.

— Butcher, J. and Freyens, B. 2010, *Policy in Action: The Challenge of Service Delivery*, UNSW Press, Sydney.

— Kelly, J. and Forster, J. 2000, *Managing Public Expenditure in Australia*, Allen & Unwin, Sydney.

Watson, E. 2004, 'Public-sector Corporate Governance: British Columbia's Best-practices Reforms', *Ivey Business Journal*, March/April, 1–8.

Watt, I. 2003, 'Commentary to the 2002 Annual Research Lecture in Government Accounting', in CPA, *Accrual Accounting in Government: A Review of its Applications, Achievements and Problems, and Proposals for Reform*, CPA Australia and National Institute of Economics and Government, Australian National University, Canberra.

Watt, I. 2011, 'The APS: Now and in the Future', speech at the National Press Club, Canberra, 22 November.

Weick, K.E. and Sutcliffe, K.M. 2007, *Managing the Unexpected*, John Wiley and Sons, San Francisco.

Weller, P. 2002, *Don't Tell the Prime Minister*, Scribe Publications, Melbourne.

— 2007, *Cabinet Government in Australia, 1901–2006: Practice, Principles, Performance*, UNSW Press, Sydney.

— Scott, J. and Stevens, B. 2011, *From Postbox to Powerhouse: A Centennial History of the Department of the Prime Minister and Cabinet*, Allen & Unwin, Sydney.

— and Webbe, S. 2008, *A Public Interest Map: Part A Report of the Independent Review of Queensland Government Boards, Committees and Statutory Authorities*, Queensland Government, Brisbane.

— and Young, L. 2001, 'Australia: Mandarins or Lemons?' in R.A.W. Rhodes and P. Weller (eds), *The Changing World of Top Officials: Mandarins or Valets?*, Open University Press, Buckingham.

Westbury, N. and Dillon, M.C. 2006, 'Australia's Institutionalised Second Class', *Australian Financial Review*, 8 December.

Wettenhall, R. 1988, 'Diversity and Change in the Statutory Authority Sector' in R. Wettenhall and J.R. Nethercote (eds), *Hawke's Second Government: Australian Commonwealth Administration 1984–1987*, Canberra College of Advanced Education and Royal Australian Institute of Public Administration (ACT Division).

— 2000, 'Reshaping the Commonwealth Public Sector', in G. Singleton (ed.), *The Howard Government: Australian Commonwealth Administration 1996–1998*, University of New South Wales Press, Sydney.

— 2001, 'Public or Private? Public Corporations, Companies and the Decline of the Middle Ground', *Public Organization Review: A Global Journal*, 1(1).

— 2003 'The Rhetoric and Reality of Public-Private Partnerships', *Public Organisation Review: A Global Journal*, 3(1).

— 2004, 'Jobs for Mates Not the Way to Go' Public Sector Informant, *The Canberra Times*, February, 4–5.

— 2004–05, 'Statutory Authorities, the Uhrig Report, and the Trouble with Internal Inquiries', *Public Administration Today*, 2 (Dec–Feb).

— 2005, 'Parliamentary Oversight of Statutory Authorities: A Post-Uhrig Perspective', *Australian Parliamentary Review*, 20(2).

— 2007, 'Non-Departmental Public Bodies under the Howard Governments', *Australian Journal of Public Administration*, 66(1).

— 2012 'Integrity Agencies: The Significance of the Parliamentary Relationship', *Policy Studies*, 33(1).

— Corkery, J. and O'Nuallain, C. 1997, 'Between Government and Management: Relationship Issues for Public Enterprise Boards: Guest Editors' Introduction', *Asian Journal of Public Administration (Hong Kong)*, 19(1).

Whincop, M. 2005, *Corporate Governance in Government Corporations*, Ashgate Publishing, United Kingdom.

Wilks, S. 2007, 'Boardization and Corporate Governance in the UK as a Response to Depoliticization and Failing Accountability', *Public Policy and Administration*, 22(4).

— 2008, 'Board Management of Performance in British Central Government', in M. McDonald (KPMG), *Holy Grail or Achievable Quest? International Perspectives on Public Sector Performance Management*, KPMG Global Public Sector Practice.

World Economic Forum 2005, *Trust in Governments, Corporations and Global Institutions Continues to Decline*, World Economic Forum, Geneva.

Yang, K. 2005, 'Public Administrators' Trust in Citizens: A Missing Link in Citizen Involvement Efforts', *Public Administration Review*, 65(3).

Zifcak, S. 1994, *New Managerialism: Administrative Reform in Whitehall and Canberra*, Open University Press, Buckingham.

Zussman, D. 2007, 'Trust in Government: Trends and Implications for Action', unpublished essay, September.

Index